WHEN GOD CHOOSES

CHOOSES

The Life of David

WHEN GOD CHOOSES

The Life of David

KEITH KAYNOR

REGULAR BAPTIST PRESS
1300 North Meacham Road
Schaumburg, Illinois 60173-4888

Library of Congress Cataloging-in-Publication Data

Kaynor, Keith, 1944—
    When God chooses.

    Bibliography: p.
    Includes index.
    1. David, King of Israel. 2. Bible. O.T.—Bib-
liography. 3. Israel—Kings and rulers—Biography. I. Title.
BS580.D3K39   1989   222'.40924 [B]   88-32550
ISBN 0-87227-126-9

WHEN GOD CHOOSES: THE LIFE OF DAVID
© 1989
Regular Baptist Press
Schaumburg, Illinois
Printed in U.S.A.

CONTENTS

PREFACE

The study of David's life is practical and relevant to us today. It is as up-to-date as this evening's news. David was faced with huge problems. Some he overcame. Some he did not. We will realize that David wrestled with the same questions we do today. Studying his life gives us perspective. Because we notice that God was gracious to David when he did not deserve it, we learn to love God and risk ourselves to Him.

A Personal Challenge: Friend, this book is written to help *you*! Writing it has greatly changed and enriched me. Consider the precious benefits you will get for your diligence in reading it:

• If you are plagued by loneliness, *study the life of David*. Read of his lonely shepherding years and see how God used them to accomplish something great.

• If you want to know who God regards as a humble servant, *notice* how David acted when he arrived at Saul's camp for the first time (1 Sam. 17:20-29).

• If you are the youngest in your family, and if your older brothers and sisters treat you like "dirt," you will be able to *identify* with David, the eighth of

Jesse's sons. You will be encouraged as you see him rise above his circumstances.

• Feel forgotten? *Travel with David* through his hidden years—all eleven of them.

• Is your schedule full? Are you always pressured by responsibilities? Then you will be able to *relate* to David's years of fugitive living, years in which he was responsible for many people.

• Maybe you work with someone who is dishonest, unjust or oppressive. Gain *perspective* for your situation by reviewing David's relationship with Joab.

• If you would protect your life against the awful destruction that passion can bring, *think through David's fall*, noting realistically the agony that lust brought him.

• If your son or daughter is creating havoc, wounding others and destroying his or her potential, you can *sympathize with David* as he sobbed: "O my son Absalom, my son, my son" (2 Sam. 18:33).

• Perhaps your mate is on a different spiritual level. You will *understand* the tension that arose between David and Michal.

Massive Amounts of Scripture: God saw the life of David as being sufficiently instructive and practical to give such a massive portion of the Bible to record his life. God saw this life as worthy of full coverage. By way of contrast to emphasize this fact, consider two other men who were spiritual greats— Abraham and Joseph. The father of the faithful, Abraham, wonderful hero though he was, was given only 13 chapters of Holy Writ. Joseph was given only 14 chapters. But the Spirit of God invested 54 chapters to report to us about this excellent man, David. Any personality upon whom God would invest this much print must be most significant. Only Paul or Moses could be ranked with David in terms of the coverage in the Bible. Incidentally, however, Paul's name is mentioned 163 times in Scripture; David's is recorded some 1,127 times. And David's 54 chapters are in addition to the

Psalms. Evidently God wants us to know this man.

A Personal Word: There have been situations in my pastoral ministry in which I would have "washed out" if I had not known of the life of my friend David and all that he went through. After meeting the Savior in Heaven, I want to meet David. Hopefully you, too, will gain from your study of this man rich insights that will enable you to be "stedfast, unmoveable, always abounding in the work of the Lord . . ." (1 Cor. 15:58).

Acknowledgments

The following fellow servants of Jesus Christ were so helpful and skillful in bringing this material to its present form:

Dr. Leon J. Wood: teacher; man of excellence; father-in-law
Mrs. Roger Jenkins: excellence in editing
Mrs. Tom Contrucci: gracious word processor

INTRODUCTION

Vertical Tennis. This is about David, a hero of the Bible. Studying his complex life is like watching a vertical tennis match. Instead of our heads moving horizontally from right to left and then back to the right, our spiritual eyes see God "serve" a set of circumstances from Heaven to earth. We watch as David "receives" (responds), and we study his "return." Then God sends His servant a new set of circumstances from Heaven's court.

What Does God Think? Many glamorous, provocative and controversial figures dominate the American scene today. What does God think about them? Since we cannot see into people's minds or know all the factors that guide their actions, we cannot be sure how God evaluates our contemporaries. But when we study a person's life as recorded for us by the Holy Spirit in the Bible, we can be certain of God's attitude toward him.

Every Christian is challenged by David's godliness, courage, faith, integrity and enthusiasm. And by seeing his sins, we are warned! Therefore, Bible biography is practical and helpful.

You Are There. A number of years ago, Walter Cronkite narrated a television program entitled,

"You Are There." The goal of the show was to re-create a historical event so that ". . . all things are as they were then, except now, you are there." The viewer would relive a dramatic moment.

Likewise, my goal is to help the reader relive David's experiences to see things as he saw them, and to know the agonies and ecstasies of this excellent man of God.

Having probed the emotions, character, viewpoint, attitudes and goals of David; having tasted what he experienced, we will apply the insight and perspective gained. The result will be believers who glorify our Savior by living godly lives.

The Goal of This Biography. Of the ten biographies in my library, F. W. Krummacher (1868) and W. M. Taylor (1875) come the closest to my writing purpose. Some of the others go far afield from the text, taking improper liberties. Others twist the Scriptures to make for exciting reading.

This work, however, seeks to be honest with the sacred text. When I am making an educated guess, there will be a "probably" or a "likely" in the sentence. I have little sympathy with those who want to sell books by resorting to sensationalism to do it. That's merchandizing the Scriptures!

However, a sanctified imagination—one that is kept in line with logic, diligent study and the text—is most helpful.

— *Keith G. Kaynor*

THE HISTORICAL SETTING

David was anointed by the prophet Samuel to be the second king of Israel. God used Samuel to preserve the nation from disintegration after a military loss to Aphek in 1075 B.C. In that battle, the Philistines captured the ark, thwarted an Israelite bid for independence and indirectly caused the death of Eli, the leader of the nation. By means of a twenty-year, herculean effort (1075–1055 B.C.), Samuel was able to reverse the spiritual degeneration of God's people (1 Sam. 7:2). Now God smiled upon Israel with a military victory, but the people wanted a king. Understandably, Samuel was hurt. He reminded the people of his integrity in his farewell address (12:3–5). Later, when the new king made mistakes, Samuel humbly rose above the rejection handed him and lamented Saul's mismanagement of the people. Had Samuel been a lesser man spiritually, he would have had every excuse to be bitter in his old age.

Though Saul had been allowed to be exalted by God in the eyes of the people, he proved to be unsuitable as a king. Shortly after a successful battle, God gave Saul a stern warning.[1] For twenty years, God waited patiently for Saul to repent. But he did not. By acting presumptuously in his dealings with the Amalakites, Saul sealed his doom (15:20–23).

God told Samuel to anoint a new king.

Mourning and Fear. "How long will [you] mourn for Saul, seeing I have rejected him . . .?" (16:1). Viewing Saul as a living dead man, Samuel's mourning for him was genuine. Sorrow, though proper, may be so indulged in that one becomes unfit for service. Samuel had an obligation to God and to others. He could not afford to consume his energies in excessive mourning. God had planned that when Samuel obeyed Him, his griefs would be sanctified to Him and thus dissolved.

"No partial affection for those who are lost can excuse neglect of those who are spared. No regret for the spiritually dead and unresponsive can apologize for inattention to the living."[2]

When Samuel left for Bethlehem to anoint a new king, he was afraid of retaliation by Saul. Therefore, he camouflaged his reason for visiting Bethlehem. That God suggested a way to disguise Samuel's purpose shows that Samuel's fears were justified (1 Sam. 16:2). Saul would have killed anyone involved in the anointing of the rival to his throne.

The opening verses of 1 Samuel 16 unveil a triangle of fear: Saul is afraid of the righteous Samuel; Samuel is afraid of the violent Saul; and the people of Bethlehem tremble at the presence of the godly Samuel. Nevertheless, Samuel obeyed the Lord's directives and journeyed to Bethlehem to anoint a new king.

Here is a chart of the historical events:

1080 B.C.	Aphek; Ark lost; Eli died; Samuel started to work
1060 B.C.	Mizpeh; king requested; Samuel stepped down
1050 B.C.	Michmash warning; David born
1030 B.C.	Saul rejected; David anointed

End Notes

1. The words of Samuel to Saul (1 Sam. 13:13, 14) sound final. Jonah's words to the Ninevites must have sounded just as "cut-and-dried." As God wanted the Ninevites to repent, He wanted Saul to repent. Then, being confident of forgiveness, Saul would have been stirred to obey.

2. Joseph Exell, ed., *The Biblical Illustrator* (Grand Rapids: Baker Book House, 1958), p. 373.

THE YOUTHFUL YEARS

CHAPTER ONE

BELIEVERS UNDER CONSTRUCTION

1 Samuel 16:1–13

A four-lane highway passes in front of the church that I previously pastored. Some twenty thousand people drive by every day. Amazingly, the Bible teaches that God is at work in every one of those lives! I am overwhelmed that He knows all about them. He knows their names, their ages, their destinations, the time of arrival and their thoughts as they drive. He loves each one of them.

Likewise, for each person involved in the anointing of David—Jesse, Eliab, Samuel and Jesse's sons—there was a special, personal lesson to be learned. All were present at that occasion, so God could weave another providential thread into their lives. Let us look at how these people were "under construction" when David was anointed as the future king of Israel.

Journey of Destiny. To an observer, Samuel's ten-mile trip from Ramah to Bethlehem would have seemed routine. God had given Samuel the family name of the next king, but He had withheld the identity of the specific individual because He wanted to bring maximum encouragement to His dedicated but discouraged servant. God allowed him time to imagine what this king would be like. Samuel's misconceptions would be corrected when God pointed out His choice. He would show Samuel that David was to become all the prophet had hoped King Saul would be.

Bethlehem was not happy to see the righteous prophet. The arrival of the circuit judge[1] stirred the conscience of the city! After the nervous introductions, handshaking, shuffling of feet and formalities in Bethlehem, Samuel relieved the guilty fears of the elders by telling them the nature of his visit: sacrifice to the Lord. Samuel called the people to make themselves ceremonially clean and then come to the worship service. The people would have gone home to sanctify[2] themselves. Since a hot meal was likely to be served after the service, ulterior motives undoubtedly brought some; guilty consciences brought others.

As news spread that Samuel was in town, Jesse, the father of David, was made aware of the call to worship. Possibly many people were told of the worship service at a public gathering place. Samuel would have inquired about Jesse and told him to be present. Since a "sheep-sitter" was found later (1 Sam. 17:14, 18–20) to free David from his responsibilities, it should be noted that he could have come with his brothers if the effort had been put forth to arrange it. Jesse simply didn't send for David. The actual worship service is not recorded, but it took place between verses 5 and 6.

Before the afternoon worship service crowd dispersed, Samuel spoke quietly to Jesse. He told him to meet him at a secret place that he had picked out as he came into town. And he was to bring all his sons with him. Samuel most likely did not tell Jesse then that one of his sons would be the next king of Israel.

The anointing of the new king occurred privately. The townspeople thought Samuel had left.

We know this for two reasons:

First, Samuel would have been continually in the presence of some admirers and well-wishers until he left town. Second, anything other than a private anointing would have shed Samuel's God-given disguise and increased the chances of Saul's wrath.

When Samuel arrived at the rendezvous, he no doubt was curious about which one of Jesse's sons would be anointed. His efforts to visualize the sons clustered around Jesse at the worship service probably focused on one well-built son—Jesse's oldest. While he waited, he may have become nostalgic about his own career—his years of victory before Saul, the ups and downs of the nation since Saul had taken over. It had been twenty-three years[3] since God's first rejection of Saul (as noted previously, 1 Samuel 13:14 was more of a warning than a final rejection). The new king was to be a "captain over his people," so Samuel was justified in expecting a grown man, a person of prominent bearing, a military leader.

After Samuel had mused a few minutes, Jesse and his sons came into sight. The oldest, Eliab, was right behind his father. When Samuel spotted the family, his eye fastened on Eliab. "Hmmmm, is this our new king? Yes, yes! He is husky and strong! Look at the way he carries himself! What manly deportment! Commanding appearance! He is surely our new king!"

This was a solemn moment—not a thing to rush. As the family came to a halt before the aged prophet, he struggled to keep his mind clear to receive God's direction. One of these youths was to be king. All stood in silence, not knowing why they were there. Jesse and his sons waited for Samuel's guidance; Samuel waited for God's.

The Vote. Jesse was about to present Eliab. The text states that the second oldest was presented second and the third oldest third, so certainly the oldest son, Eliab, was first in line to be reviewed. But before Eliab could step forward, Samuel said, "This first son is not God's choice. God has rejected him. Have your other sons walk by one by one."

As far as Eliab was concerned, no vote had been taken on him. He had not even been in the "running." Later, he had nothing to look back on for consolation. He was not only unchosen, but he was not even shown off to the prophet. He had been passed over in silence, ignored, unrecognized as the oldest. He nursed his hurt pride for some time.

As Samuel looked silently at the seven young men before him, the Lord gave him a message about one of them and gave him the principle behind His directive. God told Samuel, "I do not want this particular person—Eliab—to be king." This was a positive rejection of Eliab as a person, in contrast to the neutral disqualification of the next two brothers. God said, "Do not judge on a man's outward appearance. You see only the outward; I see the inward." Samuel had anticipated the Lord's choice on the basis of appearance, posture, deportment and bearing. In the past, Samuel often had had to evaluate character and ability on the basis of outward appearance—and in just a brief moment. His "track record" showed that he could do so quite accurately. But God reminded Samuel that His knowledge goes far deeper than human sight.

The Principle. God admonished Samuel not to "look on the outward appearance," meaning, "Do not let your evaluation stop there." There are positive and negative factors for us in this principle. Since believers are judged on their appearance, it makes good sense to give personal grooming, homes and churches sufficient attention. The negative aspect is that while some do not pay enough attention to the "outward appearance," the majority make the error of giving too much attention to appearance, at the expense of inward spiritual qualities.

The fact that the Lord knows us better than we know ourselves also has a positive and negative lesson for us. The positive is that God must give some "credit" to a believer for his desire to help others. If a person can be guilty of mental adultery (Matt. 5:28), he should also be credited for the positive things he wants to do but cannot. To want to help, give to and care for others, though one is not able to, must carry some reward. God sees *all!*

The warning seen from this verse about the Lord's looking upon the heart is that God is not fooled by excuses about our disobedience. He knows us totally. While others may exonerate us, the Lord knows the full story and has the correct evaluation.

Samuel did not know why Eliab was rejected, but he accepted God's judgment and continued his search. Abinadab was shown, then Shammah, but neither one was God's chosen for kingship. After reviewing the other sons, Samuel questioned Jesse and found that one son was absent.

David Arrives. The aged[4] prophet spoke for all present, saying that none would sit down until the remaining—and youngest—son was brought. By refusing to be seated, Samuel added urgency and dignity to the occasion. Happy is the believer who has a sense of divine urgency about him: things need to be done for God *now!* Probably the youngest of David's seven brothers was dispatched with all haste to bring him.

Breathless from running, David's brother told him about Samuel. As they hurried back, it must have warmed him to know that at least one man did not think the family circle was complete without him. As David came into view, the brothers were curious; Eliab was nursing his wounded pride; Jesse was hoping to get back into the good graces of Samuel; and the prophet reminded himself not to judge, this time, on the basis of appearance.

Just as there had been no inspection of Eliab, there was none of David—but for the opposite reason. The others had sanctified themselves; David had not. The Spirit of God indicated with as much assurance and fervency *for* David as He had *against* Eliab. David slowed from a run to a walk—and halted near Samuel. The prophet moved reverently toward David. And in majestic ceremony, he poured the anointing oil over him. David, the youngest of Jesse's eight sons, would be the next king.

God Constructing Jesse: Pitfalls of Disobedience and Parental Partiality

When all seven sons present before the prophet had been refused by the Lord, Samuel checked up on Jesse. God's sovereign appointment for David would not be thwarted by Jesse's negligence. "Are these all thy children?" Samuel asked.

The question stung. Jesse's excuse for the absence of his youngest son was that someone had to watch the sheep (v. 11). But in supplying more information than Samuel asked for, and in not directly answering the question, Jesse was defending his behavior. His defense was shabby and weak, for later he found another person to watch the sheep while David ran an errand for him (17:20).

Jesse had been "weighed and found wanting" for the following reasons: First, Samuel was the greatest and most admired man alive.[5] Second, Jesse certainly knew of David's interest in spiritual matters, and that he would have welcomed an opportunity to be near the distinguished prophet. Third, Jesse had been told to bring all his sons. He may have been merely thoughtless. On the other hand, he may have been partial and knowingly disobedient. Parents—because they are thoroughly human—have weaknesses. However, they must constantly guard against favoritism and partiality. As they value obedience from their children, they must render the same to God.

God Constructing Samuel: Encouragement

Samuel had stepped down from national leadership thirty years before when Saul became king. During those thirty years, he had watched a creeping paralysis spread over the land. Samuel had poured his best working years into this now-sinking country. Another decade would pass before Samuel would be promoted to Heaven, and when that time came, the first man he had anointed would be hunting the second. In light of the depressing forecast, how was Samuel to view his life's contribution to God and his beloved people? His remorse was doubled because he had worked so hard for the ungrateful people that he had neglected his own sons. (Did this neglect make them rebellious?) So God had a perfect reason to encourage His servant. The Lord's message to Samuel was, "Eliab looked kingly; David did not. Do not judge by appearance alone. Though you appear to have failed, do not judge your life's contribution on the basis of the current circumstances."

Emphasis needs to be placed on the last thought, and it is important to notice how God brought comfort to His servant. God controlled the amount of information that reached His prophet. He gave only the last name of the family out of which the new king would come so that Samuel could guess incorrectly that Eliab had been chosen. God then gave the perfect evaluation of Eliab. As He had rejected Eliab despite his kingly appearance, likewise Samuel was to refuse a sense of gloom and defeat despite negative circumstances. He should not give his mind over to morbidly pondering the dismal "state of the union."

Samuel had expected to anoint a military person. David did not seem like such a person, but appearances can be deceiving. Samuel did not know there would be a gap between David's boyhood anointing and his kingship; nor that David would become more of a victorious soldier than Eliab would have been. Yes, he must not assume the nation was "going under." God graciously jolted Samuel's thinking. His purpose was to shake him into trusting Him again—to lift, strengthen and encourage His faithful servant. Happy is the person who trusts God with his lifetime effort as death approaches. Such faith prevents bitterness and depression.

God Constructing David: Kingship Certain

Only minutes before he was anointed king, David did not even know Samuel was in the area. Now he stood "in the midst of his brothers" with the anointing oil running down the full length of his body. How this vindicated his character and lifted him in their eyes!

Samuel would not have gotten away without explaining his actions. Eager questions were pressed upon him! Samuel may have told young David the meaning of the anointing. Surely David would reconstruct the events of that afternoon prior to his arriv-al. Piece by piece, he would put together in his mind the special reason Samuel had sought out his family. In the days that followed, David spent many hours considering and reliving this significant moment in his life. Years later, he placed extremely high value on God's anointing of Saul, so we can be certain that he regarded his own as a life-changing event. And he accepted his God-chosen destiny: he was to be king of Israel!

An internal change in David added more evidence that he would be the king of Israel. Though he was already close to God, verse 13 tells us that the Spirit of the Lord came mightily upon David from that day forward. Certainly he could sense the Spirit's increased activity in his life. And with a growing certainty, he was convinced of God's plan for him.

Later, David would have significant need to be certain of his kingship! It is doubtful whether David could have survived the decade of fugitive living that lay ahead if he had not been convinced of his kingship. He lifted his mental focus from shepherding animals to shepherding a nation, and he began to see himself as a leader, an important person. Such thinking would carry him through the eleven years of suffering ahead.

God Constructing Eliab: Humility

Eliab had been rejected by God personally. His

pride was later evident in his relationship with David. How that sin poisons and sours! Eliab had yet to learn the New Testament truth that before honor is humility.

After anointing David, Samuel returned to Ramah as quietly as possible. That David was to be the next king became a guarded family secret. None of those involved would be safe if Saul found out.

Clearly, God was at work in the lives of all who were at David's anointing. The Lord has a personal path marked out for all who will seek and follow Him. Happiness in life is a by-product of obedience to God.

If you are a believer in Christ, you are also "under construction." Ephesians 2:10 means, "For you are right now being worked on by God." He is in the process of freeing the believer from self, pride, fear and other mental-attitude sins to serve Him joyously.

God chose and constructed David. As we study how this was accomplished, we will be better able to recognize His choosing and constructing work in our own lives as it occurs.

End Notes

1. Samuel's circuit is given in 1 Samuel 7:16 as "Bethel, Gilgal and Mizpah." His reputation as a judge was known and respected.

2. Sanctify: "to be pure, clean; hence, to be holy." The verb is translated "you begin to consecrate yourself." The point is that while people were washing themselves and preparing properly, as directed by Exodus 19:10, 14, 22, there was time to send for David, that he might attend also.

3. The figure is arrived at in the following way: 970 B.C. is the accepted date for the end of David's monarchy. Since he reigned forty years (1 Kings 2:11), Saul's rule had to end about 1010 B.C. Saul also reigned forty years (Acts 13:21). David was thirty years old when he took the throne (2 Sam. 5:4) in 1010; he was born in 1040 B.C. He must have been at

least fifteen years old when anointed (he kept sheep alone), and so the anointing is placed at about 1025 B.C. The battle of Michmash had occurred about 1048, two years after the inauguration of Saul. Samuel's first word of warning to Saul regarding possible rejection came right after Michmash.

4. Wood suggested he was seventy-five years old. Leon J. Wood, *Survey of Israel's History* (Grand Rapids: Zondervan Publishing House, 1970), n.p.

5. That Samuel was the standard of righteousness for the nation can be seen from the following: (1) In verse 11, he spoke for all present; (2) when David later sought refuge with Samuel, even the violent and moody Saul knew better than to use force against the prophet; (3) nationwide mourning at Samuel's funeral shows clearly that nothing had eclipsed his influence; and (4) Saul's pathetic attempt to reach Samuel after his death via the witch of Endor shows his undying dependence on him.

CHAPTER TWO

A MAN'S GIFT MAKES ROOM FOR HIM

1 Samuel 16:14–23

I n Europe, the factor that launches one into a "successful life" is one's family name. But the American way is that a person will be rewarded according to his own diligence, trustworthiness, effort and "hustle." In short, the American dream is, "I can make it if I'm willing to work hard." Every American student wonders if there will be a job waiting for him when school is finished. Bible college and seminary graduates ask themselves, "Is there any church that will want me as pastor?" Young women wonder, "Will the right kind of man be around to love me and to want me to be his wife?" Every person is concerned that the door of opportunity will swing open for him.

In the first chapter we noted that God has a personal plan for every believer. We now turn our attention to how a person must diligently cultivate his own potential in order to enter fully into God's wonderful plan for his life.

First Samuel 16:14–23 relates how opportunity swung wide its door to David. Here, the country youth comes to the big city. He is introduced into the highest circles of the land. The shepherd boy meets King Saul, Jonathan, Abner and the other national leaders with whom he would be associated intimately in the coming years. The practical lessons for us to learn in this section are the how's and why's of David's gift "making room" for him.

The Situation. David had been anointed because Saul, through disobedience, had forfeited the blessing of God. Some time after Saul reached the position of ultimate power in Israel, he lost the qualities that had catapulted him into it. The spiritual purity, poise and power that may lift a person upward in life can evaporate. The ship hand may talk about what he would do if he were in the crow's nest; but once he gets there, he may find it more than he can handle.

Saul was emotionally and spiritually burned out. Verse 14 states an awesome fact: "But the Spirit of the LORD departed from Saul. . . ." He would rule for about another fourteen years, but it would be without the divine endowment required to do so capably. Saul was afflicted[1] with an evil spirit to bring him to God.

The Time Factor. The Spirit of God invested the first thirteen verses of 1 Samuel 16 to report what happened in just eight hours. By contrast, as much as four years may have transpired in the remaining ten verses of the chapter, a reasonable "guesstimate" of the time period covered. Saul's servants would not have diagnosed his depression, either immediately or accurately. It could have taken months to determine that good music would help the king's troubled spirit. And while the troubles of Saul were mounting at court, David was out in the countryside creating a reputation as a conqueror of foes and as a friend of the people. It would have taken time for his acclaim to build and to reach the ears of Saul's servants. Verses 21 and 22 mention three indefinite periods of time: First, "David [attended] him"; second, "he became his armourbearer"; and, third,

Saul said "let David . . . stand before me."

God was not in a hurry to launch David into national prominence. Sterling character needs a long incubation period. The anointing raised David's status in the family, so God returned him to his lowly and lonely shepherding responsibilities to balance his newly acquired status. David may have been with his sheep for as long as two years before his talents won him an invitation to the royal court.

A Man's Gift Makes Room for Him. David was a man of high caliber. The way he responded to the loneliness of a shepherd's life is a model for all who feel ignored and forgotten. Left alone, David used the time to full advantage. He developed his musical ability. Imagine how much poorer we would be today if David had spent his time having a "pity party" instead of writing musical poems such as Psalm 23! David also invented musical instruments—would this not be the logical time for him to have done so? This musical gift—this disciplined skill—would be God's vehicle for taking him into the highest circles of the land. Wise is the person who uses the student years, the youthful years, to the full. David certainly had no idea that he would rise to the top through music, or that he would rise so quickly! None of us knows which skills we develop today will open doors of opportunity tomorrow.

Besides his interest in music, David had a sensitive and appreciative spirit. It enabled him to capture in words his outlook on life. Writing as a third party and looking at his soul through a spiritual microscope, he had a unique ability to see life from God's perspective and to record God's viewpoint. His writing style was likely formed during his pastoral years, the products of which have endeared him to godly people of every age since. His harp and pen were a hobby; his contemplative mind, a friend; and his companion, God.

A third area that was developed in these years of preparation was his fighting skill. The Philistine frontier was not far from David's sheepfold, and a long-running feud existed between the two peoples. David, of necessity, became a capable warrior. Hour after hour, during these sheepherding years, David practiced with his sling. Certainly God's providence would guide the stone that would kill Goliath, but part of the reason David was willing to face him was because he had spent a few hundred hours hitting targets no larger than Goliath's forehead. Philistine raids still posed a threat to Judaean farmers and herdsmen, especially at harvesttime. David's sling was valued protection. Victories in these border skirmishes came to the attention of Saul's servants.

At Court. At the recommendation of his court, Saul invited David to the palace. The gentle playing of David's harp might drive away the king's fits of depression. Self-control and discipline were David's allies in this promotion. He was well-liked, magnetic and handsome. He was humble, patient and honest. These Spirit-developed qualities lifted him to the highest court in the nation and kept him victorious. Truly, "a man's gift maketh room for him, and bringeth him before great men" (Prov. 18:16). God brought David there for seasoning and schooling. He would learn the workings of government, finance and management, thereby laying the groundwork for a future reign of integrity.

In conclusion, God has a unique, personal course marked out for every one of His children. He has chosen His own. Through daily obedience, each believer can know and enjoy that divinely appointed path. The Christian young lady will find her "Mr. Terrific" if it is God's will for her to marry. The Bible college student will find a church that wants him as pastor. The parent will find daily wisdom and strength to raise children. God will guide and lead. If we would please God, we must *work, work, work* to develop our abilities. And God will guide us into greater satisfaction, deeper joy and increased spiritual productiveness. David did not figure on getting into court via his harp, but he ended up riding it into the capital.

End Note

1. Notice the purpose of God in similar cases of spiritual discipline (1 Cor. 5:5; Dan. 4:16; Luke 15:17). For more on this question, see Leon J. Wood, *The Holy Spirit in the Old Testament* (Grand Rapids: Zondervan Publishing House, 1976), p. 126ff.

CHAPTER THREE

THE FINISHING SCHOOL

1 Samuel 17:16, 33–37

T rue is the saying that "our disappointments are His appointments." This proverb fits David's situation in our text. We all have had disappointments that have seemed life-engulfing. Who has not failed to make the ball team, been unable to attend a special social event because of illness or had a friend who was not true?

The Situation. As 1 Samuel 17 opens, the Philistines are gathered in the Valley of Elah for a battle with the Israelites. The date is approximately 1021 B.C., and David is about nineteen years old. He has been in court for two years and has won everyone's friendship—especially that of King Saul. Promoted to armor bearer, he now has two jobs.

The Disappointment. The Philistines were drawn up in battle formation. Saul's mind was occupied, and he no longer needed the constant musical ministry of David. The king did not have time to be melancholy once the challenge of the battlefield was thrust upon him. Since the palace had become David's permanent home, it was unusual for him to be with the sheep. But for some reason, he was not required to be with the king, not even for his armor-bearing task. When the big moment came to march off to war, David was returned home to be with the sheep! No doubt this was a keen disappointment. He wanted to be "near the action." He desired to be with Saul, his brothers and the army—at the front.

No major battle had taken place with the Philistines for twenty-seven years, and the young men were ready for a fight. Border feuding had been increasing. It was time to settle who would be in charge for the next twenty-seven years.

David wanted to be accepted by his soldiering brothers. Being at the front with them would make him their equal. When word reached David to return home, his hopes faded. And then when the soldiers—including Eliab, Shammah and Abinadab—mustered out and marched off, David felt very dejected. He found himself, once again, in the lowly role of a shepherd. Eliab felt superior when he noticed that "little Davey" was not carrying the king's armor and, indeed, had disappeared. He took pleasure in knowing that he was a fighter while David was basically a musician-shepherd. He moved in military circles while David was at home among the lambs.

Finishing School. But God had bigger plans for David than He had for Eliab. He had arranged this special time for David to be in a private "finishing school" so he would be ready for his national debut. The king-to-be was tutored on the graduate level concerning Holy Spirit power. How? God allowed David to kill a lion and a bear with very few weapons. His purpose was for David to develop self-confidence, faith and an awareness of Who is really responsible for victories. Before David would travel to Saul's camp, he must be brought to a total consciousness of God's grace that would keep him from pride at Goliath's fall. His national debut required a perfect heart.

David spent at least forty days with the sheep during his "graduate school" (see v. 16). One day, a lion darted across the field and began to slaughter his animals. Having decided he would be the best shepherd he could be, David leaped into action. He pursued the lion, struck it and killed it.

Staring at the lion dead at his feet, David must have been surprised at the physical might that had just flowed through him! The Holy Spirit's energy had been clearly demonstrated. God wanted David to say to himself, "I have just been given special might by the Holy Spirit to meet this crisis!"

How would David react? With pride? Or would he be humbled by his success? Would his worship of God be enriched? Would he accept the responsibility that accompanies success?

A few days later, a bear attacked David's flock. Again, David was ready to do battle with sanctified self-abandonment, and he overcame this beast also, in spite of his crude weapons.

God's finishing school was complete. The national debut was just ahead. Soon David would walk unsuspectingly up the Elah Valley to dispatch an errand for his father. He was headed for a greater challenge than he had ever faced. God wanted the lion and bear victories fresh in his mind.[1] When only God's eye was upon him, David came out of finishing school with a proper attitude. He had the right perspective on the victories just granted him, and he possessed the humility essential to be launched into national prominence, without becoming a casualty to pride.

Chart: David's Anointing to His Defeat of Goliath

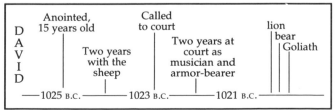

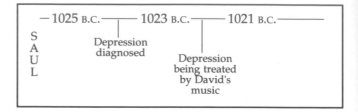

Sometimes it is difficult to say what constitutes an advantage in life. A young woman may be too attractive for her own good; a young man may be too handsome or athletic. Such individuals experience adequate human success and thus have little motivation to be successful in their relationships with God. Education makes some only more clever in evil. In David's case, God had to train and prepare him privately before He could hold him up for display nationally. The success David had over the lion and bear tested him. Success tempts one in ways that failure does not. We have seen that David's disappointment was God's appointment.

David's proper attitudes and actions on his way to the top are ones we should adopt.

First, a believer must give his schedule over to God. As David obeyed in returning to the sheep, we must trust ourselves to God.

Second, remember that God may have chosen you for an important purpose that can come only out of a disappointment. He may have more in mind for you than for others who seem to be in the limelight.

Third, when David took action to be the right kind of shepherd, the Holy Spirit brought supernatural power upon him. In obeying God, we have the ability, poise and power to be successful. David did not get power from God a week, a day or even an hour early—he got it when he needed it. When a Christian is asked to serve in some way, and when proper evaluation of one's abilities and skills has been made (Rom. 12:3), one may move ahead with the confidence that the Holy Spirit will give the victory.

End Note

1. The Sermon on the Mount urges us to fast, pray and give, but without showiness. Our Lord Jesus Christ encouraged us three times that such selfless service would be rewarded: ". . .and thy Father which seeth in secret . . . shall reward thee openly" (Matt. 6:4, 6, 18). David qualified for such reward.

CHAPTER FOUR

THE BEAUTIFUL PEOPLE

1 Samuel 17:22–29

C arol was about forty-five years old. Dark, sunken eyes peered out at life. Thin, unhealthy hair shaded her face. She was overweight. She dressed plainly. And she was *absolutely beautiful!* She had faced life at its worst and had decided that, with God's help, even that was bearable. Carol's husband had a heart condition, and their son had a serious and expensive back ailment. Yet sweetness and kindness radiated from her. What a gem!

Like Carol, David showed himself worthy of being ranked with the spiritually beautiful. While the world is searching for people with a high aptitude, God values high-quality attitudes.

News Wanted. After his soldiering sons had been gone a month or more, Jesse was eager to know what was happening. He also wanted to send them provisions, and David was ready to accommodate him. David started on the eight-mile trip up the Elah Valley to Saul's camp with the words of his father echoing in his mind, "Your brothers are up fighting with Saul." He carried roasted corn and bread for his brothers (a gift of necessity) and took cheese for their commander (a gift of luxury).

Geography. The Elah Valley runs northwest. The Philistines drew up on the west side of the valley; Saul selected the east. Jerusalem lay seventeen miles behind him. Each side was deployed on the hillsides that formed the valley; each side sought the help of gravity to add weight and speed to their arrows, spears and projectiles if the enemy should charge. Each army looked down on a central arena—a no-man's-land—which consisted of a comparatively level strip of land through which a river flowed. Soldiers from each side hurled insults at one another. The Valley of Elah (oak), though broad where David entered, narrowed so that the armies were only about three hundred yards apart.

Morale. The spirits of the Israelites were at rock bottom. For the past forty days, Goliath, the Philistine champion, had been insulting them. None dared to meet Goliath alone in combat to resolve the issue between the two armies.

Saul had been chosen king for the express purpose of disposing of fellows such as Goliath. The people had wanted someone to fight their battles for them, and Saul's size and appearance had been a qualifying factor in winning approval for the job. Now, if Saul would not face this hulk of a man, who would? Saul resorted to bribery, which indicates that defeat and apathy were rampant in the camp. Goliath's challenge went unanswered.

At the Camp. When David arrived at the camp, he left his baggage with the man responsible for it and immediately sought out his brothers. He found them among the soldiers who had gone down the slope toward the no-man's-land. As David conversed with them, Goliath strolled out to his usual position and launched his verbal barrage. As the lowest line of soldiers on the hill retreated out of

Goliath's reach, David was stunned. He had heard that his brothers and the army were fighting. Eliab, in family gatherings, had focused the spotlight on himself, with tales of valor and bravado. David waited. Surely, in a moment, someone would step forth to silence the burly enemy. But no one did. Eliab, for once, was silent.

As the moments passed, the same offer was made that had circulated for the past forty days: King Saul would give freedom, wealth and his daughter's hand to the man who would slay Goliath. There were no volunteers. Each soldier hoped the next man would take up the challenge.

David interpreted Goliath's defiance as an affront to God's reputation. All of his dealings with him were based on that premise.

When David asked about the particulars of the royal reward, Eliab could stand it no longer. Glowering savagely at David, he accused him of being only a curiosity seeker who wanted to see the battle. He insulted him and even belittled his service with the sheep. The verbal poison Eliab spewed forth reveals what Eliab thought of David. "With whom have you left those few sheep in the wilderness?"

Consider how galling Eliab's words were to David. First, he (David) had been sent home, while Eliab got to march off to the flash and splendor of a military expedition. No doubt David's self-esteem had suffered. Second, the elder brother implied that David had not been responsible with the sheep: "Did you get someone to cover for you? You probably didn't." Third, he sneered at the value of shepherding: "With whom did you leave *those few* sheep?" David was in his teenage years, when acceptance means so much. We can be sure Eliab's words cut him.

By calling David proud (v. 28), Eliab reflected his own attitude. (Liars think that most others are liars; thieves think most others are thieves; proud people see their own sin in others and hate them for it.) Eliab diagnosed David's motivation and heart attitude opposite from the Holy Spirit's evaluation

43

a thousand years later. Paul said that David was a man after God's own heart, and one who would do all God's will (Acts 13:22).

Eliab's Life. Both passages that name Eliab (1 Sam. 16:6, 7; 17:28) present him in a bad light. He was acutely embarrassed that David had found him out. He was less of a fighter than he had pretended to be. There was no battle now, and there had been none previously.

David's response qualifies him to be one of God's beautiful people. His inner strength and self-discipline showed in his actions. His mental and spiritual outlook on life freed him to respond Biblically (Prov. 15:1; 25:15) to his brother's hot torrent of accusations. He ignored the fact that his brother had not said, "Thanks for bringing the food." He humbly asked, "Isn't the situation serious enough to justify some clarification?"

Before Saul. David offered to fight Goliath. The news traveled through the camp. Saul, hearing of the offer, called David to him. It is doubtful that Saul would have considered letting David face the foe if the situation had not been so desperate. David's earnest arguments pierced Saul's doubts.[1]

Spurgeon pointed out that David did some *remembering* and some reasoning. He remembered that he had been tested before, and that it had happened while he was peacefully taking care of his responsibilities. He had met danger in the line of duty when he was in his proper place. The danger had not come because of sin on his part; it came, rather, because he would not sin by being negligent. He recalled that he had been tested in different ways—lions and bears do not necessarily fight the same way. Why should he fear *this* fiery trial, as though some strange thing had come upon him? "Is it a Philistine this time? Well, it was a bear last time, and a lion before that." He recalled the times he had risked his life before and that he had faced the attack alone. He told Saul also that he had fought with primitive weapons—weapons that were unequal to the task. God had won the victory before; He would have to do so again. David's battle tactics had been natural. He had not consulted a committee of lion-slayers or bear-trappers. His whole science of warfare had been simply to trust God to make his blows count.

David also *reasoned* with Saul. "The case of the Philistine is parallel to that of the lion and the bear. If I act the same, and since my motives are the same, so shall the results be the same: victory! It was brute force then, with the lion and bear; the same is true with this Philistine. I was alone then; so now. The sheep were defenseless then, and God's sheep seem so now."

David could have easily concluded that the cases were not parallel: "A lion or a bear—even a half-dozen bears—yes, but this Philistine is out of my league. I am a shepherd. I was never trained for warfare, so I had better let this lumbering two-legged creature alone! True, Eliab is not very kind to me—he is so proud, and he frequently puts me down. But he and good King Saul are right—I do not stand a chance against this human animal."

David could have claimed that the recent battles with the lion and bear had worn him out. "I have no energy left for such a foe. Besides, I must not press my luck. I am obligated to fight the lion and bear, but not this enemy."

Saul was convinced that David was the one to confront Goliath. So desperate—and thus persuaded—was he that he made a very special offer to David—the use of his own armor. This was significant for two reasons. First, the king's armor was the very best, and therefore held a greater possibility of assisting David to victory because of its quality. Second, it would carry enormous propaganda and morale value if it should fall into the hands of the Philistines. That Saul was willing to risk his armor falling into the hands of the enemy shows that he trusted David.

But David declined the offer. The armor was

much too big, and he was not used to it.

David also deserves to be grouped with "the beautiful people" of God because he was humble. Apparently, he shared only with Saul the victories over the lion and bear as evidence that he should be allowed to face Goliath, an even greater foe. That he would hold back this information until such a moment indicates genuine humility.

All eyes—pitying, concerned and interested—followed as David walked from Saul's presence.

End Note

1. See C. H. Spurgeon, "The Lion-Slayer—The Giant-Killer," *The Treasury of the Bible,* vol. 1 (Grand Rapids: Zondervan Publishing House, 1968), p. 659.

CHAPTER FIVE

GRACE ORIENTATION VS HUMAN VIEWPOINT

1 Samuel 17:40—18:1

C ars, people, houses and cats can be seen. Beliefs cannot. Neither can thoughts. But *how* we think and *what* we believe will control our actions, which others can see. The Bible teaches that the Christian needs an orientation to life that is based on grace, not on human reasoning. The Bible doctrine of grace (that we are saved by the grace of God, kept by His grace and enabled by His grace) allows the Christian to have the attitude, "I am nothing; but because Christ died for me, I have infinite value. His grace enables me to do what would be otherwise impossible. Whatever success I enjoy is because of His goodness to me." This is triumphant Christian living.

Twenty-five years prior to the date of our text, the nation of Israel had been enamored by the physical appearance of Saul. They had approved him on the basis of a human viewpoint. As chapter 16 of 1 Samuel opens, Samuel had lost the divine viewpoint. He was discouraged about his life's contribution to the nation because Saul, his successor, had steadily regressed morally and spiritually.

Then God moved to encourage him. When Eliab, the oldest and most able-looking of Jesse's sons, came into Samuel's view, the prophet was still functioning on human logic. He was sure Eliab was God's man but soon found out differently. In contrast to Samuel, Jesse and Eliab, David operated on divine viewpoint. He was tuned in to God.

What unbelievers would call failure, David absorbed in stride. He was looking at his life from God's perspective. He had worked faithfully in the humble role of a shepherd. His psyche had come unscathed through the potentially embittering experience of being passed over by his father. Though he was the youngest of eight children, he had not only survived emotionally and socially, but he had also flourished. If a contemporary psychologist had counseled David, he might have said, "You are the victim of circumstances. You should go to the big city, get away from it all, meet some new people and have some fun." The very hardships through which David had passed were responsible for forming his sterling character, which would carry him so high! It is difficult to say what actually constitutes an advantage in life. David was dealt a "lemon" in life, but he made sweet lemonade out of it.

David also had a grace orientation to success ("I am what I am because *God* has been good to me"). He had just graduated *magna cum laude* from God's finishing school. David could have brought parts of the lion and bear into town to show what he had done. Human thinking would have led him to do so, but he just continued caring for his sheep. David acknowledged that the Holy Spirit had given him the victories. He knew he had no basis for selfish pride.

When David came to Saul's camp, everyone there shared the same debilitating human attitude. They were afraid. No one knew that David was the only one in camp who saw things straight. It took a national crisis to reveal it. Many apparently successful people were in Saul's camp. Yet they thought,

48

The Philistine is too big to kill. But David thought, *Goliath is too big to miss!* The believer with a grace orientation will be victorious in a crisis while others are not. He will be less discouraged or dismantled by the problem. God has designed us with the potential of bringing glory to Him while going through harrowing experiences.

Whereas the events of 1 Samuel 16:14–23 may have taken as much as four years to transpire, only about one hour is described in chapter 17 (excluding David's trip to Saul's camp and the pursuit of the Philistines after Goliath's death).

David Approaches Goliath. After David left Saul, he returned to the spot where he had left the valley floor to ascend the slope diagonally to Saul's camp. Being some distance from the arena, he was able to select with unhurried care from the riverbed five smooth stones.

Then came the moment of truth. It was time to make good on his offer to defend Israel and God's honor. As an outfielder lunges at the crack of the bat, so Goliath must have whirled about to scrutinize the figure in his peripheral vision. When he saw his opponent, he mockingly promised to give David's flesh to the birds for a feast.

Goliath was an enemy who would strike terror into the heart of anyone. He was nine feet six inches tall, and as David got nearer to him, he must have seemed even taller. His armor was later weighed. It came to 126 pounds. His spear, likewise, was huge; his head alone weighed 16 pounds. What a towering hulk! Goliath induced sheer terror in his foes.

In the shouted exchange between the two, David answered all the pertinent questions: Why? Your taunting of Israel is actually an affront and an offence to God. Who? I, David, will slay you, Goliath. What? Total victory; not just over you, Goliath, but over all the Philistines. How? Not by human might, upon which you rely, but by God's power. Where? Here! When? Now!

David initiated the attack, running straight at

Goliath. His hand shot into his bag for the special rock he needed. Placing the stone in the leather pouch of his sling, David ran nearer to his enemy. He whirled the sling faster and faster over his head. He released one of the two strings holding the pouch, and the stone was hurled at great speed toward Goliath. At this strategic moment, the providence of God took over. The minute movements of David's tendons, muscles and nerves were so controlled that the stone was perfectly aimed at the one, unprotected, vital spot on his enemy—his forehead. In the supreme moment of challenge, God drew upon the hundreds of hours of practice David had invested in learning great accuracy with his sling. God also called upon the youth's faith and courage, and He intensified all these qualities and abilities so that victory was achieved. Through the Spirit's superintending, there was no lack of precision. The stone smashed into Goliath's skull, knocking him unconscious to the ground.

As David ran toward the fallen Goliath to stand on his body and cut off his head, the watching Israelites, delirious with the nectar of victory, charged across the no-man's-land and put the Philistines to flight.

Review of David's Changing Status. David's stock had shot upward when he was anointed by Samuel "in the midst of his brothers." But that was four years before. No sooner had God lifted him by the anointing than he was returned to obscurity to tend the sheep. Tested through victorious waiting, faithfulness to the task of sheepherding and growing in maturity, David rose to higher, but unapplauded, heights.

When his diligent practice on the harp won him an audience in Saul's court, he again climbed in status, in the estimation of his family and others. At court, David was more in the limelight than Eliab; but when the big moment came, again he was abased, being returned to the sheep, while Eliab marched off to the excitement of war.

The finishing school of the hills lifted David afresh; but when he arrived at Saul's camp, he was deflated by Eliab's sneers. Saul also put him down for a while, but he was desperate enough to be won over.

David's Post-Victory Status. After his victory over Goliath, David's status rose to a lofty level that he would not achieve again for a decade. He was at the very top! People from Dan (the north) to Beer-sheba (the south) had seen David slay Goliath. This was an unusual conquest, for it involved a total victory by a very young man. No one else would even attempt it, and it was all the more overwhelming because of the differences between the warriors in size, age, weaponry, ability and experience. And it came moments after David's oldest brother had told him he was a worthless person.

The victory was unique—the mysterious combination of the human and the divine had produced it. David contributed—he practiced countless hours with his sling. God contributed—His Spirit guided and enabled His servant. All great spiritual achievements come from a combination of these two factors. If a believer can totally explain his successes, there isn't much of God in them. And who wants to be limited to his own abilities?

The Post-Goliath Triumphs. David went back up the slope to rejoin the men who had not chased the Philistines westward. He was an instant national hero! People flocked around him to learn his name, question him, relive the enemy's defeat and be near the youthful hero. Saul must have come to commend him. Abner, also, would have heaped praise upon him. What a moment!

Now that God had lifted him in the eyes of the entire nation, how would David react? It is possible to win a war on the battlefield and lose it at the conference table. Therefore, it was equally possible for David to slay the giant, yet lose a battle of equal importance in his mind. How easily he could have multiplied the factors that had enabled *him* to conquer Goliath. If David had become proud, he would have been useless to God. But the private tutoring was fresh in his mind: the lion and bear victories. He knew God had given those trophies. He also knew the Lord had enabled him to hurl that stone at Goliath with tremendous speed and accuracy. Standing amidst his admirers, David won another important victory—he defeated pride.

A second post-victory triumph for David was over a vindictive "I told-you-so" spirit toward Eliab. David could have said, "This should wipe the smug grin off your face, big brother!" He could have been hard on his older brother. David did not nurture a vengeful spirit toward his brothers, who previously had had little respect for him. And future treatment of his family showed the graciousness of his spirit.

Blessed Jonathan. Along with Saul, Abner and others who surrounded David after his victory, there was another person who would play a significant part in his life from then on. It was Jonathan, Saul's oldest son, the crown prince. After Saul determined the identity of David's family so he could make good on his promise,[1] Jonathan was irresistibly drawn to David. The text says " . . . the soul of Jonathan was knit to the soul of David." A lasting and mutual friendship began that would later prove to be of supreme importance to David.

Jonathan was one of the best gifts God ever gave to David. No second-rate person, he was a man of ability in his own right. Able with the bow, capable of facing down his violent father, unafraid to champion the righteous life of David, able to inspire his armor bearer to follow him in attacking a Philistine garrison alone—this Jonathan was a man of great ability. Some twenty-seven years before, Jonathan, commanding a thousand-plus men, had broken the Philistine morale and led his forces to victory (1 Sam. 14:13–15). Jonathan enjoyed greater popularity than his father.[2]

A Surprising Fact. When we keep in mind the

ages of Saul, Jonathan and David, we understand their relationship more fully. David was about 19, Jonathan was approximately 50, and Saul had to be near 70.[3]

Jonathan's friendship was one of the few positive things David had to fortify himself for the decade of fugitive living that lay just ahead. He would need to draw strength from this, the single greatest day of his life, in the years to come.

Lessons and Observations. David experienced success because of the grace of God. We all need to be thoroughly aware that our victories are given to us by the Lord. Pride can cancel out any benefit we would enjoy from a victory. It's a constant enemy, a vicious foe, in terms of its consequences. We will be useful to God only to the degree that we are aware of His grace and give Him credit.

Next, notice the consequences of the choice Israel had made. Some thirty years before, Israel had asked God for a man to lead and fight for them in situations such as presented by Goliath. God had given the Israelites a man who supposedly met the need. Saul was approved by the people on the basis of his great physical size. God Himself wanted to be the King of the nation, but they demanded a human king. Did Israel see in the failure of Saul the thirty-year lesson God had been trying to teach them? Only the keenest, most spiritual believers would have learned this painful lesson. May God help us see the long-term lessons He is trying to teach us.

Remember, also, that believers can do what is humanly impossible only when skills are developed by disciplined training and then submitted to the Lord. While David was uncomfortable going up against Goliath with Saul's armor, he would trust his fate to his sling. Certainly, he knew that he would need the Lord to add the margin that would create victory. But one reason he was willing to step out there on the no-man's-land was because he had invested hundreds of hours practicing with that sling. David's contribution toward victory was a large one! God does not normally give great victories when believers make minimal effort. A person must develop his abilities; he must discipline himself and strive for excellence.

The second part of the victory formula is God's grace. As David's success depended on the sublime combination of the divine and human to do the impossible, so will ours. GRACE (God's Riches At Christ's Expense) enables the Christian to do the impossible. It is the link between human frailty and the Almighty. Although God's people are faced with many "giants," they can be dispatched as His people function in the power of the Holy Spirit.

Fourth, the friendship of Jonathan and David is also instructive. We tend to think that our friends must be near our own age. While this is normally true, it is not always the case. A more important factor in a mutually helpful friendship is an equal commitment to God. In a church, one may find a young firebrand being seen and serving alongside a fifty-year-old. They get along well because they are equally dedicated. They enjoy each other and serve well because their level of commitment to Christ is the same. Thus David and a man old enough to be his father—Jonathan—had an excellent relationship. Sometimes we mistakenly look only among people our own age for friends, when God may have in mind a much younger or older companion who will meet our needs.

David would carry these precious truths into the agonizing years ahead of him.

End Notes

1. Some think Saul had forgotten who David was. However, all he was searching for was a certainty about David's family. His purpose was to get the information he needed to make good on his promise.

2. First Samuel 14:44, 45. His popularity caused the people to reject Saul's foolish leadership and protect him against his father's thoughtless decree.

3. These ages are determined as follows:

1090 B.C.	Saul was born.
1070 B.C.	Saul was 20, so he could father Jonathan.
1048 B.C.	Battle of Michmash. Saul was 42, Jonathan at least 22; 1 Sam. 13:3.
1028 B.C.	Amalekite battle. Saul was 62, Jonathan was 42.
1021 B.C.	Goliath killed. Saul was 70, Jonathan was 50. David was 19.

THE FUGITIVE YEARS

CHAPTER SIX

GOD'S 'SNUBBING POST'

1 Samuel 18 and 19

When a wild animal is being trained, the trainer often utilizes a snubbing post. A horse is tied to a very strong post with a thirty-foot rope. Each time the horse, in its struggle, gets the slightest bit nearer the post, the slack is yanked in. As the horse continues to buck, twist and resist the rope, the animal is drawn in, bit by bit, until its nose is right down against the foot of the post.

Many times for our own good and growth, God allows us to be in a situation we cannot avoid. There's no way around it. Consider these examples in which only God can help: (1) A person finds himself in the hospital with a three-week stay staring him in the face. (2) The car refuses to run, so you have to humble yourself and ask arrogant, old Mr. Jones for help. (3) A couple wants children, but the doctor says they will never be parents. The couple's only hope is God's special intervention. (4) A self-centered husband has to learn to pray to God when his teenage daughter is on drugs and the heart-broken parent knows he cannot reach her. He has been only a nominal church attender and indifferent to furthering the gospel. But now he needs the Lord desperately. Such people have been brought down to God's "snubbing post."

Many times in life we believers are "closed up unto God." We are drawn to Him in ways that force us to discover how great and merciful He really is. By placing us in situations that force us to turn to Him, God gives evidence of His love for us. A superb example of this happened when Pharaoh's chariots were charging down upon the Children of Israel. The Hebrews were backed against the Red Sea, and neither flank held a chance for safety. The *only* thing they could do was to look to God. Then Moses spoke his immortal line, "Stand still, and see the salvation of the LORD" (Exod. 14:13). Then, and only then, when the people were desperate, did God open the Red Sea. In 1 Samuel 18 and 19, David was brought to God's snubbing post.

Saul Becomes Jealous. David's killing of Goliath brought momentary rejoicing to Saul. The king promoted David, retaining him permanently at court. As the young man continued to behave wisely, the Lord lifted him in the sight of all, including the court parasites.

When the nation turned out en masse to greet the victorious army, the women memorialized David's victory in song. The lyrics of the new hit tune attributed ten thousand victories to David, while it ascribed only thousands to Saul. This created an undying jealousy in the king.

Jealousy, the fear of being replaced, is a stifling, crippling sin based on a human viewpoint. It opposes the grace orientation to life. Saul's guilty mind (for not having been able to handle Goliath and then being shown up by a mere youth) darted to the ultimate results of David's popularity: "And what can he have more but the kingdom?" (18:8).

An Overview of the Fugitive Years. David became very popular in Israel. The people had tired of

Saul's whims and despotism. More than twenty years before, in the sight of the other leaders of the nation, the people forced Saul to back down on one of his leadership decisions (1 Sam. 14:44, 45). Hence, they had already lost respect for Saul and rejected, to some degree, his leadership. Goliath's propaganda campaign of forty days and forty nights dissolved the respect that had remained for Saul. The nation was ripe for a new king. One would have expected David to be wooed and courted by the people and for Saul to be replaced within a few weeks. But this did not happen. A Hollywood script-writer would be disappointed. God's ways are not man's ways.

It is always important to note what the Holy Spirit selects as sufficiently significant to record in Holy Writ. A total of fourteen chapters are invested to report the next eleven years, David's fugitive life. The Holy Spirit regarded these years of David's life as very important, for He caused them to be recorded in detail.

The Life of David

Fugitive Years	Monarchy Years
14 chapters to report the events of about 11 years	38 chapters to record the events of 40 years

What is the point? It is as if God is saying, "Knowing David's years of hardship is more important than knowing his years of comparative ease. What I am doing *in David* during the fugitive years is more important than what he will do *for Me* in the monarchy years."

Throughout the remainder of 1 Samuel David will be sorely tested. Will all things work together for good (Rom. 8:28)? Let us follow David's steps, experiencing his trials with him.

David's fugitive years were God's graduate school of character-building for His future king.

They were also God's gracious, patient hand of invitation extended to Saul in hope that he would repent. Saul likely decided God's inactivity was His permission to continue as he was. Not so. Likewise, we can misinterpret God's inactivity. Evaluating our continued pleasant circumstances in life in this way abuses God's patience and mercy.

Patterns of Deliverance. Three distinct means of deliverance are seen in 1 Samuel 18 and 19. Each one moves David closer toward God's snubbing post—total dependence on God. In 1 Samuel 18, David is attacked eight times. He repels each of these attacks through personal qualities and abilities.

In 1 Samuel 19, David was dependent upon others to save him. The pattern reaches its climax in the closing scene of 1 Samuel 19, with David's being forced to depend only upon God. God gradually moved David from self-reliance to God-reliance. He shows all His children His greatness and love by placing them where only He can meet their needs.

David Delivers Himself

Eight Attacks. Saul's mind leaped to its last stronghold ("I am still king") when he first became jealous of David. Besides indicating his guilty feelings, this shows that, even at this early point in their relationship, Saul felt threatened by David.

God permitted an evil spirit to trouble[1] Saul. Some misunderstand what this "evil spirit" was. Several factors about this incident need to be kept clear: (1) The text says this was a spirit being, not just a guilty conscience or a bad attitude. (2) First Samuel 16:14 speaks as though the power of the Holy Spirit was exchanged for the influence of the evil spirit. God was party to the exchange. (3) God's involvement was passive in the allowing of this evil spirit, while Satan was actively involved. God *permitted* it but did not *initiate* it. Satan did. (4) This action was allowed by God only after years of waiting for Saul to repent and obey Him.

62

Saul purposely sinned for many years. Failure over a period of time to repent, combined with fear, jealousy, lack of faith, pride or hate, may lead to demon influence.

The day following Saul's first wave of jealousy, David was in the king's presence, playing his harp to soothe his mental condition. As David stroked the heavenly harp, the hand of Saul toyed with a javelin. F. B. Meyer well observed: "Happy had Saul been if he had trodden the Hell-born spark of jealousy beneath his feet, or extinguished it in a sea of prayer."[2]

Suddenly Saul hurled his javelin at David! This man so recently delivered from Goliath acted insanely toward his deliverer. That the javelin sped harmlessly past David to vibrate in the wall like a tuning fork speaks volumes about David's agility and nimbleness.

Saul's second attack against David was less obvious. When word of his actions spread around the palace, Saul feared David's ascendancy all the more. And he came up with a different approach—promoting David. While this may seem contradictory to Saul's purpose, at least four factors appealed to Saul and were to his advantage in making David a regimental commander (eight hundred men were under his direction): (1) The excuse to station David elsewhere, hence removing him without increasing the rumors of his own bizarre actions. (2) The hope that David would be killed in battle without Saul's being personally responsible. (3) The outward restoration of David to a place of honor and recognition for the purpose of sapping the palace gossip of its strength concerning his berserk attempts on David's life. (4) The hope that a sudden promotion to the dizzying heights of influence and prominence would lead David to some rash act—the penalty for which would, of course, be death.

But the promotion neither turned David's head in pride nor triggered a traitorous act. Instead, David became increasingly successful in his military leadership. He was likely happy to be away from the moody, fickle-minded king. At this point, David was in control. He viewed Saul's two attempts on his life as fits of madness.

Saul's fourth attempt on David's life was also indirect. He provided David with a motive to return to the battlefield by offering him something that was already rightfully his. Apparently feeling that he could no longer delay in making good his promise to give his daughter to the one who killed Goliath, Saul offered Merab to David. One condition, however, was attached: "Only be a valiant man for me, and fight the LORD's battles." Two things are noteworthy about this condition. First, Saul wanted to lure David out to battle again, hoping he would be killed. Second, Saul was out of fellowship with God and was a top-notch hypocrite. David had been fighting the Lord's battles for a long time, while Saul was opposing God's purpose in his life and the nation's. The king's hypocrisy was especially ugly in that he was hiding behind God, falsely identifying his causes with the Lord's.

The fifth attempt upon David's life and character was Saul's effort to provoke him to some impetuous act by withdrawing his daughter from the promised marriage. After David had twice met the requirements for the hand of Merab, Saul capriciously gave her to another man. Many factors could have combined to push David into some headstrong reaction: the king was cheating him; he had earned the daughter's hand twice; he was well liked and he knew Saul was not; and he was a national hero. Yet David continued to be humble, meek and unassuming. He still had a beautiful spirit; he lived with a grace orientation to what was happening to him. He looked to God to place him on the throne in His own time.

The degree of danger into which David was lured is unknown. But we can be sure he experienced keen disappointment when Saul betrayed him. He must have had a spiritual wrestling match with himself. David was aware that marriage to the king's daughter would strengthen his claim to the throne. But he trusted God and controlled himself.

David's relationship to Merab, Saul's oldest daughter, was a sensitive matter. There is some evidence that she was given to Adriel the Mehalathite because she was not attracted romantically to David. If so, this was the first defeat he had experienced in a great while. Everything else he touched "turned to gold." Affection, or lack of it, in a relationship is a force that can build or break a person. The self-image is at stake. We all want to be regarded as desirable.

The sequel to Saul's betrayal of David occurred thirty years later, when David gave direction for the appeasing of the Gideonites. Saul violated the treaty Joshua had foolishly made with them, and God's honor suffered as a result. To make things right, God gave orders that seven of Saul's descendants were to be hanged, to atone for Saul's mistreatment of the Gibeonites. David had the gruesome task of selecting the seven. Five of the seven were Merab's children. Some Bible students suppose David was retaliating against Merab for having rejected him many years before. However, it is possible that few of Saul's relatives were still alive, making it impossible for David to select any others than Merab's children. The battle of Mount Gilboa had killed Saul and his sons.

Saul made a sixth attempt against David's character through Michal. Having lost all natural affection for his own children, Saul held out his second daughter as bait to David. He knew what he was giving away, but David did not know what he was getting. The king demanded for Michal a higher price than he had for Merab, in terms of valiant deeds, and he intended Michal to be a millstone around David's neck.

The temperament of his new bride proved to be a heavy weight for David to bear. Chapter 19 records a lie she told that left David in a bad light. In the future, God cursed her body (she would have no more children, and it is not certain she ever had any) for despising David's spiritual enthusiasm (2 Sam.

6:23). Only once during the remainder of her life-time did David act positively toward Michal. And motives other than love may account for even that one favorable action. Saul gave Michal to David so that "she may be a snare to him." And she certainly was.

In Saul's seventh assault on David, he induced the court servants to lie to David to try to convince him that the king genuinely wanted him for his son-in-law. The purpose, again, was to lure David into more dangerous exploits, with the hope he would be killed. David was getting a rapid education in court intrigue. He was not stupid; he knew their purpose. So David's challenge was to resist the temptation to operate on their level—deceiving and baiting others to their death.

Saul's deceitful servants are a classic example of the proverbial third-party-caught-in-the-middle problem. They lied for someone they disliked and disrespected, to someone they liked and admired so he would be destroyed. Saul's fickle feelings caused much concern to all court personnel. Rumors of his latest and most bizarre behavior buzzed through the palace. All felt insecure. A whim of the king could fell any of them. If his son Jonathan was not safe (1 Sam. 14:44), no one was.

The servants were weary of catering to the king's imagined persecutions and problems. They had waited a long time for someone who would ease their situation. David had been successful in sooth-ing Saul in the past, but now the patient was threat-ening the doctor. David had won the admiration and affection of these servants (18:5). What mental agony it must have been for them to lie to this guileless young man! Then, to rub salt in their wounded consciences, David chided them for act-ing as though Saul's offer were not important. David acted very honored that the king should still want him in the family.

The eighth effort of Saul to be rid of David was indirect: the demand for one hundred Philistine foreskins as a dowry. When David returned in a short time with twice the amount required, Saul's dread of him increased.

First Samuel 18 records eight attempts on the life or character of David. The key to deliverance was always the ingrained character of David. In each case, escape came as he drew upon internal resources: patience, modesty, caution, maturity, forethought and faith. He did not lose his temper or lower his personal code of ethics to compensate for the treatment he was receiving. Saul's behavior toward him was never an excuse to be anything less than what God wanted him to be.

These eight attacks were getting David closer to the snubbing post of total dependence upon God. The pressure has been turned up considerably. His life is now under constant threat. His every action must be weighed, lest he unwittingly give Saul any seemingly legitimate reason for eliminating him. He lives under pressure, yet he has not lost his faith in God; he is triumphant and he has a good attitude.

David Is Delivered by Others

In 1 Samuel 19, the pattern of deliverance changes. It is one thing to sense antagonism and to ward off hatred's onslaughts by one's own ability and spiritual depth, as David did in 1 Samuel 18. It is another matter when one must depend upon other people for deliverance. God's help for David in 1 Samuel 19 did not come by means of sterling qualities from within himself, but through people surrounding him. In this way, God moved David much closer to the snubbing post of absolute dependence upon Himself.

People are basically independent. Therefore, David's forced dependency upon others was a trial to his lofty spirit. By this time in his life, he was accustomed to winning battles; he was a self-reliant individual; his name was respected; and his opinions influenced many. To have to rely on others was contrary to his natural inclinations and desires.

Saul no longer bothered to try to hide his murderous intentions: he plainly ordered the palace personnel to slay David. God brought help—and hence dependency—to David through Jonathan and Michal.

Jonathan's Assistance. While David was still unaware of Saul's open solicitation of court people to kill him, Jonathan made plans to defend his friend. After giving Saul a night to cool off and change his mind, Jonathan advised David to hide in a field near the palace. They agreed that the next morning Jonathan would ask his father to go for a walk in that field. Jonathan would maneuver Saul near enough to David's hiding place so that he would be able to hear their conversation.

The plan succeeded. As Jonathan reminded Saul of David's valor against the Philistines and his excellent record of service, Saul relented. David then emerged from his hiding place to join the two men. But in so doing, Jonathan revealed his great respect and allegiance to David—and this put some distance between himself and his father. Saul's good will turned out to be short-lived. But for the moment, David was restored to his minstrel position at court.

After an unknown length of time (between verses 7 and 8), David again so distinguished himself in battle that he awakened the enthusiastic admiration of the people. This new success upset Saul's mental equilibrium, causing him to slide toward imbalance. This was the pattern: a wartime situation required the valor of David; God gave him victory; victory caused the people to love David more; their praise of him caused Saul to be insanely jealous; Saul persecuted David (see 1 Sam. 18:5–12; 18:30—19:7; 19:8–10). Why did this pattern recur? Military prowess was the basis on which Saul had been selected as king some thirty years ago. And he was failing in his supposed specialty.

Michal's Assistance. God placed David in a position of dependence a second time. When David returned to his work as court minstrel, he was again within range of Saul's javelin. And it was not long before it was hurled at him again. David fled to his home, which was soon encompassed by Saul's men. This incident very likely provided the historical setting of Psalm 59: "Deliver me from mine enemies, O my God . . . for, lo, they lie in wait for my soul. . . . They return at evening: they make a noise like a dog, and go round about the city." Displeased with his poor throw and impatient for David's death, Saul sent messengers to break into the house and take David. At Michal's urging, however, David slipped out a window to some unguarded spot below and scurried off to safety.

David Is Delivered by God

David's third deliverance—the one that climaxes chapters 18 and 19—was an escape from Saul himself. After fleeing from his home, David went to Naioth, two miles away. His purpose in going there was to seek protection and counsel from Samuel. He was most apt to learn "why" and "what next" from the aged prophet who lived so near to God. Hopefully Saul's respect for God's man would keep him from barging in and taking David. The prophet, however, really had very little with which to protect David, except his reputation. In going to Naioth, David placed himself in a situation where only God could help him. He was getting close to the snubbing post. He knew that now God would have to roll up His sleeves and show His power, or he would be killed.

After David fled to Naioth, Saul sent a band of soldiers to apprehend him. But, miraculously, they were distracted from their errand and joined in the worship in progress. When they did not return, Saul sent another detachment of men. The second group also went under the Spirit's control and ignored their assigned mission. When this second wave of soldiers did not return, Saul was irritated and decided to take care of the matter himself.

Picture Saul fully armed and furious about the soldiers never returning. As Saul approached the place where he knew Samuel and David were, however, the Spirit of God began a convicting work in his mind that shattered his plans. The closer Saul came to Naioth, the greater the pressure from the Spirit of God to face his wickedness. The scene is comparable to that of a hunter being charged by a large, angry animal. Lifting his rifle, he takes careful aim, for he knows his life may depend on the accuracy of his shot. He shoots and hits the animal, but it is still charging. He shoots again. Finally the furious animal collapses a few life-sparing feet away from the hunter. The nearer to David that Saul got, the more overwhelmed he became. As truth bore into his mind, he faced himself honestly and fell down near the worshipers. In a stupor of despair and remorse, the king lay on the ground with his outer garment removed. Most likely, he told to any who came to attend him about his misery and about how wrong he was in wanting David's death. The people asked, "Is Saul a prophet now?" No! They knew Saul was not a prophet, and the question was satirical. Everyone knew of Saul's tirades. The point is that God has the power to make even a demon-dominated man act like a righteous person to protect one of His chosen servants.

Remember the fascinating television program "Mission Impossible"? The thing that distinguished this adventurous, crime-fighting series was that the bad guys were always defeated from the inside. Success never came from greater numbers of soldiers or detectives overpowering the evil ones. The victory was won by means of superior plans, brains, weapons, disguises or secret mechanisms. Overcoming Saul had to be an "inside job," because as king he had great military strength. Samuel could not talk Saul out of his wrath. God had to subdue the vengeance-bound king. And He did.

Conclusion

The outstanding lesson for David in the successive deliverances was that he could depend on God. In the end, he was drawn right down to the snubbing post of being dependent upon God's help. Previously, David had known God's enablement to kill a lion and a bear. Then he was enabled to gain victory over a person—Goliath. Eight assaults against him followed, but he got himself out of every one of them.

As his life was increasingly being threatened, David found himself having to depend on people (Jonathan and Michal). In the final move, God bypassed altogether human agency in accomplishing safety for His future king.

Neither David with his agility, sterling character, forethought or self-control, nor gracious Jonathan or Michal, kept David safe. God wanted David directly dependent upon Himself. Clearly, God arranged David's circumstances to result in such a relationship.

One of the most difficult tasks for a believer is to "stand still, and see the salvation of the LORD" (Exod. 14:13). There is a vast difference between saying, "God gives me strength," and "God *is* my strength" (1 Cor. 1:30). God's people will find themselves in situations where they can turn to no one but God. God will force us to experience His greatness! The near side of such an experience is unpleasant, but on the far side such a lesson is a spiritual treasure!

End Notes

1. For a careful treatment of this matter, see Wood, *The Holy Spirit in the Old Testament*, p. 126 ff.

2. F. B. Meyer, *David: Shepherd, Psalmist, King* (Fort Washington, Pennsylvania: Christian Literature Crusade, 1970), p. 50.

CHAPTER SEVEN

TO NOB
OR
NOT?

1 Samuel 20—21:9

T he believer must know God's will so that he can do it. This is very important! What was God's will for David following his deliverance from Saul? Under the pressure of God's convicting power, Saul faced himself honestly. He fell down in a stupor of despair over the shambles he had made of his life. But David had seen Saul like this before, and he knew it would not last. What should he do now?

David sought to find out if Saul was determined to kill him, or if his attacks were simply heightened spurts of malice and jealousy. He devised a plan with Jonathan to determine what was in the king's heart. David is to be highly credited for wanting to be certain of Saul's intent. Often, we assume a person is looking down on us, or we conclude the other fellow has a pride problem. We read motives and attitudes into his tone of voice that are not there. Satan wins the victory when believers do not invest time and effort to discover the true attitudes of those who offend them.

David and Jonathan's plan was simple: While David absented himself from the new moon feast, an event he was expected to attend, Jonathan would watch his father's face and listen to his response to the excuses given for David's absence. The key verses of 1 Samuel 20 are verses 9 and 33: "If I [Jonathan] knew certainly that evil were determined by my father to come upon thee, would I not tell it thee?"; "Whereby Jonathan knew that it was determined of his father to slay David."

Jonathan discovered that his father was unalterably set on murder. When he made excuses for David's absence, Saul became furious and hurled his javelin at him. Jonathan fled to warn David through a prearranged, nonverbal signal. When Jonathan's servant left him, he was free to see David face to face. Being a tender, sympathetic man, he could not part from David without a proper farewell. A touching scene follows. Both men were deeply moved, realizing that their friendship must go "underground." The Bible records only one more meeting between these two close friends before Jonathan was killed in battle. From then on, David was left to fend for himself.

But what should David do now? Yes, he had enjoyed a marvelous deliverance at Naioth, but could he count on God to do it again? To what degree was he responsible for his own safety? Should he employ his own strength and cunning to get away? Could he trust that, after he had used all his natural abilities, God would do what was needed supernaturally to insure his well-being? On the other hand, why not stay at Naioth where he had totally depended upon God and experienced victory? Should David go to Nob to seek the advice of the high priest? To Nob, or not—that was the question.

No matter how we might evaluate David's actions and yearn to coach him from our safe, three thousand-year-later perspective, what he did was clearly recorded: "Then came David to Nob to Ahimelech the priest" (21:1). Nob was a city of priests; the tabernacle was there. Nob, Gibeon and Jerusalem form a tight right angle. David had about four miles to travel before the sun went down and the Sabbath began.

Some of David's biographers have suggested that he was wise to go to Nob for the following reasons: (1) The event was referred to with approval by Jesus in the Gospels (Matt. 12:3, 4; Mark 2:25–28). (2) God did not specifically forbid such a move, and since finding God's will is, to some degree, a matter of trial and error, going to Nob was as wise a choice as any. (3) David needed the high priest to inquire of God what he should do through the use of urim and thummim, and the obvious place for this was Nob. (4) During his future years of exile, one of David's chief complaints was that he was banished from the house of the Lord (Ps. 84:1, 2, 10; 42:3, 4). Who would deny him this last spiritual comfort? It would be nice to vindicate David, to let ourselves be convinced by these arguments. But none of the arguments above are conclusive. And we are told later that David regretted his visit to Nob (1 Sam. 22:22).

David here loses some of the beauty of spirit and transparency of character we have come to expect of him. The pressures now upon him show him to be "a man subject to like passions as we are"—rather human, after all.

David's first downward step was the lying involved in his scheme with Jonathan (see 1 Sam. 20). Compared to what Saul was trying to do to him, David's misdeeds seem to be nothing. However, God has very high standards for the individual He is going to lift to unlimited power; exacting performance is demanded. Having been lied *to* by Saul (18:21) and the servants (18:22); lied *for* by Michal (19:14); and lied *about* by Michal (19:17), David adopted the same manner of dealing with life's difficult situations. He had lost his tenacious grip on certain facts: "Samuel anointed me to be king; God has a purpose in my hardships; God's nature, plus His stated purpose for my life, require that I shall not die." Both Saul and Jonathan knew that David would be the next king (see 1 Sam. 23:17). But David was operating at the panic level. He had forgotten his normal orientation toward the grace of God.

David Arrives at Nob; Ahimelech Trembles

When David arrived at Nob, Ahimelech, the high priest in charge of the tabernacle area, emerged from the sanctuary with the week-old bread used in the religious services. It must have been in the early evening, about six o'clock. When Ahimelech saw David, he trembled in fear. Saul's condition was known over the whole land. His persecution of David was common knowledge, and Ahimelech hesitated to get involved.

David was unwise to go to Nob for the following reasons.

First, he put Ahimelech in an awkward spot.

Second, he lied to the high priest. David told Ahimelech that he was on a secret mission for Saul and had left the palace in great haste—without time to be properly attended or to pack food. By doing so, David applied a "situation ethic." He assumed that his situation was of such a serious nature, such a dire need, that the greatest good (getting food, information and a weapon) could be accomplished by resorting to a new standard of conduct—lying. This illustrates the basic approach of what is called in America "situation ethics." Proponents of this old immorality (not "new morality") use such extreme, ridiculous examples in arguing their view that they invalidate their case.

David was under great strain. Not seeing the potential harm of telling his lie, he felt justified. Though dishonest, unprincipled action seems to meet the immediate need, it often has disastrous effects. David's apparently harmless "white lie" later indirectly caused the death of eighty-five priests and their families.

Third, by going to Nob David put a strain on the food supply. Ahimelech told him that there was no other bread but the sacred bread, which was seven days old. Very likely the priests and their families were waiting for this bread themselves.

Fourth, the inquiry to the high priest was unprofitable, for it surely was not God's will for David to go to Gath—which he did when he left Nob.

Fifth, though three gospel writers refer to this event (giving sacred bread to a nonpriest), Jesus was teaching that human need is of greater importance than perfection of ritual. He was not saying that David was correct to be at Nob. Jesus referred to this experience to vindicate His act of healing on the Sabbath.

Sixth, even though knowing God's will is to some degree a matter of trial and error, David should have known that he would have to lower his standards if he went to Nob. Naioth was the place for David, the place of God's personal intervention on his behalf.

The Nature of This Trial. David's encounters with the lion, the bear and Goliath required courage—massive amounts of it—and faith in God on a short-term basis. These were high pressure, high-intensity challenges, but they were brief. First Samuel 19, however, deals with trials of a longer lasting nature. Let's call them "medium-length difficulties." Previously, victory for David had been either immediate or within a "medium" amount of time. God had always lifted David over his enemies. But now God must have seemed far away, and the swollen hatred of Saul was unchecked. David was entering a long, long trial; he lived about eleven years as a fugitive.

To trust God while one is overcoming is admirable, commendable; to trust Him while being overcome is more so. When God allows more difficulty to come to us than we think we can handle, we often respond as David did—we adopt a human view of the situation, becoming indistinguishable from unbelievers. When fear, jealousy, pride, envy, lack of faith and other mental-attitude sins overcome us, we tend to doubt God's motives and actions. When Satan tempted Eve in the Garden of Eden, he implied in his argument that God was withholding something she would like. He said, "God does not want you to have fun; be fulfilled." He urged them to disobey God, claiming "Your eyes will be opened, and ye shall be as gods [equal with God]" (Gen. 3:5).

Satan's temptations of Christians today will have the same themes he used to jab the Savior in the wilderness temptation (Matt. 4): "Obviously, you are not the Son of God (child of God), because you are suffering. God does not love you. See how poorly He is taking care of you." The believer must, therefore, arm himself with the recognition that God's unchangeable love and concern for him was expressed at Calvary. Christ died there for his sin, emptiness, laziness and selfishness. David needed to trust God and stay where he was.

On to Gath. David insisted to Ahimelech that he and his men were ceremonially clean, and pressed for the bread. He also took the sword of Goliath that had been kept there at Nob. Then David met Doeg, a man loyal to Saul, and he was fearful. At some other time and in some other place he could have looked Doeg in the eye without shame. But David felt very awkward; he had been "found out" by Doeg.

On the morning of the first day of the week, he took the path down through a valley (later named Jehoshaphat) past the Jebusite stronghold of Zion. Turning west, he passed either through, or near, the valley of Elah, where he had killed Goliath, and he hastened farther west to the area occupied by the Philistines. David, once fearless, now carried both the sword and the mental attitude of Goliath. The weapon had not delivered the giant; neither would it help David. He figured that as a fugitive from a rival nation, he would gain asylum with Saul's constant foes, the Philistines. He was even counting on the Philistines' knowing that Saul was hunting him—so well-known was the rift between them.

Lessons and Observations

Was David finished? Was God through with

him? His impetuous act (going to Nob) caused the death of eighty-five priests and their families. That's a heavy load for anyone's conscience. And David lied to the high priest. Certainly, he was far from close fellowship with God. Like David, when we get into sin, our tendency is to feel that we have gone beyond the scope of God's forgiveness. We sometimes imagine that because our exact situation is not described in the Bible, God's mercy cannot cover our case.

Notice that even as David fled, God was graciously calling him back to Himself. How? Through the memories evoked by the sword he carried. And by leading him near the battlefield where he had conquered Goliath. No, David was not finished; God was watching over His wandering son.

"It can't get any worse!" What worse circumstances could be awaiting David in the Philistine city of Gath than he had faced each hour he remained in Judah? He must have concluded, "It can't get any worse; I might as well go to Gath." When everything seems against us; when providence seems dominant over promise, we too, may give way to the weak, human viewpoint: "I'll just coast, because things can't get any worse." But they can. They did for David. Nob was bad, but Gath was even worse!

Playing God. When David lied to Ahimelech, robbing him of a responsible, intelligent choice, he was playing God for Ahimelech and the others who would ultimately be involved. He may have wanted to spare Ahimelech any involvement in the misery of his situation; he may have thought he was doing the priest a favor, allowing him to be able to tell the king that he was honestly unaware that David was fleeing from him. However, David may have deliberately kept the priest uninformed, afraid that if he knew the situation fully he would refuse to help. In either case, David made a decision that was really Ahimelech's burden. David was a faithful, respected leader in Saul's government, an individual apt to be selected for a secret mission. Ahimelech had little reason to doubt what he told him, though he was fearful. Little did he know that he would soon die because of his involvement with David.

Like David, when we are under pressure we may claim that our situation justifies a new rule of conduct. We, too, may play God for others by giving partial, distorted, exaggerated information or by withholding data that people need to make an informed choice. When people make decisions based on full knowledge, they are ready to bear the consequences. For example, consider committee work. It ranks low in some churches. But personal observation has revealed that when a maximum number of people make an informed, all-facts-on-the-table decision, they will work for its success, or they will bear the weight of its failure.

William Taylor[1] suggested a lesson from the events of 1 Samuel 21. He says that David expected his lie to Ahimelech to be carried off by the evening breeze that swept across Nob and be forgotten. But Doeg, a scheming opportunist, saw Ahimelech help David. And when he informed Saul, the king murdered every priest, woman and child of Nob—he assumed they all were disloyal. David might well have been willing to forfeit his future riches and glory if only he could reverse his behavior and leave that lie untold. But, alas, the lie had gone forth; and having done so, it was no longer under his control. It would go on producing its diabolical fruits. David could repent and have the assurance of forgiveness, yet Nob would not be miraculously restored to existence and life.

"Believers may as well think of stopping an avalanche midway in its fall, and so save the villagers below; or stop a bullet halfway to its destructive destiny, as hope to arrest the consequences of an evil once it is done. If Sir John Hawkins, in the day he first went slave hunting on the coast of Africa, could have foreseen Gettysburg, he would likely have never gone. . . ."[2]

Some believe that sin doesn't matter because God will forgive anyway. That is a flippant and dangerous attitude (see Matt. 7:21). It is true that God forgives, but let the believer steadfastly desire to be holy. Although one may be judicially free from sin in the court of Heaven, God is not mocked; what we sow, we reap!

First Samuel 22:19–22 records the killing of all who lived at Nob. How horrible! But God was still in control. He is never taken by surprise. There are never any emergency meetings of the Trinity. The decrees of the true and living God that control human destiny were initiated before man was created. God's dealings with man take into account what appears to be chance occurrences (see 1 Kings 22:28, 34; Prov. 16:33; Job 36:22; Mark 14:30) as well as the sinful acts of men (see Gen. 50:20; Acts 3:18). Everything that has ever happened or ever will happen ultimately brings God glory. While we cannot comprehend how this can be, it is God's declaration to man.

Though we cannot excuse either David or Saul, we must recognize the unseen hand of God in the Nob massacre. David took the blame for the massacre, though the crime lay clearly at Saul's feet. But God was accomplishing His purposes through the murders. Years before, the Lord told Eli that He would judge his house by removing it from the priesthood. The slaughter at Nob largely accomplished this. Later, when Solomon removed Abiathar from the priesthood, the prophecy was completely fulfilled.

While God did not cause David to lie or make Saul react as he did, He used those deeds once they were done. God's employment of David's sins to fulfill prophecy was undoubtedly painful to his sensitive spirit.

When the Lord works His will through us, even if we have not sinned, we may feel pressure. Being used by God is not easy. Moses knew what it was to work under pressure. As he unleashed God's power on Pharaoh (the ten plagues), it was difficult for Moses to hold out. He likely had to call up all of his spiritual reserves to ward off the inclination to give in. The believer on the cutting edge of a spiritual frontier, feeling the intense heat of conflict, will turn to God for greater grace to continue the fight.

David repented of his lie and grew thereby. God fulfilled the prophecy He had given years before.

This is not one of the better chapters in David's life. He had gone to another country to escape Saul. Instead of things getting better as he had hoped, things got worse. Being chosen by God does not mean life will be easy.

End Notes

1. William M. Taylor, *David, King of Israel* (New York: Harper & Brothers, 1875), p. 108.
2. Ibid.

CHAPTER EIGHT

HOW TO 'FEEL' FORGIVEN

1 Samuel 21:10—22:2

A man was sitting in the woods with a shiny new double-bladed ax on his lap when a friend came by and asked him his plans. "I'm going to chop some wood as soon as I start to perspire," said the man.

The second man wanted to make sure he had heard correctly, so he said, "You say you are going to chop after you start to perspire?"

"That's right," replied the first man. This story illustrates the emphasis that is being placed on feeling in our culture today. Slogans such as "If it feels good, do it" are seen everywhere. Pleasure is a god that is pursued with reckless abandon.

Of all the things we want to feel, the one we desire most is the feeling of being forgiven when we know we have disobeyed the Lord. David told a lie that resulted in the annihilation of a priestly community. Then he fled to the Philistines, hoping for asylum because Saul was their mutual enemy.

David arrived in Gath, the hometown of Goliath, carrying both the sword and the mental attitude of its favorite son. But the once-popular tune that memorialized David's victory quickly labeled him *persona non grata*. He was placed in protective custody while his fate was debated. Realizing that he could easily fall victim to Philistine vengeance, David faked insanity, hoping to be released. In the superstition of that age, insanity indicated that gods were inhabiting a human body. Erratic behavior supposedly indicated the presence of a god. David convinced the Philistines that he was insane, and they didn't harm him. What an undignified moment in the life of a man anointed by the Spirit of God.[1] How humiliating to have to pretend madness by scribbling on the walls and letting saliva dribble over into his beard!

Behold how deeply into sin one who has lost faith in God can go. David's unbelief made him reckless. Disregarding both God and man, he ran headlong into sin that in other circumstances he would have never considered doing. David's sin destroyed the moment and tainted the future. When a believer gives his mind over to doubt and despair ("God 'came through' once, but can I count on Him again?" "I'm no good. I've always made a mess of things." "God helps and loves others, but He wouldn't bother with me. I'm not worth it, anyway."), he is ready for sinning on a grand scale. He rushes forward, blinded by his tears, his hands outstretched to hug a fire. When a believer strays and is disobedient, the best thing that can happen to him is failure and disgrace. The worst thing that can happen to him is what the world calls "success." If a Christian succeeds while away from God's will, he is apt to go farther from God than ever. But if he fails, he is more apt to return to his own best interests and God's.

Lessons and Observations

Notice how others were affected by his deed. The Biblical principle of Romans 14:7, "For none of us liveth unto himself, and no man dieth unto himself," is clearly illustrated here. David did what he thought best. It seemed logical and harmless, but all Israel paid the bill. David was Israel's protector. While he was sidelined because of "insanity," the Philistines resumed their raiding. There had been little or no plundering or marauding since Goliath had been killed. But with the giant-killer in their hands, the enemies of Israel were free to do as they pleased.

Consider the matter of learning and relearning spiritual lessons. Months ago, when David drew himself up to his full boyish height and fearlessly faced Goliath, who would have thought he would ever succumb to the sin of fear? David may have felt above the sin of fear. But frequently, godly people find once-conquered problems returning to haunt them. Sins that they felt were safely out of reach have arisen with a fresh surge of energy. We find that we are not above having to relearn spiritual lessons. Sinful attitudes of pride, resentment, lack of love and selfishness are deeply imbedded in our natures. The believer finds that these enemies are never far from taking charge; he dares not let down his guard. How should we respond to the discovery that we are so sinful we must learn and relearn our lessons? By mentally upgrading the value of the Savior's death for our sinfulness; by appreciating the "at-one-ment" He paid so dearly for us to have with God the Father; by casting ourselves afresh on His mercy; by being patient with others as they learn perhaps more slowly than we think they should.

Notice that one-to-one thinking is wrong. When David told Jonathan, "There is but a step between me and death" (1 Sam. 20:3), he was thinking, "Saul gets one throw with his javelin; I get one instant to avoid being killed." His vision had narrowed to the point that he thought only of two people. Human viewpoint had swept over him. He was not expecting God to act, forgetting that He had ever been involved. David failed to see that the Lord was at work behind the scenes. God is the third party to every speech, act and situation in a believer's life.

Observe that success can spoil the successful.

When a believer succeeds in his own strength, he may become preoccupied with himself and the victory. Few things will neutralize past victories more quickly than switching from the divine viewpoint (which makes victories possible) to a human viewpoint. How is the switch made? By enjoying the influence newly gained rather than rejoicing in the One Who gives the influence; by reveling in one's newly gotten power rather than worshiping the God of all power; by imagining oneself to be great instead of proclaiming that God is great; by dwelling on one's newly acquired importance instead of pondering God's all-importance.

The Puritans, for example, were very diligent. That diligence resulted in prosperity; prosperity brought comfort; comfort led to complacency; complacency hastened moral decline; and moral decline invited judgment and destruction. May God give us the grace to handle our successes properly so that we may avoid this cycle.

If we put ourselves into spiritual "neutral" after a remarkable accomplishment, we will experience defeat and embarrassment, like David. The life of the believer—how much he glorifies God and enjoys Him—depends in large measure on a stable mental orientation. We must view success from God's perspective. Stability is a blessed ability.

The Right Response. While David was acting insane, he was busy praying to his all-powerful God. In his debasing situation, brought on by his lack of faith, he turned to God. Fear and impatience were swept aside as he laid hold of the true and living God!

When the Philistines became convinced that "gods" were inhabiting David, they released him. He fled to an old sheep-herding haunt—the cave of Adullam. It was about nine miles east of Gath, halfway to Bethlehem.

In the days following his escape, David wrote two songs (Psalms 34 and 56) about the experience. These two psalms are not cheap moralizing or pleas-

ant platitudes from someone comfortably at ease in
Zion. They are the concentrate of molten drama, of
life and death. They express a childlike meekness
and a delight at turning to God anew. David speaks
as one who is weary of himself, as one who is glad
to have God take over the responsibility of his life
again. He exudes total confidence in what the Heavenly Father allows in his life and faith in ultimate
victory. Never again did David commit the sin of
fear on such a large scale. His return to Israel's cave
of Adullam was also a return to spiritual health.
Bethlehem's favorite son was God's man once again.

But How Does One 'Feel' Forgiven?

When believers are obedient, they have no reason to suspect that God will interrupt the pleasant
cycle of His leading and their following. They tend
to be confident that God is indeed overseeing circumstances and arranging situations in their lives to
accomplish His perfect will. Daily obedience produces tranquility of the soul and spirit.

But what if one sins and disrupts this cycle? Will
God put him back on the spiritual track? How soon?
How much, in terms of adverse circumstances, will
He charge his child for his sins?

What lay ahead for David? We left him in the
cave at Adullam. He just had a spiritual revival. He
had found a good place to hide; food was available;
scarce supplies had been a problem since his flight
to Nob; he was familiar with the land (he had led his
sheep over every square yard of it for years); the
place held precious, sacred memories for him; he
had been close to the Lord here; he had sympathetic
friends nearby.

David wrote of his rededication to God with a
childlike delight. However, it's one thing to write
rejoicingly of God's mercy based on confidence
drawn from past experience and to know that God
has judicially absolved you of guilt, but it's quite
another matter to "feel" forgiven, to "feel" restored
and to recognize again God's loving hand of favor

through daily events. In retrospect, we can see that God was again smiling upon David. But this restored favor may have been most difficult for him to be aware of since three negative things crashed in on him shortly after his arrival at Adullam: the news of the Nob massacre, the bad natures of the men who came to join his forces and renewed family tensions.

David received the very bad news of Saul's revenge on the priests when he was hoping that *any* news would be good. At a critical moment while he was desperately trying to sense God's love and renewed favor, to feel forgiven, David heard the tale of horror.

The Three Negatives. The apostle Paul wrote of salvation as being instantaneous. But James wrote about a saving faith that works and can be seen by people. James said that it may take some time for a person to demonstrate genuineness. When David repented, he received forgiveness, instantaneously, in the court of Heaven. But God has a second kind of forgiveness that flows through people and daily events to confirm to us that we are back in His good graces. People can bring a healing touch; they can be the agent of God's reassurance. It was for this "feeling" that David hungered. News of the Nob massacre produced the very opposite effect.

A second factor that clouded David's personal revival and hindered his feeling of forgiveness concerns his family. Informed of David's whereabouts and in light of the Nob massacre, Jesse felt he had no choice but to leave Bethlehem for fear of Saul. At any moment the king's wrath could be directed against his family. The logical thing to do was to join his son. Old family tensions arose as David's family joined him. None of them had asked for a fugitive existence in the rough wilderness hideout. Bethlehem had been comfortable. Jesse and his sons felt uneasy about joining a fighting band of unproved ability. It was all very risky—just the kind of situation to make people nervous and keep everyone "on edge."

A third factor that dimmed David's spirit concerned the men who joined his band. The text says they were motivated by three factors: distress, debt and discontent. Generally, people are in such a condition because of their own failures. Many of these men were the dregs of society. Could David rely on them? Could these men amount to much? As much as ten years later, David still had among his men some who were described as "wicked men and men of Belial [the devil]" (1 Sam. 30:22). The sanctified imagination can re-create the spirit and lifestyle of these men. This would have been discouraging indeed!

The Positives of His Situation. But God was smiling upon David, and as he looked for the positives he would "feel" forgiven. First, there were sympathetic people around him. That people—any people—came to him was encouraging. Instead of an angry Saul or the frightening Philistines, David was now surrounded by people who had at least one thing in common—distrust of Israel's king. He must have sensed that God was giving him a new start. Being around friends after a period of isolation or exile is refreshing. The mind is distracted from old mistakes. Positive opportunities flood the heart.

And God had not brought ordinary people as companions. While some were undesirable, others were of sterling quality and high caliber—men of skill. From those who sought refuge with him, David formulated a faithful nucleus that would remain with him for the next half century. This band, called "David's Six-hundred,"[2] never lost a battle.[3]

Of David's inner circle of thirty mighty men, Scripture does not say any joined David in his earliest days at Adullam. But very likely, God sent him some top-quality men immediately. On what basis can we conclude this? Because men of character are the first to object to injustice and forsake its habitat. Diligent and conscientious men are the first to be willing to pay the price of exile for their principles. Those with the greatest repulsion at Saul's actions, those with the keenest perception of God's program for Israel, those who were most in touch with the moods and attitudes sweeping across the nation, those most highly principled—they are those who would have come the soonest to David. Yes, clearly, some excellent men joined with him— a token of God's favor and restoration.

The Hebrew words[4] in verses 1–3 translated "distress," "debt" and "discontent" are either neutral of moral implication or passively imply no fault. While some of these men were scoundrels, others had been unjustly disinherited, exiled or exasperated by the paranoid Saul. That justice was highly valued in David's reign indicates its absence during Saul's. False accusations such as 24:9 no doubt alienated many good men. There were legitimate reasons for an exodus of men who joined David.

David knew by his standing with the people that God was smiling upon him. The king's foolish and unjustified actions were undermining public confidence in him. While his reputation was eroding, David was gaining credibility.

Political figures try to be suave, composed and self-controlled. Only when pressured do they drop their polite approach and speak their views in everyday language. In 22:7 that is exactly what Saul does. Saul accuses David of bribing his men because he knows he would do so. As a thief thinks all others are thieves, and as a liar thinks everyone else is a liar, so Saul accused David of a practice he had used to some advantage himself! The king had apparently redistributed wealth to create favorites for himself. This also drove men to David.

Another clue to encourage David regarding his full restoration to the Lord concerned the Nob massacre. It is unlikely that the people blamed it on David as much as they did on Saul. They had come to regard Saul as an accident looking for a place to happen. Any blame that originally hovered over David was shifted to Saul as his unreasonable actions continued. The public response gradually built in intensity, though concealed for fear of retaliation.

Conclusion on 'Feeling' Forgiven

The biggest issue about forgiveness is not positive circumstances or how the believer feels about it, but what God says about the subject in His Book. There is a point at which the Christian must choose to believe God about forgiveness. It is nice if there are pleasant things that confirm God's favorable attitude, but our feelings are not the major factor in being restored to God. First John 1:9 must be known and believed, or there will be no lasting "feeling" of forgiveness. "If we confess our sins, he is faithful and just to forgive us our sins, and to cleanse us from all unrighteousness." To whom is God being faithful and just? To the believer? No! When God forgives a repentant believer, He is being faithful to what He is as our Heavenly Father. Forgiveness is part of His nature. That is what He is like. He is being just with Himself, for Christ died for the sinner's sin.

Sometimes believers think, "I can understand how God loves us when we obey Him, but does our Father remain gracious, merciful, loving and forgiving when I sin repeatedly?" If a Christian sins, repents and plans for victory, then stumbles into sin again unwillingly, he may be certain of God's grace toward him. God's nature does not change—His love, mercy and grace remain constant. In fact, it's only man's weakness and wickedness that calls forth God's graciousness and mercy. "Mercy" can operate only in times of human failure.

Forgiveness comes into play only when we have done something to need it. If there is no failure, there is no need for God's gracious forgiveness.

Our Father has chosen an unusual way to conquer us. He overwhelms us by forgiving us in situations where we do not deserve His grace. The Savior continues to stand beckoning us with nail-pierced, outstretched hands to turn to Him. In this way, He crushed the willful spirits of His own children.

91

The believer must, therefore, repent of all known sin, put Romans 13:14 into practice and believe that he has been forgiven. One must resist Satan by refusing to feel guilty once the sin is confessed and steps have been taken to learn new habits. One must believe he is forgiven and live in that confidence. When guilty thoughts arise—and they will come— a person must reject them, cease "yielding their members unto Satan" for his destructive working and refuse to allow such thoughts to lodge in the mind. The "feeling" of being forgiven will follow the rejecting of Satan's fiery darts.

So what was David to do next? Nothing! God created the next scene—it remained for David but to recognize his Father's gracious treatment and live in light of His smile.

Like every other blessed possession of the Christian, feeling forgiven is entered into by faith. Faith will cash the check of God's promise of mercy!

David's experience is worth knowing—and reliving.

End Notes

1. The leader of a nationally known youth seminar credits David for his creativity. He says David so impressed the pagan king that they later became good friends. David is not to be admired, however, for the whole situation. He was ingenious in solving his problem, but he should not have been there.

2. The figure is given in 1 Samuel 22:2 and 25:13 as 400. As time passed, more and more men came to David, and the figure of 600 is given (27:2; 30:9).

3. This elite force never lost a battle, but they did suffer one strategic withdrawal as recorded in 2 Samuel 15:13–16.

4. "Distress": *matsaq*—to be besieged, to press, to assail; "to be in debt": *nasha*—to bite, to be a usurper; "bitter of soul": *mar nephesh*—exasperated.

CHAPTER NINE

GOD'S CARE AND DELIVERANCE

1 Samuel 22:3—23:29

T his text depicts the continued care of God for the man He was grooming to be the most godly, just and effective king Israel would have until Christ reigns in the Millennium. In this section, God's precise timing delivers David. May we become more convinced of God's care and grace so that we may be stable and consistent soldiers for our Lord.

First Samuel 22:3–5 relates that David sought a protective place for his parents, that he tried to remain in Moab to avoid Saul and that God sent the prophet Gad to David to instruct him to return to Judah. Note a few details about these three matters.

Family Protection. That David cared for the safety and well-being of his parents and family is commendable, especially in light of the constant danger that confronted him. Moab was selected as the place of asylum for good reasons. David's saintly grandmother was a Moabite. Ruth and Boaz may have lived long enough for David to know them personally.

So David journeyed to Moab and went before the king. His request contains the highly significant phrase, "till I know what God will do for me." Three things should be noted. (1) David recognized that God's program might call for him to be a fugitive for a long time. (2) He realized that God Himself would accomplish His own purposes, without David's might or cunning. (3) David had confidence in God's plan—and he accepted what the Lord was presently allowing in his life. Yes, David was still sure of God's favor.

David Told to Return. Some time after David and his family were settled in Moab, the Lord sent him back to Judah by means of the prophet Gad. First Samuel 22:5 is the first mention of Gad in the Bible; henceforth he is associated with David whenever he appears in the narrative. Gad was with David for sixty years and was one of his biographers.

David was pleased that God had bothered to send a messenger to him. Gad had to make a long journey to deliver the Lord's message. God had "footed the bill" to bring him a direction. How wonderful! But the message itself may have caused David to be less than enthusiastic because God told him to go back to Judah.

Three reasons can be given for God's directive. First, God was giving Saul more time to repent. Since the righteous young man was a constant reminder to Saul of his own wickedness, his return to Judah represented God's longsuffering toward Saul. That God kept reminding Saul through the presence of David is a tremendous display of His love toward the disobedient king. We must marvel at God's stewardship—he used David to rebuke Saul, and Saul to build up David. Second, some areas of self-will in David's life needed to be purged. They would surface only with time and pressure. Do we not all discover distressing things about ourselves as life moves along? Third, David needed to lay a basis for his future kingdom by protecting Judaean farmers and herdsmen. So David returned to Judah, hiding in the forest of Hareth.

A person came to David who was to be of great help over the next fifty years—Abiathar, the new high priest. When his father was killed in the Nob massacre, Abiathar fled to David, bringing the ephod that made direct communication with God possible. It came through "urim and thummim." The Hebrew words mean "lights and perfections." Probably the stones on the high priest's ephod glowed in response to "yes" and "no" questions addressed to God by the high priest.

Keilah: David's First Campaign

First Samuel 23 is the sequel to chapter 19. Both chapters end with God's bringing deliverance to David at the last instant. The apparent purpose of the Holy Spirit in recording the events of chapter 23 was to reemphasize man's need to trust God. Though both chapters end in victory, chapter 19 begins with David's being afraid—and thus out of God's will. So to show us that it is possible to conquer fear, the Holy Spirit records this twenty-third chapter—it begins and ends with victory.

David had led military expeditions on many previous occasions, but always as Saul's servant. Now, however, he launched out with his own untried troops. It was harvesttime, and news reached him of Philistine raids on the town of Keilah. David felt responsible to do what he could. He was not so engrossed with his own problems that he forgot those of his people.

Several factors must have entered his mind as he weighed the matter. These factors are an intriguing blend of the kind of opposites that make up a normal day for us. We see here the chocolate-vanilla swirl of "self" and "others," and the truth that "When I would do good, evil is present with me" (Rom. 7:21). David did genuinely want to help the besieged city of Keilah; however, he also needed food and supplies for his six hundred men. He may also have felt a need to make up for his pretended insanity before the Philistines, which may have enboldened them to resume the raids. Balanced against the "duty" factor was his hunger to experience the total spiritual restoration that a military victory would represent. If David won the battle, it would be clear that he was on excellent terms again with God. David also needed to prove his men in actual combat in a small-scale battle and against an enemy of his own people. Replenishing his food supplies came at the expense of calling attention to his whereabouts.

Wisely, David sought the will of God. This always sounds easy to do! It is the spiritual thing to do! But so prone are we to run our own lives that we must surely give David credit for seeking out God's guidance. The Lord's direction quelled the fears of David's men, who were afraid of being caught in a crossfire, and he quickly traveled the three miles northward to Keilah to engage the marauding Philistines. The enemy was roundly beaten, and David entered the city as its deliverer.

Bitterness Beaten. David had prayed for God's direction. The victory was won, and much cattle and spoil were safely secured by his men. As David entered the city to the praise and thanks of the people, he must have wondered, "Is this the way I am to be placed on the throne—city after city coming over to me?"

David had greatly helped the people of Keilah. He had looked to God, and the victory came. He had been dependent on the Holy Spirit. But dependence upon the Holy Spirit does not mean you cannot do what you can for yourself. For example, David had to be constantly thinking about the wiles of Saul. As he entered the city, he had to look immediately for a way to escape in an emergency. He had to think, "What shall I do right now if five of Saul's men rush me from behind?" His mind had become as active and calculating as a computer, always figuring the odds on how soon informers would share with Saul his whereabouts. He would think, "Can I get the job done and retreat again to the wilderness before Saul arrives? I have raided that direction four times now in the last two months; will Saul be expecting me there? How long will our present food supply last? How are the women and children? Will Saul try to capture some of the women and children and use them for bargaining purposes? I was seen a week ago going into that superb hideout. Is the man who saw me still loyal to me, or has Saul bought him? My men went down to the well at Engedi two days ago—did people loyal to Saul see them and follow them?" Thinking and figuring were ceaselessly going on in David's mind.

David knew that someone would soon tell Saul he was at Keilah. What would David's next move be? Could he count on the people of Keilah to support him? How much time would he have? How could he find out if the people were sufficiently grateful to him to defend him against Saul?

When Saul heard the news of David's being in Keilah, he wrongly concluded that God had given his enemy over to him. Behold how warped and twisted one's conclusions can be! What strange interpretations one can place on circumstances when one is not right with God!

Again David turned to God in prayer! He called for Abiathar, the high priest of Israel, and made inquiry to the Lord through him. He learned that King Saul was coming to Keilah and that the townspeople planned to turn him over to the king. What embittering news. But David's response shows that he was still operating on "grace orientation" rather than "human viewpoint"—he was still looking at life from God's perspective, knowing that the Lord could place him on the throne at any time. He did not demand his rights! Even though the people of Keilah owed him their well-being, their material possessions and probably even their lives, David neither claimed his reward nor sought to collect any of their debt to him. And he was too gracious to place the Keilahites in a position of having to choose between himself and Saul.

Glad to have his food supply replenished, David fled to the wild, uncultivated land lying between the mountains of Judah and the Dead Sea—an area honeycombed with caves.

Jonathan Comes to David

The events of the next ten verses (23:14–23) could easily have taken a year to transpire. We conclude this on the following basis: (1) the implication of verse 14 is that Saul sought David hard and long and unsuccessfully; (2) a time lapse would be required for David to acquire the reputation with Saul as being one who ". . . dealeth very subtilly" (v. 22); (3) different hiding places are referred to in verses 14 and 15; and (4) Saul's unwillingness to immediately pursue the Ziphite tip-off (vv. 19–23) shows that he had made many fruitless trips to catch David, and therefore he was hesitant to charge out after him on meager information. The more often he went out after David, the more obvious was his floundering.

The rivalry between Saul and David was quietly dividing the tribe of Judah; it was a leading item of interest on people's tongues. Everyone knew what was going on! There was no way the king could make sorties every day for weeks and months (as verse 14 states) with three thousand men, without people knowing about it! Saul looked stupid!

Stabbing in the dark! Uselessly Saul had followed one blind lead after another. How foolish he looked!

After some months of this deadly game of hide-and-seek, Jonathan came to see David in the wilderness of Ziph. Jonathan—beautiful-spirited Jonathan! His loyalty to David was a known fact, so it was no problem for him to find the fugitive. Each man found in the other the affection he had not been receiving from his own family. The meeting of the two was important, for in it (1) Jonathan openly restated his belief that David was to be king and that he was to be second in command; (2) David was assured that Jonathan was not making a bid for the crown in his absence; and (3) for the first time the hunted was able to look out through the eyes of the hunter.

The text says Jonathan "strengthened [David's] hand in God." How did he do so? What could Jonathan say to encourage David? I am convinced that Jonathan explained to David the human side of verse 14, ". . . but God delivered him not into his hand." Jonathan gave his embattled friend a full intelligence report! He told David how many times Saul had come back to the palace worn out and looking incompetent. David questioned him about how many hiding places Saul knew about. Which ones were still undetected by the crazed monarch? Who had come to the palace recently with information to sell or trade for royal favors? Who was still loyal to him? David may have questioned the crown prince: "What does the king expect me to do next? What happened a few weeks ago when . . . ?" I am sure David had a sanctified knee-slapping laugh over the frustrations of Saul to capture him! And Saul's hesitancy to charge after David based on the information from the Ziphites (a group within the tribe of Judah) was a testimony of how God had been working against Saul. This news David fully absorbed into his soul. And how it nourished him!

Truly, his hand was strengthened in the Lord. After they renewed their agreement, these good friends parted—never to see one another on earth again.

Deliverance at the Eleventh Hour

Greatly encouraged by Jonathan's visit and aware of the Ziphites' willingness to sell him out to Saul, David moved farther south to the wilderness of Maon.

David did not know that Saul had renewed his pursuit. The betraying Ziphites led Saul to Maon with deadly accuracy. When David saw them coming, he was on a conical rock citadel atop a hill.

Suddenly Saul had the rock nearly surrounded. David had the high ground but did not want to fight. Winning would have been difficult, since he was outnumbered 5 to 1. Doom seemed inevitable! David fled down one side of the mountain while Saul charged up the opposite side and sent men around both flanks to encircle his prey.

But David had a Deliverer of whom Saul had taken no thought. Just at the critical moment, the sequence of events God had set in motion hours before and had progressively maintained was injected into the situation. A messenger arrived, urging Saul to come immediately north to repel a Philistine invasion!

Consider what was involved in God's rescue of David in this manner. First, some Philistines had to decide that the time was right to raid Israel. While they came to this conclusion in their own minds, God was ruling and overruling to accomplish His will. Second, an Israelite runner had to be dispatched to get help from the king. Third, when the runner received news of the king's absence from the palace, the Lord had to have on hand someone who knew where Saul had gone. Fourth, the runner had to have additional directions when he arrived in the wilderness of Ziph to know to continue south to the Maon area. Fifth, and most critical of all, a narrow plus or minus factor was involved regarding the arrival time of the messenger. In just a few more minutes, David would have been dead. Yet if the messenger were too early, David would not have seen the power of God freshly displayed on his behalf. The Lord brought the news of the Philistine invasion at just the right moment. God controls all things; those who obey Him discover this significant truth.

While it is possible God had greater purposes for David than for us, He is still no less concerned for you than He was for him, and God has chosen every believer. By knowing the Biblical account of David's life, we can better know David's God and enter more completely into His chosen course.

CHAPTER TEN

THE PRESERVATION OF AUTHORITY
Part One

1 Samuel 24

C hapters 24 through 26 of 1 Samuel form a single unit. One major theme runs through all three chapters: the preservation of authority. Chapter 24 records David's first chance to kill Saul; chapter 25 records the temptation of David to kill a man who somewhat deserved his wrath; and chapter 26 records David's second opportunity to kill Saul. The most important lessons to be gleaned from this unit of Scripture concern the proper way to respond to human authority, how to change that authority without forfeiting God's blessing and how to preserve authority for the benefit of future generations.

The *Pax Romona* (Roman peace) was made possible by one central, all-powerful, absolute and impartial authority. When that absolute control broke down and the Roman peace died, the Western world was plunged into one thousand years of darkness.

Authority in America is being challenged! The Vietnam War and Watergate have left the nation heroless. We have been deeply disappointed in our national leaders. Satan has mounted a sustained attack to undermine authority wherever it is found. Parents, police, civic leaders and school officials are battling for control.

The Christian should regard authority as his friend (see Rom. 13:1–7). The concentration of power in the hand of a man allows civilization to survive. Someone must lead! But what can be done when that person in authority goes astray? Sons and daughters have had to deal with prodigal parents! Congregations have had to rebuke deacon boards! And deacon boards have had to deal with strong-willed and dictator-type pastors. Employees have had to confront their bosses. How does one handle delicate matters and retain God's blessing? How can authority be preserved while changing the person with the authority? These three chapters in 1 Samuel supply us with some practical answers to these questions. David handled his situation in such a way that authority was preserved for his future monarchy.

The Quality of Our Relationship with God

First Samuel 24—Saul's Life Spared. Chapters 23 and 24 of 1 Samuel are tied together by a location (Engedi) and an event (pursuing the Philistines). After defending his land, Saul returned to his insane goal of destroying the king-elect. He set out after David with three thousand men.

Surely David had lookouts posted, so Saul's presence in the Engedi area did not take him by surprise. As Saul approached, David weighed the situation: should he run or hide? He elected to hide. But his blood must have frozen in his veins when Saul's columns halted outside the very cave in which he was hiding. Saul walked into the darkness of the cave. Temporarily blinded by the dark, he had no idea that David and his men were there. David and his men were paralyzed with the realization that if Saul were to sense their presence and call his men, all would die. The seconds must have seemed like centuries, the minutes like millennia. Then someone whispered to David, "It's the Lord's will to kill him." Here was a clear case of justifiable homicide.

As long as Saul was unaware of David's presence, the young fugitive was in complete control. He held the scepter of life and death over Saul.

God normally uses the momentum of each victory to help us achieve victory in the next phase of refining. His stated goal for this process is that we be conformed to the image of His Son—so says Romans 8:29.

Just how does God make us like His Son? How does God draw forth those qualities (the fruit of the Spirit—Gal. 5:22,23) that even the Lord Jesus learned through suffering (Heb. 5:8)? The refining of one's faith—the maturity of one's life—*and the enjoyment of Christ by the believer is in direct proportion to the attractiveness of the alternatives that he rejects to obey the Lord.* David was faced with a choice. Consider how advantageous it would have been to David to dispose of Saul. The list of factors for doing so was longer and more attractive than the list for letting him escape.

Kill Saul: **Advantages**	**Spare Saul:** **Advantages**
1. David would become king.	1. He would avoid violating the Biblical prohibition against murder (Exod. 20:13).
2. He and his family could settle down in peace and safety.	
	2. Authority would be preserved for future generations.
3. Pressure from his wearymen, tired of exile and eager to enter into their inheritance, would cease.	
	3. He would win public approval and God's favor by not taking things into his own hands, and he would gain potentially unlimited respect and national affection for *later* as a result of self-control *now!*
4. Israel was suffering militarily and economically. David could solve these problems; thus he could view his coming to the throne as his patriotic duty. This factor, because of its apparent unselfishness, could have weighed heavily in his mind.	
5. The nation would welcome him as its hero and liberator.	

Kill Saul: Advantages

6. There would be immediate relief from persecution.

7. Saul had been trying to kill
   David for months. He would
   do so now if he could. So why
   shouldn't David kill him, now
   that he had the chance?

One simple act—for which he would be commended by most of his men—would place wealth,
power and fame within his reach. The case for
taking the king's life had two strong arguments:
sovereignty and Scripture. It was clear that God, by
His sovereign power to rule in the wills and minds
of people, had brought Saul to the place where
David could easily kill him. Saul felt a body urge at
just the right moment to incline him to walk into the
privacy of this cave—this particular cave. The
moment was ripe for David to put his fugitive life
behind him. With just one stroke of his sword, he
would be free! Second, an oral promise had been
made to David by God that He would deliver David's
enemies into his hand. His men now whispered a reminder of this to him.

Twentieth-century people want immediate
gratification. The result? Instant coffee, instant po-
tatoes, solid-state tuning for instant-on television
pictures and push-button phones with redial. This
"get what-I-want-when-I-want-it" impulse tempted
David. If he took Saul's life, all the above would be
his *now*. If not, only God knew when he would
become king.

Having controlled his men and his own ambi-
tion, David slipped toward the sleeping king with
knife poised. It was a golden opportunity—and
David made use of it. He did not kill Saul. He merely
cut off a portion of his coat so that he could prove
later that he had been near enough to Saul to kill
him.

David's Victories. The anointed fugitive won
three important victories by sparing Saul.

1. *Personality* vs. *Position*. Wisely, David separated mentally the *person* of Saul (how unjust, wrong, ungrateful and inconsistent he was) from the *position* Saul held by virtue of God's appointment. David undoubtedly had little regard left for Saul as a person; yet he did respect very highly the fact that God had placed him in the top position of the land. Bill Gothard points out how relevant this is. A teenager says in disgust, "Why should I listen to my parents? They tell me not to do certain things, but they go out and do the same things themselves." This young person is failing to distinguish the difference between personality and position. One must always separate the shortcomings of an individual's personality and actions from the position he holds.

2. *Self-Control Merits Future Rulership*. David's self-control in the cave surely won the undying respect and admiration of most of his men. The nucleus of the fighting force that was to stand with David through a half-century was present. They saw their leader make a decision based on principle rather than expediency, and they were aware of the alternatives. Saul's men, also, would soon know that David spared the king when he had no human reason to do so. David's godly response in sparing the life of Saul resulted in his having unlimited power over the nation later. Proverbs 16:32 describes the virtue David employed in sparing Saul: "He that is slow to anger is better than the mighty; and he that ruleth his spirit than he that taketh a city."

3. *Victory over Impatience*. In sparing Saul, David also won over his impatience. The waiting was made doubly galling by the madness of Saul, yet he could bear it because he knew he was innocent and honest. He would never let it be said that he came to the throne by assassinating his predecessor. The Lord had not indicated that it was His time for David to ascend the throne. The Lord's promises to David for victory over his enemies were general and likely in reference to traditional ones—such as the Philistines.

Saul Confronted

After David cut off a portion of Saul's coat, he slipped quietly away until Saul woke up and left the cave. As he waited, he was smitten by his conscience for rendering even this slight discourtesy to the king. Feeling self-conscious, David acknowledged to those near him that he had been wrong.

Eventually Saul awoke and left the cave. Allowing a sufficient no-man's-land to develop between them by pausing a few moments, David took the courageous and humble action of following Saul out of the cave. Outside stood three thousand of Saul's most loyal men. They had obediently waited for their king. When Saul emerged from the dark coolness of the cave, they stood erect. To their amazement, seconds later, the hunted one walked out of the same patch of darkness. Calling to Saul, the fugitive stooped, bowing his face to the ground. It is significant that no soldier moved to apprehend him.

In the exchange that followed between the two, these points were made by David: (1) You, Saul, have foolishly listened to the gossip at the court that I am trying to hurt you. (2) I have just spared your life, which proves that I have no ill design against you. (3) The part of your coat which I hold in my hand is visible proof, for if the things of which I have been accused were true, I would be holding your head, Saul, instead of your coat. (4) God delivered you into my control. (5) He will judge between us. (6) You think I am wicked because you are. (7) Compared to you, I am like a dead dog along the side of the road—a mere flea—and kings do not normally concern themselves with such.

Saul answered these points with the following: (1) I admit your righteousness. (2) You will be king someday. (3) Promise me that when you become king, you will not destroy my family.

Thus Saul was momentarily restrained from killing David.

Timeless Lessons from This Situation

Several admirable qualities are seen in David's behavior. First, leaders rise above their own comparatively small sins and continue to lead and to be used by God. David felt he had sinned in cutting off part of Saul's coat. (He was sensitive to sin, even though the world would regard his act as a mere trifle in comparison to the barbarities Saul was heaping upon him.) What did David do to clear his conscience? He faced it. Then he acknowledged to those who had seen him do it that he could have handled it better. But he did not go into a spiritual tailspin and say to himself, "I am so sinful; how could I ever correct anyone else? I am so wicked." No, David rose above his own indiscretion. And he went on to confront the king's much greater sin! He knew that Saul's sin was "eating him up." Through David, God confronted this poor wretched man; he was brought face to face with the love and patience of God, as it shone forth through the deeds of the hunted man. David rose above his own needs and reached out to Saul.

Sometimes parents are so aware of their sins that they feel hypocritical about correcting their children. But this attitude amounts to abdicating God-given responsibility. Or in a church discipline situation, some will say, "Who are we to judge? We are all sinners." While it is possible for parents and churches to be too harsh, it is also possible for them to shy away from doing what is right because of the unpleasantness involved. Leaders rise up, overcome their own sinfulness by handling it Biblically and lead on!

Second, authority was preserved. With perfect candor, utter transparency and genuine humility, David pried from this intense situation benefits for the nation of Israel. By not taking Saul's life, he was laying the foundation for his own long and prosperous reign. Authority was preserved as an institution of their culture. It remained a working part of the machinery of Israel, and it was still there when

David came to the throne in God's time. Later, when David was driven from Jerusalem by Absalom, Shimei shouted to him that this was happening because of his shameful treatment of the house of Saul (2 Sam. 16:7, 8). David knew this accusation was false. There is no softer pillow than a clear conscience, and David would later be glad he had spared Saul in the cave.

Third, bitterness was beaten. How easily David could have given himself over to a bitter spirit. He had slain Goliath when no one else would try. He had fought and won battle after battle from which Saul's administration received most of the benefit. He had always been faithful to the king— yet Saul was still trying to kill him! Not growing bitter was no small victory! Bitterness, basically, is a failure of faith—failure to believe that God can and will turn our deepest hurts into something glorifying to Him and good for us (Heb. 12:15).

Subdued and tamed, Saul returned north. Since David had no confidence in Saul's repentance, he went back into hiding. And with him went a vital win over Satan's program to destroy authority in the nation of Israel.

CHAPTER ELEVEN

THE PRESERVATION OF AUTHORITY
Part Two

1 Samuel 25

"S trap on your sword" shouted David. "We'll kill 'em all!" That's the pulse of 1 Samuel 25. Samuel's death is recorded at the opening of this chapter. The date is approximately 1015 B.C., five years before David became king. The passing of the venerable Samuel was a huge loss for Israel. Brought up at the tabernacle in Shiloh, called early in life to a heavy responsibility in God's service, this man had won the respect and affection of the nation. By redeeming the priestly office that had sunk into contempt by Hophni and Phinehas, administering evenhanded justice among the tribes, establishing the school of the prophets and living the truths he taught, Samuel ". . . was among them to the last as an uncrowned king, to whom, in all seasons of perplexity, they instinctively turned for counsel."[1]

With the exception of the first verse of 1 Samuel 25, the entire chapter records the second test in this 1 Samuel 24–26 thought-unit, which has been titled, "The Preservation of Authority." It is one thing to spare a king, whose position was given to him by God. But what about an ungrateful, selfish man who is so stupid that even his own wife freely admits it? If David can be enticed into taking Nabal's life, when the opportunity again presents itself to kill Saul—as it does in 1 Samuel 26—then he will have set a precedent and may slay the king! If David comes to the throne with the blood of his successor dripping from his hands, so may David's successor achieve the throne. And authority will have lost immeasurably by being merely might and force, rather than the authority that flows out of integrity and character. The caliber of Israelite government and civil peace for future generations was at stake in David's response to Nabal.

David's Request. In order to understand David's frame of mind, skip dinner. The problem of supplying six hundred men with food seems to have been the catalyst for the explosion in 1 Samuel 25. Men do strange things when deprived of adequate provisions. Since David's guerrilla band could not stay in one place long enough to harvest crops, raising food was an impossibility. What was the solution? Likely, an unwritten agreement was made between David and the resident farmers of southern Judaea—protection from marauding bands and Israelite enemies in exchange for supplies. The enemies of Israel in the area made David a welcome guardian.

Thus it was with some degree of confidence that David sent ten men to a farmer who had benefited from his protection: Nabal of Maon. David told them to greet this farmer graciously and state their request with courtesy. David waited to receive whatever Nabal saw fit to send. By sending ten men, David indicated how much he hoped for and felt was appropriate. One wonders, however, how long everything that ten men could carry would last six hundred men. Two days? Four days?

David's men sought Nabal out, greeted him appropriately and appealed to the custom of the day. The harvest season was a time of generosity. They asked Nabal to verify with his own men how protective David had been, and they requested some food—whatever Nabal cared to give.

Essence of the Insult. Life is a series of relationships and interactions with people. Therefore, our Bible study should focus on the interactions of Bible characters so that we can learn what God wants of us, what we are to avoid, whom to emulate. Conversations recorded by the Spirit of God should be the special object of our scrutiny.

Notice 1 Samuel 25:10 and 11. Nabal flatly refused to give David anything. His insulting remarks contained three separate lines of response:

1. Pretended ignorance of David: "Who is David?"

2. Discredit of David: "There be many servants nowadays who break away from their master."

3. Greed: "Shall I take my bread and my flesh... and give it unto men whom I know not whence they be?"

Thus, David's generous protection was being ignored by the one who had benefited most. His motives and circumstances were completely misinterpreted.

Each of these three responses of Nabal warrants examination. For Nabal to *pretend that he did not know David* would have been hard to bear for several reasons. First, it is one thing to suffer if people know you are suffering, if your integrity is known and people side with you because they know the injustice you are laboring under. It is another matter to suffer under the illusion that others know of your hardships, and then discover that people do not know about it. David overgeneralized on the basis of the single response of Nabal and concluded, "I am forgotten! People do not even know I am suffering! No one knows I have protected their livestock! I have worked hard for them for nothing!"

Second, this scene was not so far removed in time from the hour of David's national debut against Goliath so that people should forget their deliverer! "Has Nabal forgotten that God delivered the whole nation through me?" thought David. This rejection

111

cut deeply into his self-esteem. Nabal knew who David was! How selfish for him to pretend otherwise! Everything Nabal owned had been riding on the stone in David's sling some years before. The Philistines would have owned it all if it had not been for David's faith, courage and obedience to God. Yet he pretended as though he owed David nothing!

The second barb in Nabal's response was equally devastating to the weary fugitive: *he accused David of being rebellious.* Nabal implied that David was a rebel cruising around for a handout. He would not support such a person. By so accusing him, Nabal discredited David and evaded his responsibility toward God's future king. Having a master in those days involved two things: a home and authority. Little else on earth would have pleased David more than having a home, a single place where he could settle down in safety and peace. Yet here was this selfish man accusing him of not wanting the responsibility. And if there was one thing David could never be accused of, it was of being unsubmissive to authority. He had borne patiently with the oppressive authority of Saul. Nobly he had carried himself these many years though people spied on him and sold their secrets to Saul, though people took from him with no intention of reciprocating. And though abused by others, David remained right with God and unresentful. But this current insult was too much for him to take!

Third, Nabal had *hidden his greed under a pious show of loyal devotion to law and order.* His wealth had not endowed him with common sense or kindness. The man with full pockets and an empty cranium is, everywhere and in every age, a Nabal. The text says he was "great," but it was the meanest type of greatness—that of mere money.

David's Response. When the ten young men returned and reported to David what Nabal had said—infusing some of their own hurt pride in the report—he reacted instantly! Our hero does not shine here. So frequently in the past he had forfeited himself to God, but here he claimed his rights. Bent upon revenge, David strapped on his sword and stormed back the way his men had just come. The wall of self-restraint, built by the long habit of looking to God, crumbled in a moment of fury. Nursing his anger to full capacity, David and four hundred men set off to take by force what Nabal had refused to give willingly. F. B. Meyer captured in words David's thinking as he marched toward Carmel: "There is no reason for this man to treat me so! He has returned evil for good, and added reviling and reproach! It is intolerable; I must assert myself and let this neighborhood see that I am not going to be trifled with! I will bear from the king what I will suffer from no other living man."[2] David was going to destroy Nabal.

Abigail: As Wise as Nabal Was Stupid. At this point in the narrative, we are introduced to the wife of Nabal—Abigail. When the servants heard how uncouth Nabal had been to David's men, they went to speak to Mrs. Nabal. This is a clear indication that the stupidity of Nabal was common knowledge, an accepted fact. Since Nabal was by now off on a drinking binge to celebrate his harvest, Abigail rose to give David what he had requested from Nabal. Some Bible teachers say Abigail was wrong to take the initiative to solve this problem. But this argument ignores the judgment God soon brought upon Nabal.

Rapidly estimating how much food ten men could carry, Abigail sent it on donkeys in the direction David's men had departed. Then she followed the supply train.

As David and his men continued toward Nabal's estate, Abigail hastened in his direction. In the providence of God, she intercepted him and poured the cool water of earnestness, logic, warmth, personal charm and confession on his hot wrath.

As she made the following points, in abject humility Abigail called David back to his better self: (1) She asked that Nabal's sin be upon herself,

113

confessing that he had been wronged. This acknowledgment went a long way toward easing the tension. (2) She asked to be heard, and because she was still alive, she assumed her request was granted. (3) She repeated the admission that David had been sinned against by her husband and amplified Nabal's uncouthness. (4) She pleaded that she was unaware David's men had come to Nabal. (5) Then she lifted David's sight from the merely human level of reacting to a wrong by saying, "The Lord has restrained you from taking vengeance into your own hands." (6) She gave him the food. From the first instant the laden animals came into view, the men had counted on consuming the food they carried. Everyone knew Abigail was "for real." She had food! (7) Then Abigail requested David's forgiveness. (8) She said, in effect, "God will establish you as king over the nation. You will not want to have done this which would ruin your reputation when you reach that high position." For David to retaliate would be to come down to Nabal's level. Since the man is a fool, his words are beneath contempt. It would be much more in harmony with the high-mindedness of the poet-hero to take no notice of Nabal's rudeness, but rather to let him rail on. Who was Nabal, that David should get so unglued? (9) Abigail let David know she realized he was fighting the battles of the Lord. This reduced his anger and let him know that most knew of the injustice under which he was suffering. (10) She acknowledged the ongoing persecution, but added that, as God could not die, neither would he. (11) She made a veiled reference to David's victory with the sling. (12) Speaking in the prophetic perfect tense, she said, "You are glad now [that you are king] that you did not kill Nabal."

When the wise woman concluded her plea, David was completely defused. His arguments for vengeance had melted before her more careful reasoning. His hunger and that of his men would be satisfied by the food now in hand. Instead of claiming his own rights, they were freshly yielded to God.

114

David thanked the Lord for Abigail's wisdom and returned to his camp.

Lessons and Observations

First, we see that God keeps people from sin and its scars—a great evidence of His mercy.

Suppose a house is on fire. We are glad if firemen, through heroic efforts, can save the building from total destruction. But wouldn't it be better if there had been no fire?

A man is sick. He is rushed to the hospital. White-gowned experts speed him into an elaborately equipped room. He is operated on by specialists. We cheer as they report that, through investment of vast amounts of money and effort, these men have gained the knowledge that has spared the man's life. But wouldn't it have been much better if the gentleman had never become ill?

We should never plunge into sin just to experience being pulled out of it. It is a great mercy of God when He keeps us from sin.

Sin has a hardening effect! It becomes easier to sin the second time! One sin becomes a stepping-stone to a greater iniquity. A trace of habit remains—an inclination to do wrong; an attraction toward evil. Sin is irreversible. David was a different man after his great sin with Bath-sheba. Never can a person blot out his past, even though he has been forgiven of it.

It is dreadful to know that there will be some in Heaven who, prior to their conversion, were the agents of confirming others on the pathway to Hell. One may go back to the old crowd and spread the case of Christianity before them. But he may experience the agony of seeing logic, passion and tears flow past them without any effect. One may refute the arguments he previously used but be unable to make the hearers feel the force of the case.

To summarize, God kept David from taking vengeance upon Nabal. Had his rage gone unchecked, he would have regretted it. But God—

being the merciful Father He is—did not allow him this foolishness. After all, He had plans for David that would be altered significantly, should he stoop to vengeance. Believers should yield their rights to God and then let Him return them as privileges as He sees fit.

Second, we learn that comparatively small things may suddenly overwhelm and defeat us, even though greater trials have been handled victoriously. David had been victorious in faith as he hid month after month from the fallen king. He had restrained himself and his men, again and again, from venting their feelings upon King Saul. He was braced for Saul—but then came Mr. Nabal's cutting insults. All of the spiritual braces built up by months of thinking and praying and trusting God about Saul were unmovable. The spiritual truth he had marshalled to handle Saul triumphantly was so firmly in place, he could not apply it to Nabal's insults. He was ready to take vengeance upon the fool. So he gave in to the most unhallowed rage! Little things may provoke us to anger because they are deemed too small to take to God, and we attempt to handle them in our own strength. More than once a believer has carried, with nobility of soul, the ache of being cheated out of a large sum, but then reacted vitriolically to being cheated of a paltry amount.

Conclusion

While Nabal was wrong in pretending not to know David, we can understand his fear. Everyone knew that the whole priestly community at Nob had been annihilated for aiding David. And David must have realized later, as he reflected on Nabal's denial, that part of his refusal had been that David had "played God" for Ahimelech. But David was desperate for food and exhausted from being chased. Maybe Satan was pressing his attack. God was very displeased with Nabal and showed it just ten days later by sending a fatal heart attack upon him. Though David was discredited by Saul's administration and though he was unestablished, he was God's choice to be the next king. God did not want him to starve—and, besides, he had earned what he asked for! He was not an unprincipled marauder. God had invested a great deal in grooming this man for the throne. Nabal should have been courageous and stood with David.

The indifference of some believers makes it hard for others to stand for God. Many are nonparticipants who act as if they have no investment in what happens! How foolish to fail to stand with those who are battling for godliness and holiness. In Nabal's case, it was downright fatal!

Two significant matters remain in 1 Samuel 25 that invite comment: David's interpretation of Nabal's death and his marriage to Abigail.

The Jewish mind had a pat formula for interpreting calamity—"God is punishing you because you have sinned." Thus Job's would-be comforters urged him to confess his sin so God would ease up on him.

Accordingly, when Nabal died ten days after Abigail had met with David, his diagnosis was, "... the LORD has returned the wickedness of Nabal upon his own head." To so conclude was a matter of human assumption, not a statement of holy writ. There are Scriptural illustrations of disaster not being the result of one's own sin, such as Job, Naomi and Hannah.

A particularly instructive passage about this is Luke 13:1–5. In this passage and in Matthew 7:1 and 2, our Lord speaks about the human tendency to equate personal difficulty with sin: "He is having a tough time because he is so sinful." While that may be true, it may also not be true, and it is not our business to judge.

When troubles or disasters come, a person should search his heart: "Father, are You allowing me this problem in order to pressure me to stop sinning?"

And what should the attitude of others be about this person? Luke 13 and Matthew 7 teach that the reaction should be one of contrition, brokenness, humility, repentance (as needed) and love. If believers can "weep with those that weep"—even if they have hurt us—and win their trust and friendship, we may gain the privilege of later influencing them for Christ.

From our vantage point, with the whole Bible in front of us, we can safely conclude that God was, indeed, most displeased with Nabal and dealt with him accordingly. And we read the inspired record of similar cases of God's punishment upon evil people—the plague that killed twenty-four thousand (Num. 25:1–11), the drought and famine of Elijah's day (1 Kings 17) and the death of Herod Agrippa (Acts 12:23). But for David to conclude that God was judging Nabal was inappropriate. Certainly, to speak about it would not endear him to Nabal's relatives and friends, though it is humanly understandable.

Shortly after the death of Nabal, David sought and obtained the hand of Abigail in marriage. He must have been most impressed with her the one time they met. She was a beautiful woman. Some time thereafter, Ahinoam of Jezreel also became David's wife. Since the Bible indicates that God the Father has claimed Israel as His Bride, and that God the Son has taken the Church as His Bride, it is clear that one mate is God's ideal. Having one mate preserves on earth the picture of the reality of Heaven: the Father has one bride; the Son has one bride.

American culture today looks askance at having two wives at one time but thinks little of multiple divorces and remarriages. So we dare not look down our noses at David. David enjoyed a short-term gain—he became heir to Nabal's holdings, so the supply problem was solved for awhile. But the long-term benefits would not prove to be what was hoped for. Except for a brief reference to the fact that Abigail was the mother of David's second son, Chileah (2 Sam. 3:3), she disappears from the Biblical narrative as one turns the page to 1 Samuel 26.

End Notes

1. Taylor, *David, King of Israel*, p. 154.
2. Meyer, *David: Shepherd, Psalmist, King*, p. 105.

CHAPTER TWELVE

THE PRESERVATION OF AUTHORITY
Part Three

1 Samuel 26

S ally Morgan fought her parents at every turn! She battled against her own best interests to gain her independence. The first thing that came along with a pair of pants on it—she bought. He was a one-way trip to get out from under her parent's authority. Years later, when Sally's own children were becoming young adults, she wondered why they did not respect her and recognize her authority! She got what she had wanted years before—freedom from authority—but in the process she had shattered her own potential for being an authority. The Lord gave her her request, "but sent leanness into [her] soul" (Ps. 106:15).

The Sparing of the Camp. Chapter 26 concludes the three-chapter unit that deals with authority in Israel. The major point of 1 Samuel 24, 25 and 26 is that Satan tries to get David to come to the throne with a tarnished authority—one of might and muscle, not integrity. If the blood of his predecessor were dripping from his hands, his monarchy would be of low quality.

As David returned to his camp, he felt happy and also a bit sheepish about his march of vengeance. He was glad, indeed, to see his larder full, yet embarrassed at his momentary loss of self-control.

Once again the Ziphites, eager to curry Saul's favor, informed the king of David's whereabouts. The text gives his location as the same "hill of Hachilah in Jeshimon," where he had experienced the marvelous deliverance recorded in 1 Samuel 23.

Three thousand chosen men had moved into the area with Saul—likely the same men who had witnessed the cave incident. Again, the manhunt was on! David was declared "in season."

Informed of Saul's return, David led a night reconnaissance mission to survey his camp.

Abishai and Abner in Saul's Camp. David asked, "Who will go with me to Saul?" The man who responded was destined to continue with David for the next half-century. He was Abishai, one of the three sons of David's sister, Zeruiah. This daring mission surely welded their souls together in confidence and trust.

Having been on maneuvers with Saul, David knew exactly where to look for him among the tents. Treading his way through the sleeping camp, David reached the insensible Saul. Beside him was his cousin Abner, the captain of Saul's forces for some twenty-four years. Abner's name has appeared only once in the Biblical narrative prior to this, at David's national debut against Goliath.

Saul slept quietly, his forces deployed around him. Confident and secure, he expected to capture his prey soon. God's patience had made Saul conclude that he was right to hunt David. The king's spiritual blindness was deepening! Likely he interpreted God's inactivity as approval. As Jonah slept in the hold of the tossing ship, as Samson dozed in the lap of the deadly Delilah, as Sisera slept in the tent of Jael, so Saul was wrapped in slumber in the wooing hands of the patient God of the universe.

Again, David was faced with a choice: to kill or

not to kill Saul. How strangely things combined to make the wrong course of action appear right. Both the promise and the providence of God seemed to call for instant and complete vengeance!

The Cave-Sparing Contrasted to the Camp-Sparing. There are some significant differences between the time David spared Saul's life in the cave (1 Sam. 1:24) and this experience in his camp. First, there is a difference in *how* the confrontation was initiated. In the cave, Saul came to the place where David was hiding. The situation was thrust upon the fugitive—he did not ask for it, nor arrange it. The camp situation, however, was David's choice.

Second, David's innocence was now clearly known. Saul could have honestly thought David was really his enemy at the cave-sparing, but there could be no honest doubt in anyone's mind by now.

Third, consider the escape factor. David could have killed Saul; yet, sooner or later, the troops outside would have investigated and David would have been found out. At the very least, everyone would have learned that the fugitive had taken vengeance upon Saul. Sparing Saul's life at the camp was different, for all were under a heavy sleep sent from the Lord, and no one would have known who had killed Saul.

Fourth, the result would be different. In the previous case, if David had slain Saul, he might have been killed by the soldiers who waited outside the cave. If enough of Saul's soldiers favored him, he would have lived, but his reputation would have suffered. The foundation for a reign based upon justice, righteousness and integrity would have been reduced. But if the king's killer went undetected in the camp, the house of Saul would be considerably weakened. David would stand a good chance to become king, and Abner would be greatly embarrassed, since he was in a position to profit most from the king's death. He might even have been accused of killing the king himself!

Some unnamed men of David's fugitive band

had previously suggested that it was God's will for Saul to die. Likewise, once within the camp, Abishai so interpreted God's providential arrangement of the circumstances. He offered to slay Saul for David, perhaps thinking that though David would not kill Saul, he would let someone else do it. As they stood over the sleeping Saul, Abishai asked for just one swing. The King James text does not communicate as strong a feeling as Abishai had. Paraphrased, Abishai was saying, "Give me just one swing, and I will not need a second stroke." Abishai was capable of ending the king's life with one strong move of his powerful arm!

A Supreme Moment of Self-Control

All of David's reasons in favor of avenging himself still existed, and in even greater intensity, because of the additional suffering he had endured since the cave-sparing. Another element of almost irresistible dimensions had entered the picture: David had cast his pearls before a man who had shamefully treated him. Saul had abused his precious kindness and had turned on him in a repeated effort to gore him. To spare Saul again—wasn't that just sharpening the sword by which he might one day be slain?

Many reasons for him to kill his persecutor flooded his mind. David was a mighty man of valor; he was accepted in the hearts of the people; he knew God had rejected Saul and that he was God's designated successor. Yet the greatest of all inducements to slay Saul—the most magnetic and attractive of all the advantages—was opportunity. When unprincipled men are confronted with opportunity, they serve their own purposes. And the very existence of opportunity often nudges people into doing something they never intended to do. Opportunity! It makes up for any lack of logic and provides sufficient impetus for whatever is desired. Few have sufficient spiritual strength to resist. And of all opportunities, none are so strong and work so powerfully upon the will as those that seem to come from God. It will everlastingly be to David's credit that he did not let himself exceed the bounds of rigid integrity. No doubt, God arranged for Saul to be at David's mercy; but not for the purpose of taking Saul out of the scene of life. No, God used this situation to further refine David's self-control and trust in Himself. He also used it for Saul. The Lord's goal was that David be a healing agent for Saul's sin-sick soul. And the fugitive's self-restraint was to be the basis for his future reign in Israel. David was content to leave the controversy between himself and Saul to God. He would not rashly push the conflict to its conclusion.

It was a golden opportunity—and David made a golden use of it. He would not gain success through a wrong or questionable method. Nor would he use Saul's body as a stepping-stone to the throne. Though the right way may take longer, it is safer. And when one gets to the destination, he has the satisfaction of an approving conscience and a favoring God.

David's answer to Abishai's offer had considerable thought behind it. His refusal to allow Saul to be slain was based upon his conviction that God had placed this man on the throne. Twice, David called him "the Lord's anointed." Saul had an imbalanced personality, but his position came from God—and David respected it. As David thought about Saul's anointing, his own anointing must have been keenly held in mind through all his fugitive years.

Taking Saul's spear—the emblem of his sovereignty—and his water bag, David and Abishai slipped out of the slumbering camp. Positioning himself safely out of reach yet near enough to be heard, David woke the whole camp, shouting to Abner.

A Rebuke of Abner. David must have had something definite in mind about the man to whom he addressed his taunting remarks. At this point, we know four things about Abner: (1) He was Saul's cousin;[1] (2) he had been Saul's leading general for

125

approximately twenty-four years; (3) he was present when David slew Goliath; (4) he had not been sufficiently impressed with David to learn his family name.

Looking ahead in the books of Samuel brings forth other factors.

For seven years following the death of Saul, Abner would seek to pump life into a dying dynasty. At the end of this seven-year period, he was guilty of a sex sin against the puppet king. Abner had the most to lose in terms of prestige and position during the time David was winning battles for Saul. In 1 Samuel 24:9, David told Saul that someone was telling lies about him, poisoning Saul against him. In light of the threat David posed to Abner's generalship, wasn't he the prime suspect for the spread of such lies? And one other thing is kind of "fishy"—how did Abner survive the battle of Mount Gilboa that killed all the other ranking members of Saul's inner circle?

It is probable that God wanted everyone awake to hear the shouted exchange between David and Saul. Once Saul recognized David's voice, Abner dropped out of the conversation. Abner had been thoroughly humiliated by David in front of the whole camp. David rebuked him for failing to guard the king, but the real intent of David's remark was aimed at more serious and hidden matters.

Verses 18–20 contain David's contrite and transparent remonstrance both for and against Saul. Rarely do we see such a commendable demonstration of patient endurance, such a determined effort to overcome evil. The same innocence and faith in God that toppled Goliath broke through Saul's insanity and blindness. It wrung from him the penitent cry, "I have sinned." And Saul's soldiers—some of whom had undoubtedly served previously with David when he was in Saul's good graces—must have come to admire him as a man of tremendous character.

Saul's last words to David (vv. 21, 25) were a benediction, a vindication of David's character and

126

a prediction of his future glory.

Lessons and Observations on
1 Samuel 24–26

The most crucial lesson to glean from these pages of God's Word concerns (1) the proper way to respond to authority; (2) how to change that authority when the person abuses his power and becomes unfit to lead; (3) how to remove such an unfit ruler yet retain God's blessing; (4) how to preserve authority for the next generation of society.

God prepared David to lead Israel with virtually unlimited power by testing his response to Saul's abuse of authority. The preparation consisted of a threefold challenge to David's faith. That David respected God's placing of Saul on the throne so much that he would not take advantage of the opportunity to slay him in the cave was test number one. Test number two was whether or not David would tolerate Nabal, a greedy, selfish, brutish man. In this second situation, though weakened, David did not take vengeance upon Nabal. Test number three was his undetected presence at the side of the sleeping Saul. David passed all three tests with excellent spiritual marks. And the experiences caused him to think carefully about how he would employ his power as the future king of Israel. He vowed he would never be like Saul. The fiery trial refined David.

Once I was asked to oversee the voting process of another church. A pastor had been liked by some, not by others. He was voted in by a questionable means and the church erupted in the weeks following—the police were called in to settle a battle as to who was going to preach one Sunday morning. It was a mess!

Sally Morgan wondered why her adult-aged sons and daughters had little regard, appreciation or respect for her. Here are two examples of people who did not know how to wait on God to change things properly.

If David could come through those years of high tension, low resources, desperate flight and hardship with confidence in God, a cheerful spirit and a love that continued to forgive, he could make it through anything. You may be facing some awesome challenges—maybe the greatest you have ever faced. May God grant you the faith and self-control to preserve the potential of your future! May we never sacrifice the future on the altar of the immediate concern.

A second outstanding feature of these chapters is the grace and patience of God's reaching out to Saul through David. God was using Saul to prepare David for leadership. He was also confronting Saul with Himself through David. The Lord was longsuffering toward Saul. His mercy toward an undeserving man was great, indeed. Unfortunately, this flow of divine grace did not soften Saul at all. Because he was unwilling to yield to God's will, the righteousness of David must have been all the more galling.

After talking with Saul, David turned to go back to his hideaway and resume his fugitive life. He had no confidence in the king's repentance.

End Note

1. The probability is that Abner and Saul were first cousins, although the references in 1 Chronicles 8:33 and 9:39 would seem to indicate that Ner was Saul's grandfather, and that Abner was Saul's uncle (1 Sam. 14:49–51).

CHAPTER THIRTEEN

THE DARKNESS BEFORE THE DAWN

1 Samuel 27, 29, 30

What an unusual moment! Never before had David's character catapulted to such a high position of regard and admiration in the minds of those who witnessed his sparing of Saul. If these soldiers were the same men present when David spared Saul at the cave, as I suggest, it was *the second time* they had witnessed an amazing display of David's self discipline. He had superbly applied a truth that his son Solomon would later write: "He that is slow to anger is better than the mighty; and he that ruleth his spirit than he that taketh a city" (Prov. 16:32).

But the moment that faith wins a great victory is also often one of danger! Victory lifts one into a high place, and the wind blows much more fiercely up there than down below. It seems that the confrontation with Saul had called up all of David's spiritual reserves. This most commendable handling of Saul drained the last of David's spiritual, emotional and physical energies. When the "bill" of continued fugitive living came due, David's account was "overdrawn." His faith wavered, staggered lamely forward, stumbled and fell.

As after Jericho, Joshua experienced an Ai; as after the fire fell on Mount Carmel, Elijah suffered a lapse of faith and ran; as after the boldness of the upper room, Peter denied the Lord; so after the great victory of sparing Saul's life in the camp, David buckled under the pressure of continued harassment.

David's life, like ours, was a paradox. He was always safe, yet he had to be ready to flee at a moment's notice. He was always secure in the Lord, yet hunted by his foe. He was anointed to be the king of Israel, yet no place in the land could provide him safety for long. A gossipy person speaking to the king could set in motion the wheels of a military machine that would stalk him relentlessly.

The believer today faces similar paradoxes. Paul wrote about what he and other Christians experience when he said that we are "... unknown, and yet well known; as dying, and, behold, we live; as chastened, and not killed; as sorrowful, yet alway rejoicing; as poor, yet making many rich; as having nothing, and yet possessing all things" (2 Cor. 6:9, 10). If David went to Keilah, they would deliver him to Saul, even though he had just saved them from the Philistines; if he fled to the woods of Ziph, the Ziphites would inform Saul. He could not go to the priests of God at Nob, for Saul had spies there also. Always on the run—such was the paradox of David's situation.

David's "darkness before the dawn" is recorded in 1 Samuel 27, 29 and 30, and it is the next recognizable unit in David's spiritual experience. Except for the first two verses, David's name does not appear in 1 Samuel 28. Most of that chapter records Saul's visit to the witch at Endor. First Samuel 27, 29 and 30 report a dark time in David's life—one we would prefer to forget. Accordingly, the Spirit of God gave it scant coverage in the Scriptures. David had been a spiritual giant in the verses of 1 Samuel 26, but he shrinks in chapters 27 and 29. Only twenty-five verses record this spiritual lapse. In contrast to such skimpy coverage, the Holy Spirit assigns thirty-one verses to detail David's recovery from the sticky situation recorded in 1 Samuel 30. As best we can tell, sixteen months transpire in these chapters.

First Samuel 27:1 records David's collapse: "And David said in his heart, I shall now perish one day by the hand of Saul: there is nothing better for me than that I should speedily escape into the land of the Philistines.... " How ironic that the slayer of Goliath would seek refuge in the land of his former enemies. He who once smote the Philistines now says he will trust himself to them. Strange indeed, that Israel's former champion is about to hire himself out to be the bodyguard of the Philistine king! We have no record that David prayed to God for the grace or strength to remain in Israel. When a believer ceases praying, he is open to sin on a grand scale.

But again we must not judge David too harshly. Had we been in his spot, we would have likely given up long before. In fact, we can justify his lapse of faith more easily than we can explain our own failures of faith. David's failure is more understandable when we remember that all his efforts to be as transparent as glass before Saul—the expensive death-to-self, and the intense sincerity involved in confronting Saul and sparing his life twice—had brought no results! Nothing had changed! Saul was still king; David was still a fugitive. It's one thing to give one's best and see the effort accomplish the desired goal. But it is an altogether different matter to spend yourself to the point of exhaustion and see no change. The apostle Paul would later write of similar exhaustion, saying he was "pressed out of measure, above strength, insomuch that we despaired even of life . . . we had the sentence of death in ourselves . . ." (2 Cor. 1:8, 9).

Because of the refining process of God and the conflict in the universe between God and Satan, the believer is in a titanic struggle—one in which there are no coffee breaks, no vacations, no time-outs. When the saint grows weary and gives in to discouragement, we can imagine the gleeful cheers in Hell.

And within each believer is a traitor—the old sinful nature—ready to sell holiness cheaply, to join the world system, to do anything to relieve the pressure. Our old natures will squirm, connive and dodge until pride no longer has to die, self is given credit, ego is satisfied, reward is in hand, and rationalizations explain the past. Beware, for fear can make the white-headed saint as big a fool as the new babe in Christ.

The psalms attributed to this period of David's life—10, 13, 22, 25, 64 and perhaps 40 and 69—reflect a somber spirit; a discouraged heart.

By leaving Israel, David was saying in effect, "I know God has kept me until now, but sooner or later Saul will not miss with his javelin. After all, it is stupid to attempt the impossible. I have waited eight years [author's educated guess] for God, and I can wait no longer. God expects me to use my head too, and I think He would have me leave." Would David be tempted to look at this situation in terms of luck? There is no such thing as "luck." What the world calls "luck," or "the breaks," what they think comes from blind fate, we believers know is the providence of our Heavenly Father.

David never had the benefit of an Elijah-type miracle. Not one time did God employ spectacular, non-natural means to aid David. But *always* there was the guidance of God's loving care for His servant. A miracle is God supernaturally invading the natural processes He established for life. In contrast to that is the providence of God, in which He works quietly through the wills of people, without anything spectacular to bring about His best for all concerned. Both are equally supernatural, and both reveal His love and care—though we prefer the miraculous to the slow and providential way of God's normal activity.

In making his decision to leave Israel, David must have been pressed by these facts: (1) Saul had learned of all David's hiding places by now. (2) The constant moving was hard on the men, but especially hard on the women and children. (3) Food was hard to find for such a large body of people—six hundred men, plus women and children.

So David went to the Philistine city of Gath to ask asylum of King Achish. He had been there before (1 Sam. 21:10–15) with an unfavorable result. That he was hunted by Saul was well known, so Achish assumed that David had been totally and permanently alienated from Israel. He received the fugitive.

The immediate results must have been beneficial to David and the hundreds of people with him. Food was available; they could settle down; and, best of all, Saul would not cross the borders of another country to hunt them down. But peace like that is bought at a high price. We should also remember that our sinful minds are adept at seeing enough positive features in any situation to convince ourselves that we are in God's will. That David henceforth was to live in lies, by the sword, and end up siding with Israel's enemies, shows that he had misjudged God's will in leaving Israel.

Living in Lies. To commend himself to the good will of his protector, King Achish of Gath, David faked loyalty to him. But soon his allegiance to Israel brought about conflict. So, to get out from under the "snooper-vision" of the Philistines, David claimed that he was not worthy to live in the royal city and requested a different residence. Ziklag being made available to him, he was able to continue fighting the traditional enemies of Israel—some of whom were allies of the Philistines. To cover his marauding, David had to lie. This double life was a heavy load mentally. When a person lies, he has to be very careful to remember what he told whom. It gets hard to keep the story straight. While David totally fooled Achish and held his confidence, it was not God's best for him to live in this manner. Our psyches are not strong enough to stand the pressure of living a lie. God has purposely made us weak, so that guilt brings us to repentance.

Living by the Sword. David lived in the city of Ziklag most of the time he was outside the nation of Israel. This city had been given to the tribe of Simeon 350 years before. God had told Moses that the people of this city and surrounding cities were under the sentence of extermination for their wickedness. By annihilating men, women and children as he raided, David was carrying out the orders of God that the Israelites had failed to accomplish at the time of the conquest.

David was active in the wilderness of Shur, forty-five miles west southwest of the Dead Sea. How distasteful this must have been! All this killing of people must have been most unpleasant, and David has been severely criticized for this by twentieth-century scholars. Years later, however, when David was forbidden by God to build the temple because he was a man of war and had shed much blood, this activity was not specifically condemned by God. The difference is comparable to saying, "Since he plays the flute, he is not likely to be a tackle for the Detroit Lions football team." The nature of the one precludes and eliminates the other—though neither is wrong nor sinful.

Living by the sword was done at a high price—constant fear of being detected. In leaving Israel and adopting this kind of life, David actually only exchanged one fear for another.

Siding with Israel's Enemies

King Achish assumed David had laid aside Israel's traditional hatred for the Philistines because of the rift with Saul. It is not uncommon for people to shift sides if it is convenient and expedient. Saul wanted all Israel to regard David as a traitor—for if public opinion formed against him, he would be forced to renounce his claim to the throne.

Suddenly the problem of being a secret agent for Israel in the land of the Philistines was compounded by a resumption of hostilities between the two nations. David was in a "pickle." Would he do in battle what he had twice refused to do in one-on-one situations? One step down the wrong road can bring one into unforeseen problems.

In 1 Samuel 28:2, David told Achish that he would finally find out firsthand what a good fighter he was. But the reader senses that David's answer can be taken either of two ways—it was couched in ambiguous and vague language to veil his real intentions. Very likely David was stalling for time because he did not know what to do. When the Philistines marched off to the battleground, David was with them as a prisoner of his own claims.

In spite of David's boast that he was loyal to Achish and would fight Israel (29:8), he was greatly relieved when the Philistine warlords refused to let him and his men fight alongside them in the battle lines. Although David put on a good act and pretended to be offended that his loyalty to Achish should be questioned, he was relieved that God had rescued him.

Occasionally, the believer gets into situations in life where only God can rescue him. The result is that his worship becomes more genuine, deep and meaningful after God does just that. God rescued David because His plans for him would have been significantly damaged had David alienated his future subjects by fighting against them. Likewise, God has plans for every believer. May we not damage the potential for His best in our lives by slipping into a double life as David did.

What was David thinking as he traveled the forty-eight miles back to Ziklag? Many factors must have ricocheted around in his mind. Foremost would be a sense of relief. He was greatly indebted to God for having been kept from the conflict between Israel and the Philistines. David would not have to risk the lives of his men after all! He could relax.

Second, he was encouraged by the men who had joined him in the last sixteen months. First Chronicles 12:20 tells us that men who had the ability to direct one thousand soldiers came to David as he returned to Ziklag. Others had joined him in the preceding months. His ranks were swelled by men who were defecting from Saul on the eve of the battle of Mount Gilboa.

Third, David wondered what his future might hold. What would happen to Saul? If he won the battle, he would have a fresh grip on the allegiance of the people and would be thus assured of continued years of rule. But if Saul lost the conflict or were killed, David could be on the verge of becoming king. Unknown to David, the witch at Endor (1 Sam. 28:19) had already told Saul of his impending death.

Arrival at Ziklag

Cresting the hill before their home, David's men expected to see their families again and to enjoy the comforts of home. They had not rushed the return trip from Aphek, taking it rather in two whole days, plus a portion of a third. Instead of loved ones looking out their windows for the expected warriors, they saw only skeletons of homes, trails of smoke spiraling skyward and charred ruins and were greeted with utter silence. In David's absence, the Amalekites had come in vengeance. Just at the moment when David's prospects seemed to be improving, things looked bad again! All was lost— irreparably! His double life had caught up with him.

This was, no doubt, one of the lowest moments of David's life. He was at rock bottom. It would be another twenty years before he would face as much adversity. His wives and the wives of his men were gone, dead or enslaved. Their homes were burned. While some of the men who had joined David were capable and of an excellent spirit, others were bitter misfits who had come out of pure expediency. Such men shared little in common with what motivated David. The mainspring of their lives was selfishness, and they had little interest or sympathy for the spiritual dimension of their leader's life. These unhappy men, angry at life itself, spoke of stoning David. Some had likely opposed going north to join

136

the Philistines in the first place; others resisted the idea of taking all six hundred men because such a move left none to protect their families and possessions. For various reasons, many of the men blamed David and were ready to kill him.

In spite of the pressure on him, David was a leader! Leading can be lonely work! Those who lead spiritually in a church often find themselves operating on the spiritual frontier. Leaders are the cutting edge of progress. A godly leader encounters the old sin natures of the people he is seeking to lead on to higher ground. He makes decisions that involve some risk. Will the people accept this? Will they trust his judgment? Leadership can be lonely. The leader follows a spiritual dream that others do not yet embrace; he walks on in solitude with God until his people see the potential for progress and are willing to invest their time, energy and love. Many times a pastor is resisted by the people who will benefit the most from the leadership he is exerting. Paul wrote that leader-servants ". . . must not strive; but be gentle unto all men, apt to teach, patient, in meekness instructing those that oppose themselves . . ." (2 Tim. 2:24, 25). David was a leader, and he did what all such soldiers do if they are to lead successfully—he turned to God instead of answering people.

What Did David Do? Did he blame others? When we are in difficulty, we often think of how others have failed us and created our problem. It is interesting to notice who Adam blamed for his own disobedience in eating the forbidden fruit: "The woman whom thou gavest to be with me, she gave me of the tree, and I did eat" (Gen. 3:12). Adam actually blamed God. And David could have said, "If only the Simeonites had done their job 350 years ago, there would not be any Amalekites here. And if Saul had obeyed God [1 Sam. 15:13], they would have been dead twice over, and I would not be in this mess." How easy it is to blame others.

To David's credit, he did not blame others. If there was ever an hour to call up his spiritual reserves, this was it. He proved the reality of his faith by turning to God. In a critical moment—one in which history turns upon the hinge of a single man's actions—David proved himself fit to reign long before he was crowned. One can tell what a person really believes by what he does under pressure. Do we turn to others first? Get on the phone? Call the psychologist? Run to ____? Reach out for another human being? While God may use these people, we are to be the most familiar and at ease with the Lord in solving our problems.

David sought the Lord. The text gives marked emphasis to his actions in contrast to those who spoke of stoning him. "But David encouraged himself in the Lord." Just what did this consist of? Only one thing is specifically stated, though others may be guessed at. The text states that David was not a priest himself, and he was wise enough not to intrude into the priestly office as some did.[1] Abiathar consulted the Lord for him.

A second thing we can imagine David doing is seeking a quiet place of seclusion where he could pray and seek God's direction and help.

In addition to prayer, this "encouraging himself in the Lord" likely included the remembering of other trying situations. He thought, "I have been at death's door before, and God stepped in to save me." He also remembered previous victories that ranked in difficulty with the one he now faced. Perhaps his experience with Goliath, which had faded and tarnished with age, was gotten down, dusted off, relived and compared with his current problem. And the tests which had set the stage for the Goliath contest—the lion and the bear incidents—David probably resurrected also, as a means of encouraging himself. The child of God must be ever mindful of past challenges, for we are so prone to feel forgotten by God. Spurgeon captured this thought when he wrote: "We write our benefits in dust and our injuries in marble, and it is equally true that we generally inscribe our afflictions upon brass, while the deliverances of God are written in water."[2]

God graciously answered David with far more information than he had requested (see Jer. 33:3; Ps. 91:15). Beyond directing David to pursue the Amalekites, God promised victory over them. He also assured David that everything taken would be recovered. After telling his men of God's promise and successfully suppressing their intention of stoning him, David charged off so fast that one-third of his six hundred men became weary and had to be left behind a short way down the trail. Since it was not likely that these veteran soldiers were weary from the forty-eight miles covered in the precious three days, it seems logical to conclude that the refreshed zeal of their leader wore them out. Two hundred remained behind at a brook.

God's Providence

Since God was directing David's situation, He caused a slave of the raiding Amalekites to become ill six days prior to this time. When three days passed and the slave did not get better, his owner abandoned him to die in a field. He languished there until, in God's providence, he was found by David's men. This "chance" illness proved to be the key to David's victory and the recovery of all the losses.

The Bible teaches much about occurrences like this in life. One of the greatest texts in all of God's Book regarding God's control of all circumstances is 1 Kings 22:28 and 34: "And Micaiah said, If thou [evil king Ahab] return at all in peace, [Jehovah] hath not spoken by me. . . . And a certain man drew a bow at a venture [meaning by chance, or at random, with no target in mind] and smote the king of Israel between the joints of [his armour]." This text tells us that God, unknown to the man who drew back his bow, guided his muscles as he lifted his bow and fired randomly into the opposing army so that Ahab was shot. As God's providence had controlled that arrow's flight to fulfill Micaiah's prophecy, we must also credit only the Lord for this Egyptian slave becoming sick, being left to die and being found by

David's men. Beware of attributing such gracious efforts on God's part to "luck" or "coincidence," for God will not be cheated of the glory due His name.

The slave was sufficiently broken down and angry at his master for having deserted him to die that he was willing to cooperate with David. He guided his captors to the feasting, celebrating Amalekites. Thinking themselves safe, they indulged themselves. But David engaged them in fierce combat at sunset. The carnage continued for twenty-four hours.

Since only four hundred Amalekites escaped— and the implication of the text is that this was only a small percentage of the total force—the number of enemy soldiers must have been large. If the four hundred who escaped represented 5 percent of the total Amalekite force, they had numbered eight thousand. If the four hundred represented 25 percent of the enemy army, they had numbered sixteen hundred.

Bear in mind that David had only four hundred men! This shows that God's power was operating mightily on David's behalf. David reestablished himself as the leader of his men—there was no more talk of stoning him. By his piety, decisive leadership, magnanimity of spirit and personal charisma, he was firmly reentrenched as *the* leader. Even the bitter misfits who had been ready to stone him were whipped into line and made to contribute to the victory.

Did David Recover All? Most biographies of David make a big point of this phrase: "David recovered all." He did recover everything, just as God had said he would. But authors who are eager to make the application to the reader place in this "all" a spiritual revival for David that is missing in the text. They tell us in glowing terms that David was totally restored to the Lord. Such a claim stretches the text to the point of breaking. I do not believe David is restored to the Lord—yet. While it is clear that he enjoyed an astounding victory, recall that Ahab also enjoyed a victory (1 Kings 20:13–28) when he was not right with God. The biographers are simplistic in their discussion of this phrase "David recovered all." The reference here is to the people and possessions stolen from them.

The Dawn. I have pointed out that the Holy Spirit recorded in greater detail David's fugitive years than his monarchy years. The Spirit of God invested fourteen chapters of the Bible to report the events of eleven years of fugitive living, while He used only thirty-eight chapters to record some forty years of his reign. At our current point in the text, the building years of this mighty man of God are nearly over.

Paul wrote to the Philippians, ". . . work out your salvation with fear and trembling." What has been so carefully worked *in* by the Spirit of God into David's life during his hidden, fugitive years remained only to be worked *out* during his monarchy years. The sterling quality is now ingrained in the man, only awaiting the circumstances necessary to call it forth. For example, David refused to let the wicked men with him keep those who had been weary and stayed back at the brook from sharing the spoil of the Amalekite victory. Thus David created an "all-for-one and one-for-all" spirit among his men. His viewpoint on such matters was so well received that it became a tradition in Israel that those who tarried "by the stuff" shared equally with those who went to battle. David was setting precedents and starting traditions in many areas.

Part of the spoil from the Amalekite victory went to the cities that had supported and sustained him.

Many factors dovetailed at David's moment in Israel's history: (1) The stored-up sinfulness of Saul—his cup of iniquity was full, and he was about to die. (2) The need of Israel for a responsible and able leader—it was time for God's people to fare better. (3) David's patience—David had had about as much as he could endure, and God saw that the moment

141

had come to end the rigorous period of spiritual training. God applied 1 Corinthians 10:13 three thousand years before it was written. (4) David's apprenticeship was over—he was prepared to be king. He had passed through the fire of the Great Refiner's purifying process. God's hour of appointment to kingship was now approaching.

End Notes

1. Saul had intruded into a priestly function and had been severely rebuked by Samuel (1 Sam. 13:9–14). Later, God tolerated nonpriestly Gentiles carrying the ark in violation of Mosaic law, but struck Uzza dead for touching the ark (1 Chron. 13:9, 10). Still later in Israel's history, King Uzziah assumed a priestly function and was judged by being struck leprous, whereupon he himself ran out of the inner areas of the Temple, as the priests urged him to do.

2. Spurgeon, *The Treasury of the Bible*, p. 660.

THE MONARCHY YEARS

CHAPTER FOURTEEN

HURRY UP AND WAIT

2 Samuel 1—4:12

O ne common experience of anyone who has served in the armed forces is being told to hurry up to get some place and then to wait there. It often is a way to test obedience.

David is in a similar situation as we finish 1 Samuel and enter 2 Samuel. First Samuel 31 records the deaths of Saul and Jonathan. With Saul gone, we expect to read that David immediately ascended the throne of a united Israel. But he is "all dressed up with no place to go." It will be another seven years before he is king of the united twelve tribes. Right now, he will have to be content with ruling two tribes—and content he is.

Introduction to 2 Samuel 1—5. The opening five chapters of 2 Samuel record the ascent of David to the throne—first of two tribes and then of a united Israel. Two of these chapters (1 and 4) deal with David's reaction to those who court his favor by killing his enemies. Two chapters (2 and 3) record Abner's attempt to gain power by propping up the teetering house of Saul, then defecting to David when his plan was on the verge of failure. The remaining chapter (2 Sam. 5) records David's coronation over the nation after appropriate negotiations, the expansion of his family and some military conquests.

David's Monarchy Years (*ca.* 1010–970 B.C.)

David became the standard for all future kings. Forty years from the date of our text, he would leave a strong, efficient government. He did not inherit such a government from Saul. In fact, he was handed a difficult set of circumstances when he took over. David had seen the loose government—the narrow, sectional approach of Saul—and he wanted no part of that. He carried into his government an elite six hundred (1 Sam. 27:2; 30:9) that never lost a battle. The worst they suffered was one strategic withdrawal.[1]

David would reorganize the priesthood, and it would flourish in his era. So many priests would serve that they would have to be organized into "courses." David's administrative genius affected priests one thousand years later when the Baptist was born. It was while "the course of Abia" was serving that Zechariah entered the temple and was informed that he and Elisabeth would have a son. The priesthood became respected under David, whereas a whole priestly community had been annihilated by Saul. David also upgraded the levitical choir to a level of high honor. In short, David was a great king, to be exceeded only by the King of Kings, the Lord Jesus Christ. David inherited a war-torn, feudal collection of people and left his son a strong, cultured, godly empire. This was the golden age of Israel. Things would never be better for the average Israelite citizen.

Second Samuel 1. At Mount Gilboa, about six days before the time of our text, the Israelite army slowly and stubbornly yielded to the Philistines, falling back from the plains of Jezreel to the comparative safety of Mount Gilboa. The battle lasted all day. Darkness must have fallen before the Philistines knew the extent of their victory and before they began the gruesome work of stripping the dead of their valuables. Sometime before morning, when such a work was to start, a wandering Amalekite came upon the fallen body of Saul and saw a choice opportunity. The Philistines would have enjoyed parading the crown of Saul through the streets as a war trophy (see David's eulogy, v. 20). But the Amalekite got it first and went to see David, trusting he would be favorably received since he carried proof of Saul's death.

Before the light of morning, news of the battle was spreading. Soon those Israelites who lived nearest the Philistines would be streaming eastward. People deserted their homes, carrying whatever they could. The Philistine soldiers filled the empty villages, on the heels of the retreating refugees. When they discovered Saul's body, they hung his headless trunk and Jonathan's body on the walls of Beth-shan, an Israelite city.

The Messenger Arrives. After returning victorious from pursuing the Amalekites (1 Sam. 30), David and his men rested for two days. Meanwhile, was David thinking of rebuilding Ziklag? More than likely, he was awaiting word of the battle up north. When the wandering Amalekite who had come upon Saul's body arrived, his appearance— torn clothes, dirt on his head—told David instantly the outcome of the battle. Israel had lost! The Amalekite claimed to have killed Saul at his own request since he was wounded and was sure to die. From his years at court, David could positively identify the crown and the bracelet to support the man's story. But he did not shout with glee, as the Amalekite had expected.

A Hard Choice. Life is made up of many difficult decisions. What should be David's reaction to this man? If he accepted this fellow—be it toleration, thanksgiving or reward—public opinion would say he was cheering Saul's death. His enemies would probably claim he had arranged it. Also, to accept this fellow would be to betray his hard-won reputation of highly regarding Saul's position as God's anointed. On the other hand, to reject him did not sound like the thing to do either. The act of killing was supposedly done out of mercy, shortening his agony and keeping him out of the hands of the Philistines. Besides, the crown and bracelet proved only that this man or someone else had been in Saul's presence either before or after his death— if he was really dead. They did not prove the man's story. What should David do?

Believers today are also faced with choices that challenge our closeness with God. The believer must be in touch with God to know His will! One never knows how soon he will need information that only the Holy Spirit can provide. Having our spiritual radar tuned can become invaluable at any moment, should a crisis arise.

Though scholarly opinion is divided as to whether the Amalekite told the truth, most hold that 1 Samuel 31 contains God's description of Saul's death, while 2 Samuel 1 gives one man's fabrication.[2] Whatever one's view, as Theodore Epp pointed out, this Amalekite took his story to the wrong man. David had him executed. What he had so carefully avoided doing (killing Saul) at great personal expense, he would not be associated with now. By having the fellow executed, he made it clear to all that he did not rejoice in the death of the king who had viewed him for so long as an enemy. In refusing to be identified with or rejoicing over the death of Saul, David was applying a truth that his yet unborn son Solomon would later write about (Prov. 24:17).

The Eulogy. Second Samuel 1:17–27 records David's eulogy for Saul and Jonathan. He graciously focused on the admirable qualities in Saul in his official statement. With an eye to the better days of his early years at Saul's court, David honored him, calling him a "righteous man." All that was personal was excluded. Pink said of the eulogy, "Forgetting the mad hatred and relentless persecution of his late enemy, thinking of sunnier days of earlier friendship, David cast over the mangled corpses of Saul and Jonathan the mantle of his noble eulogy." For Jonathan, David wrote a special stanza (vv. 25–27) in which he said that his love for him went beyond the love of a woman.[3] God used Jonathan's friendship to sustain David through the dark years of persecution. That two men, thirty years apart in age, could be such good friends shows that it was of the Lord. But noble, self-sacrificing, beautiful-spirited Jonathan was gone.

David Becomes King at Hebron. In 2 Samuel 2:1 we read of a second prayer that was answered by God within one week. This time David sought direction about going into some area of Judah (previously he had asked about pursuing the Amalekites). Again, God gave more information than David asked for. Yes, David should go to Hebron. How encouraging to be the recipient of such personal, positive direction! This indicates that God and David were on excellent terms.

Verse 3 speaks of the "villages of Hebron," so it is likely that David was led to several small towns, chief of which was Hebron. God's direction indicated the likelihood of success awaiting David at Hebron.

Hebron! Blessed Hebron! Abraham pitched his tent there, sacrificed at the oak of Mamre nearby, buried his wife and was later buried there himself. So were Isaac and Jacob. Sacred Hebron! It held rich memories for David's people. It was one of those towns to which David had sent spoil, in anticipation of the hour when he would become their leader.

It appears that David arrived at Hebron and waited for the people to take the initiative in making him their king. Verse 4 says, "and the men of Judah came, and there they anointed David king over the house of Judah." Although the time seemed right for

149

David to take over, he again did not push himself forward. Pink well said that circumstances should be the last—not the first—consideration in doing the will of God. Are we not wise to wait for God to give us what He has promised, rather than taking it by our own efforts? As the believer waits upon the Lord, he will become keen at distinguishing the voice of God from the many other voices clamoring for his attention. David seems to have reached that blessed contentedness Paul spoke of in 2 Corinthians 3:5: "Not that we are sufficient of ourselves to think any thing as of ourselves; but our sufficiency is of God."

With his two wives, his six hundred men, their wives and their families, David moved into Hebron and settled down. At last, the exile was over. And the "cherry on top" was that the people made him their king. David enjoyed a second anointing—the first having occurred about fourteen years earlier!

What a grand moment it must have been for David! He was anointed king of Judah! How rewarding for him to know that he had arrived at this point of his life at the direction of God, not through willful, self-designing aggressiveness! He was prepared to be ruler; it was time.

Verse 4 tells us that David was now told that the men of Jabesh-Gilead had rescued the bodies of Saul and Jonathan.[4] We can be certain that David had been fully informed about the military defeat the nation had recently suffered. Because he had been out of the country for two or more years, he had to catch up on many things.

The coronation would not have been an occasion to rush. The diplomatic negotiations, conferences and the official business called for proper ceremony and official protocol. The fugitive had been waiting a long time, and he would make the most of this strategic moment.

Since running a nation requires many people, David would have been eager to learn about able and respected leaders other than his own six hundred. He wanted to build diplomatic bridges into the hearts and lives of the people for whom he was now responsible. He had to meet new leaders, talk with the people and establish himself with those who did not know him.

David's response to the men who rescued Saul's body is a graphic example of bridge-building. These brave men had crossed the Jordan, traveled west to the city, removed the bodies, carried them to Jabesh-Gilead, burnt them there (practically the only reference in the Bible to cremation) and fasted seven days to honor their dead king. David commended these men. While this was a conciliatory gesture toward the ten northern tribes and the house of Saul, it was also an honest act, displaying personal attitude. Commenting that the Lord would reward the men of Jabesh-Gilead, David went on to say that he would "requite" them. Some question exists about whether he was saying he would pay them money for their patriotic deed or whether the public commendation itself was the intended compensation. Either way, this attitude on David's part opened the hearts of those who were prone to be loyal to the house of Saul. That David was observant and thankful appealed to the people. It was genuine; not merely politically expedient.

Judah Crowns David. Only Judah crowned David. Somehow, ever since the conquest (*ca.* 1390 B.C.), the twelve tribes had always been divided into two sides: Judah and Benjamin in the South, the others in the North. This division now clearly showed. Tribal jealousies and rivalries would split the nation. Though David and Solomon reigned over a united nation, the division would surface at the end of Solomon's reign and continue into Jesus' day, as seen in the mutual hatred of the Jews and the Samaritans.[5] Since David was from Bethlehem in Judah, he was viewed as a sectional hero, a favorite son. The cautious attitude of the northern tribes was understandable. Everyone, North and South, knew of David fourteen years ago when he slew Goliath. But that had been a long time ago. When he defected to the Philistines, he faded from the minds of people in the North. Furthermore, throughout decade after decade, if the South was in favor of something, the North was suspicious of it. True, David had been a great hero many years ago, but there were new problems to face today. Yesterday's savior did not necessarily solve today's problems. Judah, however, knew him and accepted him.

Many of the cities of Judah had been receiving war booty from David periodically. They were eager to have a leader of proved military skill. It was well-known that David had been responsible for many of the military victories credited to Saul's administration. When he appeared on their doorstep, therefore, they were ready and willing to anoint him king.

What was the Philistine reaction to David's anointing? David had recently been a vassal in the Philistine army. It had been only a month or two since he had marched north with them to face Saul in battle. They knew of Saul's hatred and assumed that David would be eager for their friendship. They expected to be allies with the new king of Judah and to dominate him for their purposes.

Chronology

The events recorded in 1 Samuel 28 through 2 Samuel 2:3 occurred in two months or less. Now contrast that extensive coverage given this short period of time with what follows. The Spirit of God invests only about the same amount of print[6] to record the events of the seven and one-half years reported in 2 Samuel 2:4 through 5:25. Where is one to place the war between the house of Saul and the house of David within this seven and one-half year period?

Second Samuel 5:5 establishes that David was king at Hebron for seven and one-half years. Within that period, however, another period of time is marked off with a definite starting point (the placing of Ish-bosheth on Saul's throne, 2:8, 9) and stopping point (his death, 4:8). This period is stated in 2 Samuel 2:10 to have been two years long. Where is this two-year period within the seven and one-half year period? David would have sent the "thank you" delegation to the men of Jabesh-Gilead immediately after they had done their good deed. Thus 2 Samuel 2:5 has to occur at the start of David's Hebron reign. I believe the conflict between Abner and Joab (2:12ff) and the hostility between Ish-bosheth and Abner must be placed at the end of this seven and one-half year period. They lead logically to the immediate crowning of David over the ten northern tribes, which occurs in 2 Samuel 5:5. The following reconstruction[7] suggests that five and one-half years be placed in the "white space" between verses 7 and 8 of 2 Samuel 2. Following the battle in which Saul was killed, Abner (Saul's general) withdrew to the eastern side of the Jordan River, to the fortified city of Mahanaim. The scattered troops regrouped there, and in the next five and one-half years, they slowly recaptured the western side of the Jordan, pushing the Philistines westward. When Abner's strength grew to the point that he was ready to challenge David, he proclaimed Ish-bosheth, son of Saul, as king, in an attempt to appear loyal to the royal house. Abner then challenged David's forces to combat (see 2 Sam. 2:14). The rest of the events flow in the order in which they are recorded.

David included in his commendation to the men of Jabesh-Gilead the fact that he had been crowned king of Judah and Benjamin. Writers have pondered David's motives in doing so. The speculation regarding his motives ranges from a critical view (David was hinting that the northern tribes should make him their king also) to a neutral view (David was sharing a fact without a hidden purpose) to a benevolent view (he was offering to extend his banner of protection over them). In any case, Abner reacted by placing Ish-bosheth on the throne and consolidating the bedraggled and scattered elements of the house of Saul.

What about Abner?

We have met Abner on two previous occasions. In 1 Samuel 17:55 he is called "the captain of the host," and in 26:14–16, David addressed Abner, singling him out for a strong reprimand while the whole three thousand-man force listened. One other fact about Abner is interesting. How did he manage to live through a battle that killed all the other ranking people of the house of Saul? Because of David's rebuke and this unanswered question, Abner is suspect.

By placing the favorite son of Saul on a throne at Mahanaim, Abner sought to prop up the teetering house of Saul. Ish-bosheth was not necessarily the youngest of Saul's sons, even though he was called "the fourth son." He suffered that kind of status because he was born to Saul by another wife. We meet this same man under the name "Esh-baal" in 1 Chronicles 8:33 and 9:39. Though Abner laid claim to the west of the Jordan, the people there enjoyed few, if any, benefits from his struggling rule. Abner could only slowly win back the area the Philistines had taken.

What was David's reaction to Ish-bosheth's being crowned? He did nothing, leaving the entire matter to God and His timing. David was content to use the seven and one-half years to establish himself firmly in the hearts and lives of those for whom he was now responsible. Likewise today, the individual Christian is responsible for the quality of his life, work and service for God. God will open greater doors of influence and recognition to the believer who has shown himself humble in the face of success; willing, in spite of inconvenience; steady in the face of pressure; discriminating in regard to priorities and diligent for God's glory when others seem indifferent. We are accountable for the depth of our ministry; God is responsible for the breadth of it. (See chapter 2 for an illustration of this principle.)

The War between Abner and Joab. In the conflict between David and Ish-bosheth, neither of them did any fighting because their generals represented them.

David had a sister named Zeruiah. She must have been a "spitfire." Just to be mentioned in Scripture was rare for a woman, yet she is mentioned several times. Normally, only the father's name is mentioned (David, the son of Jesse; Saul, the son of Kish). But Zeruiah is mentioned, and her husband is not. She had three "go-getter" type sons—and that adds to our impression of what this woman was like. I picture her as a dominant, choleric, fiery person. Joab, Abishai and Asahel were aggressive, rough-and-tough soldiers who were thirsty for the glory that could come from successful warfare.

Joab was to be with David for the full length of his reign, more than forty years. He was an able general, but ruthless. Looking closely at Joab, we see moments of spiritual perception (2 Sam. 10:12; 24:3) and greatness, but overall we have to conclude he was a professional soldier.

Conflict between Joab and Abner arose because of Abner. He came to Gibeon (apparently to make it "Gibeah of Saul" again) to engage David's men in battle. Abner suggested one-on-one combat as a way of settling the question of who was in charge. "Let the young men play before us," refers to the terrible practice of single combat. Joab was fully ready to accommodate him, yet we see Abner's strong personality. He was an opportunist. When his soldiers lost in the hand-to-hand fighting, the situation escalated and others became involved.

One encounter is recorded with special detail because of its bearing on events to follow. When it became clear that Abner's men were getting the worst of it and there was no chance for victory, he retreated. Asahel, the youngest of Zeruiah's trio of firebrands, was a swift runner and saw an opportunity for real glory. He chased Abner. Asahel was determined to have the glory of slaying the leader of the opposing force. Intoxicated with the prospect of instant fame, he had either no weapons/armor, or he had armaments clearly unequal with those of

Abner. Surely this is an example of foolish zeal. Abner had been a soldier for two decades, while Asahel was much less experienced.

As he fled, Abner shouted back twice to warn him. The first shouted exchange established Asahel's identity as Joab's brother. Asahel was advised to get weapons to make the contest somewhat fair, should the two come to blows in a one-on-one situation. Then he was warned that he should stop chasing him, and Abner said that if he slew the weaponless Asahel he could not "hold up his head" to Joab. When the zealous young man would do neither, Abner made short work of him. When those coming behind Asahel came to where he was wallowing in his own blood, they stopped short. Each side withdrew to its headquarters, but the basis for bitter revenge had been laid. Joab was determined to avenge his younger brother's death. And, in due time, he did.

The war between David's men and Ish-bosheth is called a "long war" (3:1). The two-year period reported in 2:10 is probably the length of the war. Though a state of war existed, there were few battles. The Spirit reports only one, and the results are given in the following description: ". . . but David waxed stronger and stronger and the house of Saul waxed weaker and weaker." In this one battle mentioned, Abner lost 360 men, while David lost only 20 men— a ratio of 18 to 1.

Abner's Falling out with Ish-bosheth. As the fortunes of Saul's house turned sour, tensions mounted at Mahanaim. Ish-bosheth charged Abner with improperly going in to one of his concubines. Abner acted as though he were falsely accused, though the progression of statements (3:6–8) makes it clear he was guilty. "Abner was making himself strong in the house of Saul" (NASB). It is logical that the next verse would give us an example of how Abner was doing this, and accordingly, we read that he went in to one of Saul's concubines. In oriental etiquette, this was a step toward usurping the throne itself. Ish-bosheth was resentful and told Abner so; whereupon Abner claimed he was falsely accused and threatened to defect to David. This silenced the timid king, because he knew his rule was subject to the good pleasure of Abner. Poor Ish-bosheth! He assumed that David was his enemy. Little did he know of David's great heart. Later David would search for a member of the house of Saul upon whom he could lavish his affection as a memorial to Jonathan. Ish-bosheth could have been that person.

David's Increasing Strength. During the seven years that David was king at Hebron, the size and morale of his forces was growing. A steady stream of men joined them from the ranks of those once loyal to Saul. They were fugitives from the confusion and misery into which the nation, both North and South, had been plunged. Even Benjamin— Saul's own tribe—sent some of its famous archers to David, a token of the waning influence of Ish-bosheth and Abner. The hardy men of Manasseh and Gad, "whose faces were like the faces of lions, and were swift as the roes upon the mountains" (1 Chron. 12:8) followed his standard as well. And from his own tribe of Judah, "day by day there came to David to help him, until it was a great host, like the host of God" (1 Chron. 12:22).

Abner's Defection to David

When Abner defected to David, there ceased to be any other side. In offering to use his influence to turn the northern tribes toward David, Abner was accepting the inevitable. Abner saw David's star rising. He could not prevent it. He figured that it was better to risk being a nobody in a winning administration than to be a "big shot" in a government that did not govern anything. A proverb was circulating among the people of the South and the North that David would be king over the whole nation. As his influence and strength grew, more and more people began to favor him. People wanted a winner; they wanted peace; they wanted freedom. David held out the promise of all three.

Always keen for grasping opportunity, Abner used the accusation of Ish-bosheth as an excuse for turning on him and throwing his weight behind David. He would salvage his wounded pride at being rebuffed by this puppet king! He would make him pay!

Thus it came about, in the providence of God, that the old sinful nature of Abner became the agent whereby David became king over a united nation. David did not take the initiative in becoming king over the ten northern tribes. They came to him, courted him and crowned him. Whatever ticklish negotiations with the northern tribes were needed, they were carried out by Abner, not David. Thus, through circumstances outside his control or sphere of influence, David was on the verge of being king over a united Israel.

Michal Returned. While David did not ask to be king over the ten northern tribes, once they sought him, he was in control of the negotiations. Since he was the one sought out, he had the upper hand in the talks. God waited until this would be the case so that David could gain important concessions (taxes, support for a central government, agreement on a standing army) essential to the success of his government. How different such negotiations might have gone had David been the pursuer!

David asked Abner to bring back his wife. Michal had been taken from him many years before and had married another. Pink suggested that from David's standpoint, this would be a good test of both Abner's sincerity and his ability to get things accomplished.

The return of his former wife was David's only condition to further negotiations. This demand is interesting because of several intriguing factors. (1) Michal had been married to another man—Phaltiel—for nearly a decade. (2) This man loved her enough to follow her weeping as far as the boundary between Ish-bosheth's area and David's territory, and he returned only when ordered to by Abner. (3) When Saul condoned Michal's marriage to another man ten years before, it was an insult to David—an intentional slap in the face. (4) Michal had become a pawn to politics—an important pawn to be sure—for a son born to David and Michal would fuse the house of Saul to the house of David and thereby make David more palatable to those loyal to the former king. (5) When Michal went to become the wife of David, she discovered that he had taken other wives—but she had not exactly been "lily white" either. (6) Writers are divided about whether they loved each other. Abner forced Ish-bosheth to cooperate in returning Michal; and this signaled the end of Ish-bosheth's reign.

David's Family

The text states that David's firstborn was not born until he became king at Hebron (3:2). David was not a father until he was thirty years of age. His family was to become a disaster. His firstborn son, Amnon, would bring shame upon the family. Chileab, a son by Abigail, is unheard from after the verse that notes his birth. The third son, Absalom, was born to the daughter of Talmai, king of Geshur. Since this was one of the groups David plundered and marauded during the time he lived at Ziklag (1 Sam. 27:8), poison was in that marriage before the wedding knot was tied. As far as character goes, Absalom has to rank right next to Judas Iscariot. David's marriage to this woman was just a bandage on the surface of a deep infection. The fourth son, Adonijah, would make a try for the throne and be killed for the attempt (see 1 Kings 1, 2). The fifth and sixth sons disappear from the Biblical record after the notations of their births. A second reference informs us of the enlargement of David's family (5:13–16), adding more unknown sons to the family tree.[8] None of the eleven sons born to David after he became king over a united Israel figure prominently in the story to follow. Since the six sons born during the Hebron monarchy were older, they had the advantage in political maneuvering. Hence, the eleven sons born at Jerusalem were largely forgotten. It is noted that daughters were born to David at Jerusalem. No indication is given that any were born at Hebron, but it is likely. It was a "man's world," and women were not often mentioned.

What are we to think of David's large family? God had given specific direction about the size of a king's family five hundred years before Israel had a king. Hidden in the archives of the nation, in Deuteronomy 17:15–20, was a prohibition against the king having many wives. David violated these directives. Both Biblical history and secular history provide many illustrations of the problems that arise from having more than one wife. The Lord Jesus Christ has only one wife—the Church. David had problems because of his many wives.

Abner's Death

In speaking for David to the ten northern tribes, Abner likely made much of his proved military skill. He promised deliverance from the Philistine threat once they were under David's protection. Abner appealed to them: "Ye sought for David in times past to be king over you: now then do it" (3:17b, 18a). When Abner came to Hebron, Joab was elsewhere.

When Joab returned, he told David that he had been fooled or used! Unknown to the king, Joab sent after Abner to bring him back. Joab then took him aside privately as though to speak of diplomatic concerns. Then he killed him with a knife. As David's leading general, Joab had the most to lose if Abner was added to the staff. He claimed he was simply avenging Asahel's death. But his argument was very weak for the following reasons: (1) Asahel was killed in battle, an activity one goes into knowing he may not survive. (2) Abner warned Asahel twice; but Joab had no way of knowing this, nor would he

160

have believed it. (3) Hebron was a city of refuge, and Abner should have been safe until he was tried by the elders. Joab was guilty of murder. No question about it!

What did David do about having a murderer as his chief-of-staff? Not much! The king's humanity is evident in how he handled this situation. We have come to expect perfection from David, so we are understandably disappointed here. True, it was a most difficult situation, but as Taylor suggested, for a ruler to be weak is to be wicked.

The following factors made this a thorny and difficult situation. First, Joab had been with David through the hard, spartan years of his fugitive days. He had proved his loyalty. Second, he was a valued general of obvious skill. Third, he had influence and a following. Fourth, public sentiment favored Joab, if only because Judah had been at war with Abner for more than seven years. A harsh judgment against Joab would not likely receive public support.

But Joab had killed a potential rival! In a planned, skilled fashion, he murdered a man! David was on the spot! Everyone was watching him. How would he treat this man who had served him faithfully but had acted criminally? David himself gives us the most significant fact to understand his lenient treatment of Joab: "I am this day weak, though anointed king; and these men the sons of Zeruiah be too hard for me" (2 Sam. 3:39).

Most of us can identify with David. There are moments when we, too, are weak, drained of our ability to do right. The best David could do was to totally disassociate himself from the foul deed. He knew he did not need the help of crime to gain the throne. Having taken a stand against foul play when it would have been very convenient to do otherwise (the sparing of Saul at the cave and the camp), he was not about to damage his integrity now that he was on the verge of total monarchy. To heal the wound, David proclaimed a period of national mourning and ordered Joab to take part. He publicly announced his intentions to fast as a token of his personal sense of loss.

David's attitude is commendable in light of the fact that at the time he spared Saul's life at the camp, he sternly rebuked Abner, believing that he had stirred up Saul against him. David's attitude is also commendable because he had been at war with Abner for seven and one-half years. With one eye to Abner's funeral and the other eye fixed on the reaction from the North, David was concerned about what appeared to be a glaring instance of low morality. It must have appeared that David's reign would be no better than Saul's.

But the public must have been satisfied about David's attitude and personal innocence, based upon a statement about Joab made during the mourning period. David said of Abner, ". . . as a man falleth before wicked men, so fellest thou." While calling Joab "a wicked man" did not endear him to his general, it set the record straight, convincing people that he did not condone Abner's death.

With Abner gone, would the northern tribes be suspicious of David and turn away? Would it be more "hurry up and wait"? No, they did not turn away. The house of Saul had no champion left, and the flag of Ish-bosheth folded, almost without notice.

At this point, two opportunists decided the time was ripe to assassinate Ish-bosheth. They killed him and took proof of it to David, expecting a reward. So, for the second time in a matter of days, David had to disassociate himself from a vicious killing so that he would not alienate the northern tribes and so that he would do right. He killed the two mavericks for their murder of Ish-bosheth. Because David wanted to establish a different kind of government—one of high morals and ethics—he had to be a leader of a "new breed." Some men in his violent age would find him hard to understand. Significantly, the Spirit of God gives the majority of two chapters (24 verses) to record David's negative reaction to news he should be expected to welcome.

God does not want the believer to rejoice at the

calamity of an enemy. We're not to benefit at the expense of others. We are to reject pride when our sinful natures whisper, "They cannot get along without me." Solomon wrote, "Rejoice not when thine enemy falleth, and let not thine heart be glad when he stumbleth; lest the LORD see it, and it displease him, and he turn away his wrath from him" (Prov. 24:17, 18).

Hurry Up and Wait

God had been grooming David for the throne for more than a decade. Many times, when God is going to do something significant, He waits a long time. For example, Abraham did not get a son until he was 100 years old; Sarah was called barren before she became a mother; and Noah worked on the ark for at least 100 years.

In many ways, David had been ready to be king for a long time. God arranged his spiritual growth, and he cooperated by obeying Him. Then came several years of being ready "in the wings." David was about to hear his cue—the waiting was over! We, also, can trust our Father that our waiting will end when He has accomplished what needs to be done for our next stage in serving Him. God has chosen us too!

End Notes

1. This occurred when Absalom revolted against his father (2 Sam. 15).

2. How does this conflicting report affect the doctrine of inspiration of the Scriptures? Inspiration does not require everything in the Bible be true, only that it be accurate. Satan is quoted in God's Word. Satan did not speak the truth, but since God wants us to know our enemy, He made sure that what Satan said was reported correctly.

3. Some have sinfully twisted this beautiful statement to make it support homosexuality. Since the Scriptures condemn homosexuality and show God's power to rid mankind of that vice (1 Cor. 6:9, 11),

David could not have been a homosexual and still enjoy the blessing of God as he did. Later sins would show David to have a normal, heterosexual preference. While guilt and shame stalk the homosexual, David gives no indication of ever being hounded by such feelings.

4. The victory that had launched Saul into public acceptance was the deliverance the Lord brought through him for Jabesh-Gilead some forty years earlier. It is highly commendable that these people would honor Saul, repaying the debt so long afterwards. This is genuine gratefulness!

5. This mutual contempt was a recognized thing in our Lord's day: "Can there any good thing come out of Nazareth?" (John 1:46).

6. First Samuel 28—2 Samuel 2:3 contains 110 verses, while 2 Samuel 2:4–5:25 contains 105 verses.

7. Taken from Taylor (1874), who acknowledges that he had first seen it in an earlier work by a scholar named Kitto (pp. 191, 192). This view is contrary to Maly's.

8. The Solomon mentioned is not the one who later becomes king.

CHAPTER FIFTEEN

KING AT LAST

2 Samuel 5

A s we approach 2 Samuel 5, we come to a new era in David's life. This chapter records David's coronation over a united Israel. How gratifying it must have been for the northern tribes to continue to seek him even after the embarrassing murders of Abner and Ish-bosheth! Representatives from the ten northern tribes, totaling 339,600 (1 Chron. 12:23–38), came to Hebron and asked David to become their king. The basis for their appeal is given in the following paraphrase: (1) "We are a part of your heritage; we are of the same ancestral stock." (2) "You were the real leader of Israel even when Saul was still alive." (3) "The Lord has said that you are to feed and lead His people." David was finally receiving the credit that was long overdue.

The text adds, ". . . and David made a league with them." Of what did this "league" consist? Having seen the mismanagement of Saul's government, David wanted the arrangements made clear prior to his acceptance. This agreement was essential if he were to have a successful government—taxes, a standing army and a central government. David needed guarantees of the people's submission to his style of government as well. Leon Wood suggested that the northern tribes may have had to make concessions to Judah so they would be willing to share their king. No price was too high to pay in exchange for deliverance from Philistine pillaging and tyranny.[1]

Vindicated!

A special moment had arrived for the long-time fugitive! One era was ending; another beginning. His integrity was being vindicated. His men had wanted to kill Saul in the cave and later in the camp, and he had refused to let them. Now his men saw their leader honored highly. His judgment on countless matters was seen to have been correct. Both friend and foe had to think more highly of him now than ever before. He is now king in his own right; he is no longer overshadowed by Saul. David has emerged into the sunshine of full national recognition without manipulation, maneuvering or scheming. He had come there by God's appointment. Seldom has a ruler climbed the stairs to the throne with a conscience as clear as David's. It was for this moment of harvest that David had sown precious seeds of self-control in his dealings with Saul. David must have also been extremely grateful that God had kept him from taking vengeance on Nabal. This was his hour! All the sacrifice—the years of hurry and worry, hustle and hassle—were now paying rich rewards. David could not know what we know—that the next thirteen and a half years—would be the finest of his life.

A Coronation Psalm. Psalm 101 is attributed to this moment in David's life. It is a song about being the right kind of leader—zealous for righteousness, purity and justice. The psalm expresses the responsibility of those God can use: those having a clean heart and life, open to God, aiming to operate government on a high moral and spiritual level and avoiding wicked counselors, slanderers and opportunists.

David likely had a particular revulsion for opportunists, like Doeg, who caused vast injustice, misery and hardship. Three phrases in this psalm indicate David's extreme displeasure toward wicked informers: "whoso privily slandereth his neighbour"; "he that worketh deceit"; and "he that telleth lies." Doeg brought David much trouble because of these practices. When he told Saul that the priests of Nob had helped David, Saul slaughtered all the priests and their families. Doeg sinfully used his observations to personal advantage. He wickedly ignored Saul's violent nature and was unconcerned about the use Saul might make of the information.

Psalm 101 goes beyond describing correct outward living, penetrating the thought-life and motive behind every action. For every believer—as well as for David—the thought-life is strategic in our spiritual warfare. The Bible teaches that "as a man thinketh in his heart, so is he" (Prov. 23:7), and that "out of the abundance of the heart, the mouth speaketh" (Matt. 12:34). What we give our minds over to is very important. If a believer is fantasizing about power, renown, sex or is full of self-pity, he is fueling his own spiritual defeat. Thoughts produce feelings. Many believers are controlled by emotions rather than faith and facts. "Feeling" plays too large a part in some Christians' lives, while obedience is downgraded. We feel "down," however, because we let our minds dwell on negative thoughts or criticism we have received. Since our minds and wills control how we feel, we must constantly challenge ourselves to hold in our minds the grace of God, His goodness to us and the positive aspects of our current situations.

The challenge of 2 Corinthians 10:5 is powerful ammunition for defeating the "blahs" of life. The verse says, "Casting down imaginations, and every high thing that exalteth itself against the knowledge of God, and bringing into captivity every thought to the obedience of Christ."

There are many ways we can cause our minds to dwell on the greatness and goodness of God. A jogger, for example, can repeat positive, godly phrases to himself, matching the rhythm of his running: "Man of God, man of God; man of prayer, man of prayer; obey the Lord, obey the Lord; trust in God, trust in God."

An expectant, upward look is essential for triumphant living. It is here that the believer needs the freedom only the Holy Spirit can give. Enough things go "wrong" in any day to give our minds ample material for self-pity, fear, selfishness, pride or jealousy. But the Spirit of God produces supernatural peace and grace as the believer yields his mind and will over to Him. David provided an excellent example for us with his personal job description (Ps. 101), as he challenged himself on the eve of his monarchy.

The Forty Years of Kingship

The monarchy of David has three clear periods: (1) the years of conquest, as reported in 2 Samuel 5–10; (2) the years of peaceful rule, but awesome family troubles, recorded in 2 Samuel 11–20; (3) the years of declining strength and the co-regency with Solomon, recorded in 2 Samuel 21 through 1 Kings 2:11.

The Years of Conquest, 2 Samuel 5—10. The early years of any organization or movement are special. As it reaches upward for its goal, the effort is characterized by a strong spirit of optimism and willingness to sacrifice. Accordingly, the first years of David's monarchy were characterized by zeal, transparency of spirit and earnest purpose that were unique even in David's pure life. He could not know that these were to be his best years. Everything he touched "turned to gold." Great anguish of heart was ahead, but right now—and for the next thirteen years—he would enjoy the best period of his life. His abilities were at full flex; his capacities rose to meet every challenge; his military brilliance brought maximum results. And the nation cheered him on.

Second Samuel 5 records the conquest of Jerusalem, Hiram's establishment of diplomatic relations with David and twin victories over the Philistines. Chapter 6 reports the arrival of the ark in Jerusalem. Chapter 7 informs us of David's desire to build God a house, God's counterpromise to David and his subsequent worship. Chapter 8 reports military action and concludes with a list of David's cabinet. Chapter 9 tells of David's gracious treatment of Saul's posterity in honoring Mephibosheth. And chapter 10 shows what happened when a well-meant gesture of sympathy was misunderstood and led to war. Chapters 5, 8 and 10 record military accomplishments, and 6, 7 and 9 deal with spiritual matters.

What God Sees as Important. Although these were David's best years, the Spirit of God does not give them much space in the Bible. In comparison to these six chapters, titled "The Years of Conquest," the next period of David's monarchy, the years of peaceful rule but grave family problems, is given almost twice as much space. The two periods of time are nearly equal, but the Scripture allotted for each is vastly different.

Hence, what is God saying to us? Again, the Holy Spirit did not record each victory David rolled up on the battlefield. Instead, summary statements are given on what took months to accomplish. For example, we read: ". . . And the LORD had given him rest round about from all his enemies . . ." and ". . . it came to pass, that David smote the Philistines, and subdued them . . ." (7:1; 8:1, respectively).

God is more interested in what He is doing *in us* than what we are doing *for him*. Our greatest messages for the good of others and God's glory come out of personal failures that are rebuilt into testimonies of His transforming power. While Satan tries to

169

use our defeats to bring us down to a suicide's grave,[2] God uses our weaknesses as a platform on which to demonstrate His power to encourage and heal. I believe the Spirit's purpose in recording these experiences of David is for us to see God's love flowing toward David when it is clear he did not deserve it. We, then, are made sure that God loves us even when we are unlovable. Armed with this wonderful truth, we are stirred to yield in obedience to Him, thereby priming the spiritual "pump" for richer experiences with God.

The contrast between the amount of Scripture given to the two periods (years of conquest *vs.* years of peaceful rule and grinding family problems) comes into sharper focus when we realize two facts: (1) Even within the six chapters about the years of conquest, only 47 of the 122 verses deal directly with war. (2) The years of peaceful rule and family problems—a unit of ten chapters—are given 319 verses. And almost all of them deal with David's sin with Bath-sheba and the repercussions, God's judgment, of that sin.

A Capital Is Selected

When one-third of a million people arrived in Hebron to ask David to become their king, he was very pleased. It was no small demonstration of their desire! Consider what it must have cost the people in terms of inconvenience, travel, lodging, meals and time away from home responsibilities. They very much wanted David as their leader. Some 120,000 people came from the east side of the Jordan River. People came from the northernmost tribes— Issachar, Zebulon and Naphtali—and that was impressive. But the most gratifying delegates, no doubt, were the twenty thousand men from the tribe of Ephraim. David's own tribe, Judah, had been Ephraim's rival for centuries. Their support indicated that the nation had indeed been won over to his banner. By waiting until the public was clamoring for him, David placed himself in a powerful position at the negotiation table. Because the tribes anticipated either long negotiations or an immediate favorable response from David, the 339,600 brought provisions. Agreement must have been reached quickly, and a three-day national feast followed.

Once the celebration was over, the king got about the business of leading. It is unknown whether David immediately sought to channel the energy and enthusiasm of his new subjects, or whether some time elapsed between his coronation and the taking of Jerusalem. But we can be certain that much thought had gone into selecting a site for the new capital. The location of a nation's capital is important since it needs to capture the affection of the masses and serve as the center for its visionaries.

David had observed closely the shortcomings of Saul's pro-Benjamite government. All of Saul's officers, capital and elite forces were of Benjamin. David knew that a government with a broad base was essential for success, so he avoided an exclusively Judaean government.

Hebron had been responsive to him during his fugitive years and was an attractive possibility. He had married into the line of the godly Caleb by taking Abigail to be his wife. But Hebron was a city of Judah and thus would not do.

The northern tribes would be more responsive if the nation's capital were moved out of Judah's territory. They would resent too close an association with the tribe or anything that smacked of Judaean pride. David would avoid giving the northern tribes ground for saying, "David just wants to absorb us into his own tribe." Neither did he want his capital in the geographic center of the nation, since that would be in the domain of one of the northern tribes. Such a location would alienate those who had crowned him seven years earlier when he was comparatively unknown and unappreciated.

Careful thinking marks a mature leader. Leadership has been defined as "seeing the consequences of actions further into the future than those you are attempting to lead." Thinking through your actions and anticipating people's reactions is a characteristic of any of God's chosen. David wisely decided on a city that belonged to no tribe, but which all tribes could have a part in acquiring. The city was near enough to Judah to favor her slightly, but new enough to capture the interest and involvement of the northern tribes.

The ideal location was the city of Jebus, located eight miles north of David's hometown of Bethlehem. He had, undoubtedly, walked its streets as a boy and was familiar with it. Up until this time, it had been nothing special. Though Joshua had taken it at the time of conquest (1390 B.C.), it soon slipped back into Canaanite hands. David renamed Jebus "Jerusalem" (meaning "city of peace"). The fortunes and fame of Jerusalem and David were henceforth linked together.

The Jews had long known that God would place His name somewhere, that He would be identified with some specific location in the Promised Land. But it was not until David became king that the Lord was willing to do so. The Israelites had been in the Promised Land for 380 years. Since the Jewish people occupied the land of Palestine only until A.D. 70, those 380 years represent almost one third of their total time in Palestine. Why had the Lord delayed claiming a spot?

It seems that God would have wanted any place identified with Himself to start on a high plane. The place must quickly win the world's acknowledgment, and it must be worthy of His person. It must be a place of maximum credibility so as to draw the most attention to the truth of Himself. It should have an aura of honor, awe and stability. When the right time and the right man came, God was willing to identify Himself with a specific city. That God waited so long shows His attitude toward David!

Mocked by the Jebusites. David would very much have wanted a strong victory to establish himself as king before taking on more risky projects.

172

But taking Jebus would not be easy.

As David's soldiers approached the massive city walls, they were mocked by enemy soldiers on the walls. The city was well fortified and seemed unconquerable. A double reference was intended in David's mocking of the Jebusites: to the gods and to the guards. David disdainfully referred to their gods as "blind and lame." The gods—idols—were placed atop the wall so they would appear to be viewing David's soldiers below. The Jebusites sneered in return, "You say our gods are blind and lame; well, even if they are, they are still strong enough to keep you out." They also boasted that even blind, lame guards could protect their city against the motley crew of soldiers David had brought.

Generalship up for Grabs. David motivated his troops by proclaiming, "Whoever leads in taking this city shall be my number one general." The following reasons may have been in David's mind. First, Joab had greatly embarrassed the new king by killing Abner, and David may have felt sheepish about handling the matter weakly. Putting the generalship up for grabs would have reminded Joab of his displeasure. It would keep Joab in a subordinate position. If he wanted to retain the job, he would have to show himself capable.

Second, David appealed to the northern tribes for allegiance. He was opening the highest position in the nation to both the northern and southern tribes on the basis of performance. Joab rose to the challenge and led the way in taking the city. One wonders how many would have dared oppose him, in light of what he had done to his former rival.

Jerusalem. The new "city of peace" would come to have a sacred history. There Abraham was surprised to find a godly individual, the mysterious Melchizedek. This city would hear the preaching of saintly Isaiah and righteous Jeremiah. The God-Man, Jesus Christ, would pray here in Gethsemane, be judged in Gabbatha and die at Golgotha. Here the Holy Spirit would fuse believers into the Body of Christ at Pentecost. And it shall be from blessed Jerusalem that the glorified Lord Jesus will rule the world during the Millennium.

After taking the city, David increased fortifications, built himself a permanent home and received ambassadors from the city of Tyre. As the diplomatic relationships were established, the king was granted international recognition.

God Lifted the Nation

By taking Jerusalem and receiving ambassadors from Tyre, David became conscious of being established by God as king for the benefit of the people. He saw God's mighty work in making the nation united and strong. The Lord was putting Himself on display again through His people. He demonstrated Himself as the only true and living God. His people "came into their own." Their lot greatly improved.

The period of the judges (1390–1050 B.C.) was the greatest opportunity for prosperity and peace that any people have ever been offered. With God as the ruler of the nation, minimal taxes and no standing army, the potential for Israel to be a model nation to the entire world as the representative of God was without parallel in history.[3] Israel failed to obey, however, not realizing the favorable opportunity God held out to them. That was 380 years before David's day, and God was ready to trust His people again with world success. He had painstakingly prepared "a man after his own heart" through whom He would lift His people to a place of prominence in the world. Through David's leadership of Israel, the world would come in contact with God. Thus David saw more in his rise to power than material benefits for himself. He distinguished himself from other kings—he recognized the higher royalty of God and saw himself as a mere human agent through whom God was working.

David's excellent attitude is articulated in Psalm

30. Theodore Epp commented that David's spirit was far different from Nebuchadnezzar's when he looked out over Babylon and said, "Is not this great Babylon, that I have built . . . for the honour of my majesty?" (Dan. 4:30).

Epp added that a beautiful home, costly furniture and extensive possessions will do no harm to those who, as they survey them all, turn to God and say, "Thou hast girded us with gladness, to the end that my glory may sing praise to thee, and not be silent" (Ps. 30:11, 12). Happy is the Christian who sees more in the promotions of God than mere personal benefits. Every believer has been chosen to have at least one spiritual gift[4] so that he may be God's agent for good as he travels through this troubled world. Do not squander your energies and abilities on yourself, because happiness and fulfillment is a by-product of using your gift(s) for the glory of God.

David's Family. The record states that David's family expanded considerably once he became headquartered in Jerusalem. Previously (2 Sam. 3:2–5) we were told that six sons were born to David by many different wives while he lived at Hebron. Now we learn that eleven more sons were born to him in the first ten years at Jerusalem. This was *not* God's best for him. Multiple marriages caused multiplied problems. These eleven sons are forgotten with the turning of a page. None of them are mentioned again in the Biblical narrative. Being younger, they were the lowest in the family power structure. Because they were unable to jostle their older half brothers in the quest for recognition and power, they were soon forgotten. The three sons who figure prominently in the family troubles (Amnon, Absalom and Adonijah) were all born during the Hebron monarchy. David sinned in taking more wives, but the sin was likely caused by following the customs of other kings and a matter of pride rather than sexual desire. The size of a king's harem was an acknowledged measure of his power.

175

The Philistine Perspective. When they heard of David's capture of Jerusalem, and possibly of Hiram's diplomatic overtures to the new king, the Philistines attacked the infant nation. A nation divided in loyalties (Saul *vs.* David) had served their purposes. They would not have waited long to attack, not wanting to give David time to consolidate his army and government. He had been a vassal bodyguard to their own king about eight years before. They felt he was indebted to them for the political asylum they had granted him. The slaying of Goliath about fifteen years earlier was all but forgotten. The Philistines expected to add David's nation to their sphere of influence without too much trouble.

David's Perspective. More than any other factor, the Philistine threat had forced the nation to see David as their king. And he knew why they wanted him. This was the Gordian knot he must slice through to justify his monarchy. But he did not have long to ponder this foreign policy problem, for the Philistines brought it right to his doorstep. While he had been king of Judah only, they let him alone; but now he was laying claim to much of the territory they had taken from Israel in the battle of Mount Gilboa (1 Sam. 31).

Anticipating the battle, David returned to the cave at Adullum (the "hold" of v. 17). This was west from Jerusalem and closer to the enemy. No doubt, David's six hundred men were with him, and very likely his army now included some of Saul's elite troops. They must have been astounded to see for the first time the sentry system, the water supply, the escape routes, the lookout posts and other military secrets that had enabled David to elude them when they were with King Saul.

The Philistines prepared for battle at Rephaim, just south of Jerusalem. Their goal was to divide David from the northern tribes by slicing through the middle of the nation, thus cutting in half the infant unity of the country. One Philistine garrison was stationed at Bethlehem (2 Sam. 23:14).

The Victory. This was a very important battle. A loss would be devastating. David must win; he had been made king to handle this very problem.

David's first concern was to make sure of God's direction. In view of 2 Samuel 3:18, God's *general* direction was clear, but David must know the particulars. *When* should he engage them? Was *now* God's time? Timing is always important. Elijah waited until the correct moment had come on Mount Carmel before asking God for the fire; God waited until "the fulness of the time" to send His Son; and the Savior was content to let the Holy Spirit teach the disciples what they were not ready for when He was on earth.

God's time had come to deliver Israel. He gave a splendid victory in the first battle. When measured against Saul's inability to free Israel from the Philistine domination, the victory is all the more striking. It gave a great boost to the new king.

Bethlehem's Well. Unwilling to let their domination of Israel go so cheaply, the Philistines approached the same location for a second battle. Sometime between these two battles, or perhaps associated with them, came the events of 2 Samuel 23:13–17. These verses tell us that while David was "in the hold" at Adullum, he offhandedly expressed his desire for some clear, refreshing water from the well in Bethlehem, his hometown. While he never intended his request to be taken seriously, some of his loyal soldiers—out of zealous love for their leader—traveled to Bethlehem, located the well while avoiding the Philistine soldiers, obtained the water and returned to Adullum. David was overwhelmed that these men had put their lives in jeopardy to get him this water. He refused to drink it although he was grateful for their zeal and love.

The Second Victory. In the second battle, God Himself was the commanding Tactician. While the

177

enemy was the same and the location was the same, God's directives to David were different. Believers may find themselves in similar situations where they have been victorious before. Yet the Lord is still to be sought and obeyed.

David was told to circle around behind the enemy and wait until the wind was blowing through the trees. Previously, he had been directed to "Go out and get 'em." Now it was "Wait, and move when I show you." The wind would show David that God Himself was marching in front of his men to smite the Philistines. David should then move forward and finish the job. How exciting and reassuring for him to get such specific information about the battle! For a believer to realize that the God of the entire universe is guiding his life is very important. What peace, confidence and strength this gives a soldier of the cross today.

Lessons for Us

How Much Does Victory Cost? What must believers do to have spiritual success? How much prayer, work and sacrifice is required? As we study the Bible, we find the answers. It takes from nothing to everything. A case where God required His people to do nothing is given in 2 Kings 19:35, where 185,000 Assyrians were killed by God. David could and did do nothing to be delivered from King Saul (1 Sam. 19). But most of the situations we meet in life are ones in which we must exert ourselves in the power of the Spirit and doggedly pursue our objectives. The believer needs to bear in mind that while God can do anything, believers should not be discouraged when steady plodding is called for. David was not given this 70 percent "God's effort" and 30 percent "his effort" victory until he had battled through eleven years of fugitive living. Even our Savior "learned . . . obedience by the things which he suffered" (Heb. 5:8).

One does hear "barroom to the pulpit" testimonies occasionally. While we rejoice in such instances of God's mighty grace, those with a testimony less dramatic should not be jealous of or feel inferior to those who have had a more spectacular experience with God. Though unable to tell of a particularly exciting conversion experience, those saved early in life do not have to wage constant battle with former sins, as those saved later in life often do. They never feel the "pull" of well-entrenched sins, the downward drag of past wickedness.

The Bible tells us that all Christians have great potential. No one is predestined to a shabby Christian experience. We all share in the joyous miracle of salvation, the wondrous grace of God. Normally, success does not come suddenly. God cannot trust many of us with it. It is a heady commodity. For every "barroom to the pulpit" testimony, dozens of God's precious saints give accounts of victories that came from "slugging it out" in the trenches of daily spiritual battle.

Reasons for Victory. David had been patiently waiting in line before the throne of grace for a long time. God saw that it was time for victory. A second reason for David's instant rise to power was that God had a large place in His plans for him. Every believer is special to God and chosen by God, but He does have a larger place of service for some than others. The Savior told a parable about the wise use of talent in Matthew 25. The man who was lent five talents gained five more—a 100 percent increase. The man who received two talents gained two more—also a 100 percent increase, but the first man's 100 percent increase was much larger.

Believers must be careful not to envy those to whom God gives a larger sphere of influence, more spiritual fruit. There is a higher price to be paid by the Christian who would be used of God more than others. Take Paul, for example. We would enjoy the glamour of his spiritual life—conversion through a personal appearance of the risen God-Man, a three-year course in the desert with private tutoring by the Lord, being caught up to the third Heaven. But we would not be interested in all the suffering he endured (see 2 Cor. 11:23–30). The glories and victories of every Christian's life are balanced with burdens, pressures and responsibilities.

For eleven years, David had been a persecuted nobody; now it is his hour. God made it so. The twin victories over the Philistines gave him a solid grip on the leadership of the nation.

Not Far, but Far. In establishing his capital at Jerusalem, David was not moving far from where he grew up. Bethlehem was only eight miles from Jerusalem—but what a change had come about in him! David did not move far geographically, but he had traveled a long distance politically and spiritually. He was more experienced, wise, obedient, faithful and ready to lead than when he had lived in Bethlehem.

Write It Down . . . Pay Attention. It is good for Christians to keep an account of God's major dealing with them. Remembering *how* the Lord opened certain opportunities, *what* took place, *why* people felt as they did and *when* things unfolded can be a big help in determining God's will for the future. By paying close attention to what God has done in the past, we can sharpen our "spiritual radar" to know His will. Such a journal helps us count all the ways our Father has been good to us, and notice His chosen paths. A spiritual journal is a way to say, "Father, I am serious about paying attention to what You are doing in my life. I want to be a good student of life."

Psalm 30 is attributed by some to the occasion of David's coronation. He wanted to preserve the moment. God told the people to take careful note of the events so they would be able to tell the yet unborn generations what certain customs meant (Deut. 6:20). And, in Deuteronomy 17:18, we learn that a king over God's people was to make his own handwritten personal copy of the law. We should pay close attention to what God is doing in our lives.

By taking notes, we prepare ourselves for victory in times of pressure and satanic attack.

Conclusion. David was entering the best years of his life. Before the horrible years of family crisis came, the nation enjoyed thirteen years of excellence under his leadership.

Believers need to notice that the "good guy" does not always finish last. To obey the Lord, do His will and then leave the results to Him is success. David was keenly aware that God had lifted him for the benefit of His people. And He had lifted His people to bring glory to Himself. David's humility of spirit would be the channel through which God would empower the man and the nation to enjoy a golden era.

End Notes

1. Wood, *A Survey of Israel's History*, pp. 263, 264.

2. Satan seeks to turn our guilt into a tool for our destruction (2 Cor. 7:10).

3. For an excellent treatment of the potential of the Judges period, see Leon J. Wood's *Distressing Days of the Judges* (Grand Rapids: Zondervan Publishing House, 1975), pp. 45–70.

4. A spiritual gift is a God-given capacity to bring about spiritual growth, insight or help in the life of another believer. Your gift is for the benefit of someone else. I believe the "lists" given in 1 Corinthians 12 and Romans 12 do not include all possible spiritual gifts, and that a believer may have more than one gift. Certainly, David had more than one; so did Paul.

CHAPTER SIXTEEN

BEING NEAR TO GOD— GOD'S WAY

2 Samuel 6

The one outstanding question after reading 2 Samuel 6 is, "Why did God judge Uzzah with such harshness?" The chapter also tells of God's judgment on Michal, the daughter of Saul and wife of David. The actions of these two people who brought judgment upon themselves were opposite: Uzzah's was one of overzealousness as he unwisely steadied the ark; Michal's was one of underzealousness in being apathetic to her husband's spiritual enthusiasm. It seems strange to us that Uzzah, the zealous one, received greater punishment—he was killed by God. Second Samuel 6 warns us of the need to be near to God in His prescribed way—and illustrates the consequences of not wanting to be near to God.

The Motive. David wanted to bring the ark of the covenant to Jerusalem. He is to be commended for wanting the worship of Jehovah to be central in the life of the nation. By bringing the ark to the capital, he hoped to demonstrate to the people that any successes they experienced were based on a correct relationship with God.

Chosen Men. David gathered together all the chosen men of Israel for the purpose of bringing the ark to the capital. Their number was large—no less than thirty thousand. For David and his key advisors to know so many men means that the tentacles of his government were spreading into all areas of the nation. Searching out skilled, knowledgeable people to run a nation is no small part of governing well. One does not have to know all the people personally, but a leader must know some people who will know qualified people.

The Ark: Construction and Contents. The ark of the covenant,[1] a box of wood measuring 2' x 2' x 4' and overlaid with gold, inside and out, was the most sacred piece of furniture the nation had been instructed to build. God had given specific instructions on the construction of several pieces of religious furniture to Moses on Mount Sinai, and the ark was the most important. Basically a container, it held three things: (1) the contract written on stone—the Ten Commandments—that formalized God as Israel's God and the Israelites as His people; (2) the golden pot of manna, which commemorated God's provision for Israel during the forty years of wilderness wandering; and (3) Aaron's rod that budded, which showed that he was God's choice for the priestly office. At each end of the gold lid, statues of a kind of angel called "cherubim" faced each other, their wings arching over their backs and joining overhead. This lid was called the "mercy seat" because it was of this place that God had said, "... there I will meet thee, and I will commune with thee" (Exod. 25:22). The high priest would have communication with God there, and from there he would hear God's pronouncements of mercy.

The Ark: Its Meaning. The ark represented the presence of God among His people. God had strictly forbidden the making of any image of Himself. But people like something visible—a representation of God's presence—so God graciously directed that an

184

item—in this case an ark—be built.

That it did represent God among His people can be verified by two events in Scripture: the crossing of the Jordan and the taking of Jericho.[2]

The Jordan Crossing. When the infant nation of Israel was ready to cross the Jordan River into the Promised Land, God showed His presence by the way He directed things. The priests were to carry the ark directly toward the water. God wanted the people to think, "God is leading the way." When the feet of the priests came to water, the river rolled back. A three thousand-foot space was kept between the priests carrying the ark and the first people to cross the dry riverbed. This space was likely commanded by God to enable people to see what was happening. The mighty God wanted people to say to themselves, "God is leading us in triumph over this barrier that has stood in our way—He is with us." The ark was carried to the midpoint of the riverbed (the most dangerous point, should the waters flood them), and it remained there for all to see as they came to it in crossing. Then it followed them and was last to come up from the riverbed.

Jericho. When the Lord was about to destroy the walls of Jericho, He directed that the ark be carried at the head of the procession on each of thirteen circuits the nation made around the city. The ark was the symbol of God's presence.

History and Treatment of the Ark. The ark, a portable worship center, remained with Israel through the forty years of wandering. After the conquest, it was respectfully maintained for two generations (*ca.* 1390–1340 B.C.) until there arose a "generation that knew not the Lord" (Judg. 2:6–10). During the period of the judges (1340–1050 B.C.), worship associated with the ark diminished. The priesthood degenerated. Tribal wars raged. And the spiritual life of the nation was at a low ebb.

185

In the battle of Aphek,[3] the ark was taken from the tabernacle[4] and captured by the Philistine enemies. But when plagues broke out upon them, they hastily sent it back. It was returned to the Israelite city of Beth-shemesh, but remained there only a short time. Finally, it came to rest in the care of the house of Abinadab in Kirjath-jearim, where it remained for about seventy years, during the times of Samuel, Saul and Ish-bosheth. Eleazar, a son of Abinadab, was charged with its care.

Going for the Ark

On the appointed day, the thirty thousand guests gathered in Jerusalem for the eight- to ten-mile trip west to get the ark. Having invested considerable time getting ready, David would not want anything to go awry. When all were in their places, the procession started out. First Chronicles 15:16–24 lists the musicians and singers involved. It was to be a day that would be remembered—but not in the way David wanted.

The Disaster. When the procession arrived, two grandsons (or great-grandsons) of Abinadab, along with others, were ready. These two, Ahio and Uzzah, were honored to be near the ark as it was transported. Since they had cared for it and were familiar with it (the ark had been in their family possession for several decades), they were the logical choices to tend it. When the ark had been placed on a cart, the procession started back to Jerusalem. Some distance down the road, however, rough ground and God's displeasure caused the oxen pulling the cart to stumble. They jolted the cart so violently that the ark was in danger of falling off. Uzzah, walking near the ark, had to make an instant decision: (1) Should he reach up and steady the ark? (2) Should he let it fall? Each choice had good and bad aspects. If he let it fall, he would be accused of being lazy and unconcerned. People would think he was ungrateful for the honor of being near the sacred ark. And if it fell, the joy of the procession would be dampened. The king would be unhappy. Since the ark was old, very dry and brittle, it was sure to be damaged. On the other hand, God had commanded that the ark was not to be touched. Poles had been attached to it so that it could be moved without being touched. These and other factors undoubtedly ricocheted through Uzzah's mind in the split second he ran to the ark. Uzzah reached up to steady the ark. A moment later, he was in eternity! God had struck him dead!

The procession ground to a halt. One can imagine people hurrying to the side of the fallen man. Word spread back through the ranks, "Uzzah is dead." David was stunned. The joyous vitality of the throng disappeared. Harps, coronets, cymbals, psaltries and timbrels became silent. Those nearby stood quiet, shocked into silence. Those in the back spilled over the edges of the road, attempting to see why the column had stopped. Then the crowd flowed around the dead man, leaving a wide berth lest something happen to them, and went home. Total disaster! The king gave hurried directions to bury the body and take the ark to the nearest home, and he left the scene. The ark came to rest in the home of a man named Obed-edom. The location where Uzzah died was renamed "Perez-uzzah" (meaning "outbreak against Uzzah").

David's Reaction. The text says that David's first reaction was displeasure. He was upset at God for the death of Uzzah. We do not know what was in David's mind, so it is risky to judge. Because we know our own sinful minds, however, we may conclude that this disruption stung David's pride. His programs had always been a success. Whenever you become angry with God, you are in danger of despising "the chastening of the Lord" (Heb. 12:5). The second reaction of the king was fear. Pink wrote:

There is a slavish fear which springs from hard thoughts of God, and there is a holy and laudable fear which issues from lofty thoughts of His majesty. The one is a terror produced in the mind of apprehensions of evil, the other is a reverential awe of God which proceeds from right views of His infinite perfections. The one is the product of a guilty conscience, the other is the fruit of an enlightened understanding.[5]

There was likely some of each kind of fear in David's reaction. He was frustrated because he was sure it was God's will for the ark to be in Jerusalem. After he had cooled down, he knew his heart was right with God. Why had this happened?

Desiring the Presence of God. David longed for the presence of God. He knew that his rule must be anointed by God's involvement. He knew he served at God's good pleasure—he could be replaced at any time. Any victories won were viewed as products of God's grace. David's administration was dependent upon God's smile of approval. He wanted to be obedient to God. Having the ark in Jerusalem would focus the worship of the nation.

Christians of our day need the same awareness of God's presence—the sense of belonging to God and the security of being abandoned to God. Those living with a God-consciousness are powerful tools in His hand.

When David Livingstone was to be granted an honorary degree at the University of Glasgow, the administration and others expected that all the students would receive him with bubbling enthusiasm. But the appearance of Livingstone—a gaunt veteran of twenty-seven years under the African sun, one arm rendered useless by the bite of a lion—and the reputation of this venerable man of God caused the students to receive him in awed silence. All were stirred as he said, "Shall I tell you what supported me through all these years of exile among a people whose language I could not understand, and whose attitude toward me was always uncertain and often hostile? It was this, 'Lo, I am with you alway, even unto the end of the world.' "

As a child needs to know that Mother and Father are near, the child of God needs to be constantly aware of the Lord. This will keep the Christian separated from sin, encouraged in difficulty, comforted in the daily grind and strengthened in the challenges of his spiritual warfare. It is wonderful that God is looking over our shoulders. Knowing He is with us causes us to "[perfect] holiness in the fear [reverent trust] of the Lord," favorably reflecting our Best Friend.

What Went Wrong?

All who saw Uzzah die on the road and those who heard about it must have wondered what went wrong. Three factors should have caused Uzzah to make the right choice: *samples, sovereignty* and *Scripture.*

Samples. Previously, God judged His people harshly for violating His sanctity. "Sanctity" may be defined as God's separateness from sinful humanity. Consider some samples of such judgments:

Nadab and Abihu offered "strange fire" to God and were killed for doing so. The essence of this disobedience (see Lev. 10:1–7) was the use of fire that was taken from or kindled by a source other than that which God had designated. Possibly they had let the fire on the altar go out, and God had directed that it was never to stop burning. Thus, they had to get fire from a nonsacred source to continue worship ceremonies.

These men had had long association with priestly activities and were themselves the guardians of the ceremonies that were to demonstrate the sanctity of God. They knew better. Although they were sons of Aaron, just recently promoted into the priesthood, they were expected to offer worship in the prescribed manner. Because of their father's lifelong priestly service, possibly they had become careless through overfamiliarity. Or perhaps their promotion filled them with pride.

Er and Onan. These were two sons of Judah, both killed by God (Gen. 38:7, 8). The Bible says simply that Er was wicked. And Onan refused to provide an offspring for his brother by his brother's wife. Both men were critical links in the ancestry of the Messiah, so God did not tolerate their actions. God's program was at stake; therefore, the judgment corresponded in harshness with the potential privilege and blessing that was theirs.

Moses. We are accustomed to thinking of Moses as being next to perfect. He was a great man whom God used mightily. But there was a time in his life when ". . . the LORD met him, and sought to kill him" (Exod. 4:24–26). The basis of His anger was Moses' failure to circumcise his two sons. God meant business about circumcision since it was the indication of His special relationship with His people.

Mount Sinai. God told the Israelites that anyone, man or animal, who touched Mount Sinai would die. Moses was the only exception—he had to go up on the mountain to receive the law from God (Exod. 19:10–13).

Achan. This man violated God's directions and paid with his life. The reason for his being judged so harshly was that the conquest was in its infant stage. Standards, morale and a precedent of obedience were at stake. Later on, God might have dealt with Achan's sin less severely. But coming as it did at the start of the campaign, when proper obedience and attitudes were essential, God had to deal with Achan strongly, or others would think they could do whatever they wanted (Josh. 7).[6]

Those Who Disrespected the Ark. God slew fifty thousand Beth-shemites for their irreverent treatment of the ark.[7] They had peered into the sacred chest. The Philistines, who were comparatively ignorant in committing the same sin, got off with an illness sent from God. The men of Beth-shemesh were knowledgeable Levites, so they were judged more strictly (1 Sam. 5:6; 6:19–21).

Uzzah had ample opportunity to be familiar with each of these instances. Scripture records many

190

subsequent judgments of God upon men who violated His sanctity: the *unnamed prophet* (1 Kings 13:23, 24) was killed; *King Uzziah* was struck leprous for intruding into priestly functions (2 Chron. 26:16–21); *Ananias* and *Sapphira* died for their hypocrisy (Acts 5); *Herod* was killed for receiving worship intended only for God (Acts 12:21–23); and some of *the Corinthian believers* died early for partaking of the Lord's Table *lightly* and *irreverently*.

Sovereignty. In addition to many samples of God's judgment, Uzzah should have been aware that God sovereignly protected the ark. An unusual event had occurred about sixty-five years before. After the battle of Aphek in 1075 B.C., and after the Philistines discovered that God was plaguing them because they had the ark, they decided to send it back to Israel. But they wanted to send it back in such a way that it would be destroyed, thus humiliating the Israelite religion. Yet they feared God and did not want to be directly responsible for the destruction of something He claimed as His own. They decided to send the sacred vessel back on a cart pulled by two oxen that had never been tamed. They hoped the unbroken animals would bounce the ark off, causing it to shatter. But God supernaturally controlled these untrained animals, and, to the amazement of the watching Philistines, the oxen pulled it safely back into Israelite territory, ". . . lowing as they went, and turned not to the right hand or the left" (1 Sam. 6:1–13). God sovereignly protected the ark from the very kind of danger it was in when Uzzah reached up to steady it.

Scripture. Third, and most important, Scripture gave clear guidance about handling and moving the ark. Numbers 4:15 says that only Kohathite[8] Levites were to move the holy vessel. Numbers 7:9 reiterates this directive, saying it was to be lifted and moved by the poles attached to the rings in the side, so it would have no direct contact with sinful men. Since the ark had been in one spot for seventy years,

191

one would think Uzzah, Ahio and the spiritual leaders would have found their textbooks and brushed up on "Advanced Ark Moving." This was a grand event and should have called forth the best preparation that the Levites could give.

Uzzah's disregard for God's strict prohibition indicates a laxity in the house of Abinadab in maintaining the laws entrusted to their care. They had become overly familiar with this object associated with God and took it for granted. In doing so, they set a bad example for the entire nation. When David granted Uzzah and Ahio the honor of escorting the ark, he assumed—and properly so—that they were thoroughly familiar with the right methods for its movement.

Summary. Certainly, Uzzah did not see the matter of steadying the ark as a life-and-death matter. Approaching the teetering ark, debating the pros and cons, he concluded that it would be the lesser of two evils to go ahead and steady the ark. Had he been wise, he would have insisted before starting out that it be carried, rather than placed on a cart. But, in spite of the fact that they disobeyed Scripture in using a cart, Uzzah should not have compounded the error by touching the sacred vessel. He should have realized from history that the Lord took very seriously the violation of His sanctity. Also, the stumbling of the animals should have alerted Uzzah and Ahio to God's displeasure.

Though we are tempted to think meanly of God, we should recognize that the purpose of the priest's work was to teach, maintain and strengthen the law of God, in all its particulars, by a careful adherence to them. Their example would be highly influential—for good or ill. As guardians of the laws of God, they should have insisted upon doing God's work in God's way.

What Was So Bad about Touching the Ark?

To what does the Bible attribute Uzzah's death? "And God smote him there for his error." The New

International Version translates it, ". . . because of his irreverent act." First Chronicles 13:10 tells us what this error was: ". . . he put his hand to the ark." So what was so bad about that? Why was his action irreverent?

Touching the ark was equal to defiling God by virtue of contact with sinful humanity. As people were not to come near Mount Sinai, so no one was to touch the ark. The whole tabernacle was arranged to intensify God's holiness in the minds of people and to lead them to the conclusion, "Because we are sinners, we can be near to God only in *the way He allows*." The very arrangement of the ark and tabernacle was designed to show that God is holy, separate from sinners.

For example, a cloth fence around the outer perimeter of the tabernacle area (approximately 100' by 50') not only kept people out but also kept them from seeing in. The small percentage of the nation who were of the priestly class and who were allowed inside had to pass a brazen altar to get inside the tabernacle itself. This altar spoke of sacrifice; animals were slain upon it to atone for man's sin. Freedom to get closer to the object that represented God (the ark) was purchased with blood.

The cloth-like structure that housed the ark—called the tabernacle—was another barrier. It prevented most of the priests and Levites from seeing the ark. For the few allowed inside the tabernacle—in an area called the "holy place"—there was a washbasin that further reminded people of sinfulness. Finally, only one man—the high priest—went into the curtained-off area called "the Holy of Holies" once a year. And he could not come into the presence of the ark without the blood of a slain animal, or he would be killed. Blood to cover sin was the only means of approach to God. This was important, for God planned to send His Son to shed His blood. He would not tolerate any tampering with the procedures He had established—for they all pointed to the Lamb of God, Who would make a once-and-for-all offering of Himself for human sin.

So He could not tolerate Uzzah sweeping aside His directives that pointed to His holiness and sanctity.

Sincere, but Wrong. Uzzah was sincere, but he was sincerely wrong. It is possible for us, too, to be sincere, but totally wrong. Some people believe that it does not matter what one believes or what church one attends as long as he is sincere. How thoughtless! Suppose a man went to the medicine chest at 2:00 A.M. to take his wife an aspirin tablet. He earnestly wanted to help, but he mistakenly gave her poison, and she died. He was very sincere, but she is still dead. In the war for the souls of men, Satan will use every deceptive method he knows to keep people from placing their faith in Christ as Lord and Savior. One very effective trick in his arsenal is to promote the idea, "Believe anything you want as long as you are sincere—a loving God will not reject you." Beware! God killed Uzzah for just such casualness and presumption.

The Bible and the Blessing. Back in Jerusalem from the disastrous attempt to bring the ark into the capital, David began to work on the gnawing question: "What had gone wrong?"

Uzzah's death was not an ordinary thing. It was supernatural judgment. All recognized it as such; if they had not, Uzzah would have been replaced and the procession would have continued on to Jerusalem. But why? David wanted answers! A team of scholars was dispatched to study the matter. He probably invested some time reading his own copy of the Scriptures. In good investigative procedure, eyewitnesses would have recreated the event, piecing together the mosaic. It became clear that judgment came the instant Uzzah touched the ark. This conclusion sparked a review of the Scriptures regarding treatment and movement of the sacred vessel. This may have taken weeks for them to figure out. David did, however, come to the correct conclusion (1 Chron. 15:2).

Meanwhile, God was doing things to cause

194

David not to lose interest in having the ark in the capital. In the past and in the future (see Deut. 32:21 and Rom. 11:14), God would be good to others to cause His own to become jealous—so they would turn to Him in faith and obedience. God blessed the house of Obed-edom. Josephus, the Roman historian, tells us that Obed-edom enjoyed great prosperity because of the presence of the ark,[9] proof that God is pleased with those who would be near to Him in His way.

The Second Attempt

With the "pull" of prosperity Obed-edom was experiencing and the "push" of wanting the ark in Jerusalem, David, having studied the Bible, was ready for a second attempt. So a vast concourse of worthy people assembled at Jerusalem. This time the prescribed ritual was observed with utmost care and precision.

One can imagine the processional. The levitical choir was primed for this regal day. They may have sung Psalm 15 when they came to Perez-uzzah—it asked and answered who would have the privilege of being associated with God's tabernacle. Psalm 132 may have also been used. With musical accompaniment, a sense of anticipation and festivity, the ark was ceremoniously lifted to the shoulders of the Levites assigned to carry it. All was proceeding smoothly. When just a few steps were taken, animals were sacrificed. The king danced before the Lord in delight at the sacredness of the hour. The march was renewed. Trumpets sounded and the ark moved steadily forward. It is almost certain that Psalm 24 was sung as the procession approached the walls of Jerusalem. The processional choir sang, "Lift up your heads, O ye gates; and be ye lift up, ye everlasting doors; and the King of glory shall come in" (v. 7). The choir atop the city walls sang the part of the sentry, "Who is this King of glory?" Then the singers in the procession would answer back, "The LORD strong and mighty, the LORD mighty in battle."

After repeating the question and answer, both choirs sang the finale: "The LORD of hosts, he is the King of glory." Many believers today have enjoyed Handel's marvelous music about this scene without knowing the occasion of its first use. The psalm recorded in 1 Chronicles 16 was also sung on the day the ark arrived in Jerusalem.

It was a significant day in the nation. From that moment on, Jerusalem was the spiritual headquarters of Israel, even though Zadok continued to offer sacrifices morning and evening at the tabernacle at Gibeon. David was very pleased and showed it in song, dance and poetry.

Meet Mrs. Ice Water. After providing each guest with a meal to encourage the national celebration, David retired to his home with a heart full of gratitude. He expected the joy of the moment to perfume his home. But his wife Michal, the daughter of Saul, did not share his enthusiasm. Mrs. Ice Water poured her displeasure over the happy king by mocking his spiritual fervor. She was ashamed that he had cast aside his kingly dignity and danced before the people. She would have preferred that he review the parade from a dignitary's stand. Possibly her rejection of David's actions was because she had never seen her father involved with a similar spirit. He had never cared to honor the ark. Michal felt nothing but humiliation and chided David for acting like a commoner. Constrasting David's man-of-the-people approach with her father's proud grandeur made David come off second best.

David's response hints that there had been tension in the marriage before. His answer aims at what he thinks is her real complaint: "God removed your father from being king, and He gave me your father's throne." And he would make himself even more vile (lightly esteemed)—if she did not like it, too bad! If she did not respect him for his worship, then others would.

Many sincere Christians today have mates who do not share their spiritual interests. They will be able to identify with David.

God judged Uzzah for being overzealous. In the closing verse of this chapter, we read of God's judgment on Michal's indifference. She would have no child for the rest of her life. This shows God's supreme displeasure about her throwing ice water on her husband's display of spiritual leadership and interest. God does want people near Him.

Conclusion

First, we see the importance of being near to God in the way He prescribes. There is a right way and a wrong way to serve Him. Foolish people, people who are happy to be a law unto themselves, think God will be pleased with any spiritual crumb they care to throw in His direction. Never!!! Some would say, "It does not matter if I trust Christ as my Savior or not. God loves everyone, and if He grades on a curve, I will make it." Uzzah thought it did not matter either—but it cost him his life.

Second, notice that believers are always in danger of thinking some things in the Bible are not important. If we let small things "slide," soon there are changes that bewilder us, and we find it difficult to trace the problem to its source. For example, a person who tells "white lies" later finds that he has become spiritually color-blind.

Third, we see the consequences of being spiritually indifferent. The result for Michal was barrenness. When a person fails to develop his God-given abilities, boredom and discontent set in. Too often, local churches limp along with only 10 percent of the people bearing the load of dispatching the Great Commission. Church is viewed as a performance. Everything happens "up on the platform" while Christians sit, soak and sour in the pew. Spiritual laziness and lack of faith will end up with a high price tag—it cost the Israelites forty years of wandering in the wilderness.

Fourth, God wants us to be near Him. All of this information about the proper attitude in worship and service points out several things about our approach to God today:

We can be certain that *God does want us near Him.* He wants us to seek His company and desire His presence. Genesis 15:1 is most instructive in this connection. Abraham had just rescued Lot from a powerful coalition of eastern kings. He put his life on the line, and when he returned home triumphantly, he refused any reward from the slimy king of Sodom. But as he neared home, he began to wonder, "What do I get out of all this?" All he really wanted in life was a male heir, as God had promised. He had waited for several decades and had become rich and respected. His only unfulfilled desire—for a son—was Scriptural, logical and understandable. The text says he was afraid—and with good reason. That eastern coalition of kings could come looking for him at any time. His neighbors might turn him over to them to buy safety for themselves.

What does God say to Abraham? "Fear not, Abram: I am thy shield, and thy exceeding great reward" (Gen. 15:1). God promised him protection. And—more importantly—He said, in effect, "Abram, I want you to regard Me, My company, My Person, as your highest reward." God wanted Abraham to be near Him. And God wants us to seek Him, love Him and enjoy Him today.

The New Testament teaches that believers in Christ have the privilege of coming to God through the mediatorship and righteousness of the resurrected God-Man, Jesus Christ. Two points are important here: (1) Christ is God's appointed means of salvation. If He was what He claimed, then Christ is the *only* means of redemption. Jesus made very exclusive claims (see John 14:6). He was—and is—God. We must be careful not to think—like Uzzah—that He does not mean what He says. (2) We can always be near God. We read in the book of Hebrews, "Having therefore, brethren, boldness to enter into the holiest [meaning the Holy of Holies] by the blood of Jesus, by a new and living way . . . let us draw near with a true heart in full assurance . . ." (10:19–22). The apostle Paul expressed his thirst to be near to God in these words: "That I may know him, and the power of his resurrection . . ." (Phil. 3:10). May God develop in us the same desire.

God does want us near Him, but we must come His prescribed way. To believe ourselves smarter than God . . . to conclude that He will accept us on terms we choose . . . to determine that He will violate His Book . . . is the essence of self-will and sin. Such self-will and sin is the very problem Jesus Christ died for!

End Notes

1. The Hebrew term translated "covenant" means agreement or contract.

2. These events are recorded in Joshua 3 and 6, respectively.

3. 1075 B.C.; see 1 Samuel 4; also comments in "The Historical Situation" on p. 13.

4. The cloth tabernacle was located at Shiloh for some time. During Saul's reign, a large priestly community was at Nob—likely the tabernacle was there. Possibly after the Nob massacre (1 Sam. 22:9–19), it went to Gibeon where Zadok the high priest carried on priestly functions in the reign of David. Abiathar, the sole survivor of the Nob massacre, had fled to David with the Urim and Thummin. David viewed him as the legitimate high priest instead of Zadok, but David was content to leave the tabernacle to Zadok, allowing him to continue offering sacrifices. (See 1 Chron. 16:39 and Wood's footnote on Zadok, *A Survey of Israel's History*, p. 267.)

5. A. W. Pink, *The Life of David*, vol. 1 (Swengel, Pennsylvania: Reiner Publications, 1971), p. 306.

6. Likewise, when the New Testament church was in its infant stage in the early chapters of Acts, God did not tolerate from believers what He later put up with.

7. The New International Version (NIV) gives the figure seventy, instead of fifty thousand.

8. Levi, one of twelve patriarchs (sons of Jacob, and thus one of the founders of the twelve tribes of Israel) had three sons: Gershon, Kohath and Merari (Gen. 46:11).

9. Flavius, Josephus, "The Antiquities of Jews, Book VII," *The Complete Works of Flavius Josephus*, trans. William Whiston (Philadelphia: J. E. Potter Company, n.d.), p. 173.

CHAPTER SEVENTEEN

THE GREAT EXCHANGE

2 Samuel 7

I f 2 Samuel 6 was significant—and it certainly was—2 Samuel 7 is even more so. In chapter 6, David did something to honor God. In chapter 7, God does something for David. One of the most beautifully reverent passages in all the Bible, one of the most tender, affectionate portrayals of a relationship between God and one of His created, is here on display for us. The Spirit of God pulls back the curtains, not only to the living room of the palace, but also to the very heart and mind of the king. We are given a private view of the attitude of David. We are allowed to listen in on his conversation with God. In the first half of the chapter, God speaks to David through the prophet Nathan; in the second, David responds.

Not Satisfied. Only part of David's spiritual desire had been met by bringing the ark to the capital city. He also had a longing to build up the spiritual life of the nation. For years he had lived on the run. A permanent home had been out of the question. But once he became king, finding a home and settling down was high on his priority list. When this need was met, David became concerned to honor God. Finding himself comfortable in his own home, surrounded with peace, honor and prosperity, he became jealous for the Lord. He resolved to build some kind of structure to house the ark, the grandeur of which would be in keeping with God's majesty. Any building that God would be identified with should reflect God's nature.

David wanted to please the Lord by doing a grand piece of service. Too often, believers settle down comfortably once their own needs and desires are met. We are apt to think our successes are our own and decide we are not indebted to God. Instead, God's provision of our needs and desires should cause us to be grateful, to rally and serve so our Savior will be magnified in the minds of others.

Starting Well. In the springtime of one's Christian life, a holy fervor moves one to do something spiritually heroic. A young man turns his energies toward becoming a pastor. A young woman resolves that she shall serve God by being a first-rate Christian schoolteacher. A man already well into the business world determines that God shall be honored with his money and that he will support missionaries beyond what might be normally hoped. A newly converted grandmother fixes her mind on changing her bitter spirit and determines, with God's Spirit enabling her, that no matter how much her old sinful nature battles her, she will be a sweet believer and a submissive wife. Holy resolve backed by self-discipline and dogged determination become part of these people's lives in their efforts to please God. David was this kind of person. He set his heart on building a temple for God.

The Need for a Temple. Besides David's love for his Lord, building a temple was logical, in light of the needs created by growth of the capital city. About twenty-six thousand Levites and priests were serving the religious life of the nation. Having a facility commensurate with the portion of religious personnel that served in Jerusalem made sense.

Meet Nathan. We are introduced for the first time to Nathan, a prophet of God. Likely, he and David were close friends. Later he would be entrusted with a distasteful task, but now they seem to have had a warm and personal relationship.

Taking Nathan into his confidence, David shared, in general, the idea of building a temple. Nathan responded with enthusiasm even though he did not know specifically what the king planned to do. With great excitement of soul and joy, David dreamed of fulfilling his great vision. Some Christian leaders today question whether a person has had a meaningful meeting with God if that person has no vision or determination to serve God.

God's Refusal. The next day, however, David got bad news! Nathan returned with a message from God. God placed several questions and statements in the mouth of the prophet, the drift of which was that David was not to build the temple. However, the refusal was shared with David in such a gracious way—padded by positive statements, assurances of love, reminders of past mercies and promises for the future—that no sting remained in the refusal. Through Nathan, God tactfully and diplomatically answered David in a nebulous mist of love. So indirect was God's answer that we must read the chapter carefully to see a clear "no" to David's plans.

God's Response. A paraphrase of God's response follows: "I have never lived in a house. Have I ever asked any leaders I have raised up to build Me a house?" (2 Sam. 7:5–7). "I took you from shepherding sheep to shepherding this special nation. I will make you great and will enrich My people with peace and prosperity" (vv. 8–11). "I will establish you and your family on the throne of Israel forever. One of your sons will build this temple. I will prosper, or punish him, according to his actions, but I will never take my love from him, as I took it from Saul."

God's Reason. Years later, when the temple was about to be built, David gave a parting charge to his son Solomon. In that charge he tells why God did not let him build the temple. It was because he had shed much blood and because he was associated with conquest. Therefore, he was not the appropriate person to build a temple that would symbolize the peace, worship and holiness of the God of the universe. Other nations of David's time would have thought it "out of character" for him to build the temple.

When God Says No

It is hard for a believer to understand why God would allow a dream, a holy goal, to possess a person and not allow its fulfillment! As months and years pass, a Christian becomes aware that his dream is still on the drawing boards. A person can find himself virtually where he was ten years ago, with little of the spiritual dream accomplished.

Perhaps there have been times in your life when you offered yourself to God, your mate, your family, your employer, your church or others—and the offer was refused. To make it worse, you do not know why. Such a moment is a great challenge not to turn sour. One must wait to learn the greater purposes of God and to trust the Lord with such experiences. If you can "trust and obey," the Lord will clear your spiritual sight and enable you to see the greater things He has in mind.

We are not told *why* David could not build his temple until 1 Chronicles 22:8. However, David likely knew why at the same time the refusal came. Verse 15 of chapter 17 hints that additional information was given to David: "According to *all* these words, and according to *all* this vision, so did Nathan speak unto David."

The Great Exchange

Most authors make much of God's refusal. They focus on applying that situation to the reader. However, the emphasis of the text is on exchange: David offered to build God a building; God counter-promised to build a dynasty for David. The king offered something material as evidence of his love for God. God responded by giving spiritual enrichment and peace to David. This is the "great exchange."

What did the Lord do for David in return for his willingness to build a temple? In verses 8–11, God reminds David of his promotion and His proclamation of him as king. David again relived all the close calls he had had with Saul. And then he was happy to agree with God that he had become king for the benefit of His people. When God promised to "make thee a house . . . I will set up thy seed after thee . . . and thy house shall be established forever," David was very pleased. It was very important in Jewish culture that sons followed in the steps of their fathers. God promised more to David than he could reasonably expect. From this moment on, David's name was certain to be enshrined in the pantheon of Israelite greats. His claim to fame was guaranteed.

An Especially Comforting Promise. Beyond these promises, God added something that gave the king blessed assurance and wonderful confidence. If the son who followed David as king were to disobey, God would correct him instead of abandoning him.

Inside every believer is the potential of being a spiritual traitor. David was concerned for himself in this regard, but he was even more concerned for his family—especially the son who would become king. The ironclad promise that God would correct David's son and not discard him was significant. Most parents would do anything to ensure the spirituality of their children.

Sitting before the Lord. The king's perfumed

response is worth noting. After Nathan broke the news to David that he was not to build the temple, he went ". . . and sat before the Lord." This was no ordinary sitting, not relaxation. David's desire was to meet purposefully with the Lord, to be conscious of His presence and to worship Him.

What is worship? Worship is ascribing to God all that He is and does and reminding ourselves of His unfathomable value. It results in an ever higher valuing of our relationship with Him.

David went in to sit "before the Lord." He would do the same even after his horrible plunge into sin with Bath-sheba. We are seeing the real David in this man who worships, not in the other man who gets involved with Bath-sheba.

David knew what it was to have intimate communion with God. God intends worship to be refreshing for us (Acts 3:19). David's response can be paraphrased as follows: "I am not special, but You are treating me so and You have spoken about a long future for my children, and their children's children" (2 Sam. 7:18, 19). "You know all about me, and I know You have promoted me to glorify Your honesty in keeping Your sovereign plans" (vv. 20, 21). "You are absolutely unique, and the people You formed into a nation have become special also" (vv. 22–24). "Fulfill Your plans, so that You will be magnified in the lives of people" (vv. 25–29).

The humility David displayed is noteworthy. The first thing out of his mouth showed that he had not forgotten from whence he had come. "Who am I, O Lord God? and what is my house, that thou hast brought me hitherto?" His attitude of humility had surfaced previously (1 Sam. 18:18) and was highly commendable then. But David is powerful, rich and famous now—and he is still humble. So his humility is even more noteworthy.

That God would promise to keep David's ancestors on the throne forever demonstrates what God thought of him. Amazed, David asked, "Is this Your normal method of dealing with people?" He continued, "What can I, a mere man, say? You are

God." He then recited some of the "wonderful works of God,"[1] and ended by saying, "Be glorified by doing what You have chosen to do." Success humbled David—it did not lift him up in pride. God can trust much to this kind of believer.

Conclusion

When God says no, it is very important to trust Him. Otherwise, we will not qualify for the great exchange. God's refusals hold potential blessings—provided we can trust and ward off a sour spirit. Hebrews 12:15–17 teaches us that bitterness is a failure of faith in which a believer does not appropriate God's enabling grace.

David accepted the fact that he was not God's man to build the temple. *The Magnificent Obsession* is a book and movie about a man who caused someone to go blind. His "obsession" was to restore that person's sight. After going to medical school and becoming a surgeon, he was eventually able to do that. But that is a *story*.

Christians often must realize and accept the fact that they will never do certain things. I would very much like to be a channel of God's love in the life of a certain man with whom I served in the same church as assistant pastor and pastor. I made some mistakes with him, and he made some mistakes, and the congregation made some. His leaving was not pleasant; he was wounded. Though I tried to convince him I cared about God's blessing on him and his wife, he left without being convinced. God will love this couple through someone else—I have to accept that. God calls us to different functions in His great plan. Though the part God gives to another person may be more appealing to us than our own, peace and joy come through developing our role at God's direction.

Since David could not do what he wanted to do, he decided to do what he could do. He got busy gathering all the materials needed to build the temple. He had the delight of anticipating the magnificence of the temple.

When unable to do what they want, some people do nothing! If things go their way, fine. But if not, they do not participate. This is immature and tragic. And doing nothing is a sure way to disqualify one's self from "The Great Exchange."

End Note

1. This phrase is used in Acts 2:11. There it does not mean the gospel but rather significant deeds of history God accomplished to benefit the Israelites. This was a normal Jewish way to worship. God's miracles were reviewed by Stephen in Acts 7.

CHAPTER EIGHTEEN

WHAT THE BIBLE TEACHES ABOUT WAR

2 Samuel 8 and 10

These two chapters record the successful military campaigns of David against the Philistines, Moabites, Ammonites and King Hadadezer. The directions of these battles were west, northwest, east and northeast, respectively. Large numbers of men, massive supply lines and awesome consequences were involved. Without question, some ghastly suffering resulted from these military engagements. For example, two-thirds of the captured Moabite soldiers were killed, removing Moab's retaliation capabilities. What about the widows of these men? Or consider the consequences when David defeated King Hadadezer, king of Zobah. A thousand chariots, seven hundred horsemen and twenty thousand foot soldiers were captured. David killed all the horses, except enough to pull one hundred chariots. The luckless Syrians were hired to help Hadadezer in a second battle, and twenty-two thousand died. Having routed the Syrian mercenaries, David turned to face Hadadezer's forces. David's reputation spread still further when he crushed the enemy in the "valley of salt," where eighteen thousand were killed.

Chapter 10 reports that a neighboring king died. David sent messengers to show his sympathy and respect for the departed ruler. But the gesture was taken for a spying mission, and the new king shamed the messengers and sent them home. While this certainly displeased David, he did not take the initiative in avenging this diplomatic embarrassment. But the Ammonites, believing they had come into disfavor and assuming David would retaliate, mobilized for war. Not only did they field their own men, but they also hired thirty-three thousand mercenaries. Out of self-defense, David also prepared for war.

David won the battle—nothing unusual about that. The only thing out of the ordinary provided by this war is an insight into the personality of Joab. While Joab was not normally an admirable person, he does show excellent insight into the balance between God's sovereignty and man's responsibility. Joab divided his forces. Taking the best men to engage the mercenaries, he sent his brother Abishai to hold off the Ammonites. Joab wisely knew that if he could defeat the hired soldiers, the Ammonites would be demoralized. Joab's excellent statement comes in 10:12: "Be of good courage, and let us play the men for our people, and for the cities of our God: and the Lord do that which seemeth him good."

Joab was saying that the battle results would be determined by God, but that the means for winning would be fighting to their fullest capabilities. Joab's strategy worked: " . . . and when the children of Ammon saw that the Syrians were fled, then fled they also before Abishai . . . " (2 Sam. 10:14).

The defeated Syrians retreated north, and upon arriving home, they called together a larger force. Again, David did not initiate further hostilities. Upon hearing of the second Syrian mobilization, he rallied his forces.

The Syrians suffered the loss of 40,700 men, some of them leaders. Since Hebrew legislation forbade the use of horses in warfare, David's foot soldiers defeated mounted Syrians. The whole area became subject to David. This was a supreme moment in Israelite warfare; it likely taxed Joab's generalship to the limit. It was the greatest military triumph these two men ever shared.

The Golden Age

The reader is told that the Lord preserved David through all of these dangerous battles (8:6, 14). It was God's time to lift the nation—no need to look for any other explanation. God had invested several years of painful preparation; now He had an excellent king through whom He was going to advance the fortunes of Israel. Economically, because of the tribute money flowing into the nation, Israel was thriving. The average man on the street would be better off than ever before. People could turn to cultural pursuits, the climax of which came under Solomon.

Israel was in its golden age. Literature flourished. The arts blossomed. Abraham had lived one thousand years before this time; the God-Man, Jesus Christ, came one thousand years later. Nothing between these two events could rival David's monarchy in terms of military, spiritual, economic or political success. This golden age, which started twenty years prior to the time of our text, continued for fifty years—through the majority of Solomon's reign.

This period set precedents (see 1 Sam. 30:21–25 for an example) that became honored traditions and the means of measuring the correct way of doing things. During David's reign, Israel came the closest ever to possessing all the land God had promised to Abraham. Having a free hand, David's creative personality was bound to thrive. His skills as a musician, inventor, administrator, military strategist and man of God were drawn fully into play. *David was a great man*. And the thing that kept him on top was his skill in handling that explosive commodity *success*. God could trust David with much success because it did not lift him up in pride.

David's Cabinet. Chapter eight closes with a record of David's top advisors. Joab, the son of David's sister Zeruiah, was the commander in chief. Jehoshaphat was the official secretary. Zadok and Ahimelech[1] were the two official high priests. And Benaiah was the leader of the king's bodyguard. He was assisted by an elite force called the Pelethites and Cherethites.

David's sons were royal advisors. This gives a clue as to how much time had passed since 2 Samuel 3:2. We are told in that verse that David's firstborn did not arrive until he was king at Hebron. Surely these sons did not get the job of "royal advisor" until they were at least twenty years old! Thus, we are certain that at least twenty years passed between David's coronation at Hebron and his tragic involvement with Bath-sheba.

The Greatness of David's Monarchy

Administrative Skill. It would be almost impossible to overestimate the skill and wisdom of David's administrative work.

Spiritual Gifts. While some Bible teachers maintain that a person can have only one spiritual gift (see 1 Cor. 12; Rom. 12), I believe David had more than one spiritual capacity to bless others. The gift of "ruling" was one. The structure of priesthood David established lasted more than a millennium. Zacharias, the father of John the Baptist, was " . . . of the course of Abia," and " . . . he executed the priest's office before God in the order of his course" (Luke 1:5, 8). David was the one who established those "courses."

First Chronicles 23—27 also details the king's organizational genius. David's gift of "ruling" can further be seen in his work with the army. Of the regular standing army of two hundred eighty-eight thousand, only twenty-four thousand men were on active duty any given month. The remainder of the men were free to be involved in agriculture or commerce—therefore, no large standing army drained the national treasury.

Elite Forces. Taylor, borrowing from the scholarship of Kitto, Stanley and Blaikie, suggested that within David's fighting force of six hundred men there was an elite group called "worthies," or "mighty men." Taylor's view is that David's six hundred was divided into thirty bands of twenty men. Each band had a leader, and these supposedly were David's "thirty mighty men." However, the text upon which these thoughts are based (1 Chron. 12) is a translator's nightmare—it is not clear. So, these suggestions cannot be confirmed.

David set a "prince" over each of the tribes. And when the crown was formally handed to Solomon, he assembled all the "princes of Israel" (1 Chron. 28:1).

Education. David vigorously promoted the school of the prophets Samuel had started. Taylor noted that the preeminence attained by Solomon in all branches of education shows the advanced condition of the nation upon which he built.

That such a man as Solomon, a man of peace, letters, science and philosophy, could reign at all shows the progress of the nation under David. Solomon (his name means "peaceful") could never have reigned before David. When David came to the throne, the nation desperately needed a warrior. But by the time Solomon was groomed for the throne, times had changed—and the nation was ready for a poet-leader.

Agricultural Abundance. One of the best measurements of a nation is the attitude of its people. Are they secure? Confident of the future? Knowing there would be no Philistine marauders, David's people planted the fields. Food storage depots were in the cities and the country (1 Chron. 27:25). Davidic peace revolutionized the Israelite attitude toward agriculture.

Biblical Instruction. There were thirty-eight thousand Levites serving prosperous Israel: six thousand as officers and judges over civil courts; twenty-four thousand advancing the spirituality of the nation; four thousand maintaining the worship area by purifying the courts, chambers and items used in worship; and four thousand composing the Levitical choir and orchestra.

Some twenty-four thousand men were involved in advancing the spirituality of the nation. How? *By teaching!* A majority of these religious workers lived in the forty-eight levitical cities so they could invest their lives in the villages and towns, teaching God's prescribed manner of living. This was the strength of the nation's spiritual vitality. The common Levite in the by-ways built the God-consciousness of the nation. David knew the importance of their work, and he promoted their service.

What the Bible Teaches about War

In these two chapters, there is a good deal of war. War involves violence and killing. What does God's Word teach about war?

Winston Churchill said, "War is hell." This illustrates in part the terrors, uselessness and waste of war. But war does not come near the terror and hopelessness of Hell.

War was sired by Satan and mothered by human selfishness. What are we to think of the wars of David? How can a God-fearing Christian today work in a factory that makes bombs, bullets or missiles? As one looks at the *total* teaching of Scripture on war, several things become apparent.

First, many soldiers in the Bible appear in a favorable light. They are in good standing with the Lord and with men. God sent Peter to Cornelius so he could hear the Gospel and be saved (Acts 10). In Matthew 8, we read of a Roman centurion who requested the Lord's help for his servant. He said he was not worthy of Jesus' coming into his house. He asked Jesus to speak the healing word, believing that Jesus did not have to be present for the servant to be made well. The Lord Jesus praised the soldier, saying He had not found such great faith in all Israel.

Luke 3:14 tells of some soldiers who repented at the preaching of John the Baptist. They asked him what they should do to submit their lives to God. If God were against soldiers/soldiering, this would have been an opportunity for John to say, "Get out of the army. No person can be right with God who is associated with the violence of war!" Instead, John told them to be honest.

Second, war represents failure to obey God. Yet, God uses war. Several Bible texts[2] make this clear. Under the strain of war, people face themselves as sinners, admitting that they cannot solve their problems; pride is crushed, ungratefulness is exposed and materialism is broken. War is often God's judgment on nations.

Amazingly, the Bible says there will be war in Heaven (Rev. 12:7).

Third, not all killing is murder. "Thou shalt not kill" (the sixth commandment) should be translated, "Thou shalt not murder." God has killed people.[3] Some of God's greatest men have killed people with His approval. Samuel killed Agag at God's command. And on his own initiative, Phinehas killed an adulterous couple and was commended by God (Num. 25:6–13). God authorizes governments to kill criminals (Gen 9:6; Rom. 13:4).

Individuals vs. Government. What God forbids the individual ("Thou shalt not kill"; Deut. 5:17), He sometimes commands for the government ("Thou shalt smite them . . . and utterly destroy them"; Deut. 7:2). What a person is not to do out of anger, a nation may do without forfeiting God's blessing.

Smarter Than God. The Bible teaches that there are crimes for which the government should kill people (Gen. 9:6; Rom. 13:4). Many today do not agree, imagining themselves more merciful and wise than God. How shortsighted and foolish!

What a society values can be judged by what the death penalty is given for. If life is valued, a law will say, "Our law punishes murderers with death."

Jesus, a Perfect Environment and War. When arrested in the Garden of Gethsemane, the Lord Jesus said, "If my kingdom were of this world, then would my servants fight" (John 18:36).

The hope of believers is not in a warless world, or in a perfect environment, as liberals futilely strive for. We are fed the line: "The environment is the reason Johnny turned out bad; he cannot be held accountable for his actions." When the prodigal son (Luke 15) "came to himself," he had a horrible environment—a pig pen. Good schools, no ghettos and minority rights do not make people moral.

The environment during the Millennium will be perfect. But at the end of these years of peace, justice and prosperity, Satan will find a substantial number of discontented people and raise an army for one more stand against God (Rev. 20:8, 9). And we are told in Revelation 19:11 that " . . . in righteousness he [the God-Man, Jesus Christ] doth judge and make war."

David's Wars. How are we to evaluate the wars of David? Certainly, it would never be pleasant to kill anyone. Yet it was God's time for the nation of Israel to expand, to display God's power and righteousness to the world. Though David caused many to be killed in war, we see in his reactions to the deaths of Saul, Ish-bosheth and Abner that he had not become calloused in killing. David was exonerated for his wartime activities.

Conclusion

(1) All murder is killing, but not all killing is murder. (2) Men are sinners and can be very greedy—a major factor in the cause of wars. (3) God uses wars to accomplish spiritual purposes. (4) What one person is forbidden to do (murder another person), one may do in wartime without coming into disfavor with God. Governments are responsible to punish criminals with death when their crime deserves it. (5) According to God's sovereign plans, nations rise and fall.

End Notes

1. The text is confusing. Both the KJV and the NIV say Ahimelech, not Abiathar, was David's high priest. Yet 1 Samuel 22:16–23 tells us Ahimelech was killed and only Abiathar escaped. Abiathar, not Ahimelech, continued with David.

2. Deuteronomy 28:7 and 25; Jeremiah 25:8 and 9. There are about 235 references to war in the Bible.

3. Er, Genesis 38:7; Onan, Genesis 38:9 and 10; Nadab and Abihu, Leviticus 10:1 and 2; Uzzah, 2 Samuel 6:6 and 7; King Herod, Acts 12:23; Ananias and Sapphira, Acts 5:5.

CHAPTER NINETEEN

MEPHIBOSHETH

2 Samuel 9

David's treatment of Mephibosheth, Saul's grandson, is another high point of his life. He acts most admirably. At a time of great success, having captured the affection and the loyalty of his nation, when he was on top spiritually, militarily and financially, David thought of the shattered house of Saul. He wanted to show the kindness of God to Saul's remaining relatives.

David thought of his early life: his days of suffering in exile, the years of rejection and fugitive living, his rich fellowship with Jonathan. He greatly missed his good friend. As he mused over the good times they had shared, he thought, "I wonder if there are still any members of Saul's house to whom I can show the kindness of God." And this brings us to one of the most touching and warmhearted chapters in the Old Testament.

God's grace, mercy and love flowed through David to an undeserving man. As we see God reaching out to salvage Mephibosheth, we have greater confidence that He will also meet our needs. He has chosen us to enjoy a fulfilling relationship with Him. Notice the similarities between David's relationship with Mephibosheth and Christ's relationship with us believers:

First, Mephibosheth was hopeless. We have already met him once in Scripture. His name appears in connection with the news of Israel's defeat at Mount Gilboa (2 Sam. 4:4), when Saul and Jonathan were killed. As the word spread, Saul's family panicked. Gathering what they could, they fled for their lives. In the rush, the woman attending Jonathan's five-year-old son, Mephibosheth, dropped him. He became permanently lame in both feet as a result.

So, Mephibosheth was a cripple and a member of a defunct regime. The house of Saul had little—their possessions had been lost or confiscated. His life was in constant jeopardy. His condition seemed hopeless.

Life's challenges and hardships make humanity hopeless. Men and women are at odds with everything and everyone. An honest person will admit that he is basically selfish, proud, lazy, indifferent and anger-prone. And many reject God's solutions for these attitudes.

Second, a long time passed between Mephibosheth's accident and David's help reaching him. The twenty-year reign of David intervened. Mephibosheth was about twenty-five years old when David sought him out. Therefore, people should not think, "You can't teach an old dog new tricks." People are not dogs, and salvation in Christ is not a trick. This should encourage Christians about the salvation of their loved ones. The passing of many years does not preclude Christ's power of life-changing help and grace.

Third, David was under no obligation to serve Mephibosheth. He did not owe anything to the house of Saul. By the day's standards, it was gracious that David had ignored the house of Saul instead of killing all associated with it. Likewise, God is under no obligation to meet our needs. People have rebelled against God—by nature we reject His authority. As Mephibosheth became lame through a fall, the human race has become lame and impoverished by a spiritual fall. And God is not obliged to save us.

Fourth, Mephibosheth had nothing to give that David needed. He was in a position only to receive. But the king sought him for what he could give to him, not for what he could get from him. What an accurate reflection of our situation before God. God does not seek us for what we can give to Him; nor is forgiveness traded for future service. God does not need anything from us. While God loves us, He does not wait breathlessly for people to complete His life.

Fifth, David was kind to Saul's grandson for the sake of another. It was because of his past relationship with Jonathan that David was roused to be gracious to Mephibosheth. Likewise, it is because of God's regard for the Lord Jesus Christ—His atoning work on the cross—that He reaches out to those who ignore and oppose Him. David found a reason outside Mephibosheth to befriend him. And because of Another, God heals our blindness and causes us to believe in the Savior.

Sixth, David took the initiative in finding the helpless cripple. And he quieted his fears. Mephibosheth assumed he was on David's "black list," and he wanted to stay out of his way. And so it is with people who are not believers in Christ. They imagine God is not interested in them and even that He's against them. They foolishly crown themselves gods of their own lives. We must obey God to experience His love, but many do not see it that way. As David invested the effort to find Mephibosheth, comfort him and provide for him, so the wonderful God of the Bible seeks out people and graciously overcomes their resistance. His life-transforming power is purely a matter of exercised sovereignty, attracted by nothing praiseworthy in its object. GRACE (God's Riches At Christ's Expense), is the Lord's provision for our needs. Every person needs it. Sinful human nature cannot be changed by our efforts. Our self-centered natures are so blind that we do not see the effects of sin; nor do we acknowledge the origin of our problems or agree with God about how to solve them.

Conclusion

David is to be commended for showing the "kindness of God" to Mephibosheth. He lived in the palace and ate at the king's table the rest of his life. David's example challenges us to "put feet" to God's care for others.

CHAPTER TWENTY

CONSIDER THYSELF, LEST THOU ALSO BE TEMPTED

2 Samuel 11

Recently, I was talking with a teenage girl who attempted suicide in an effort to get away from the loving restraint she very much needed. She defiantly hurled at me, "I'll never go home!" It echoed something Peter had said in the Garden of Gethsemane, "Though all others forsake you Lord, I will not." There was a spirit of pride in both the teenager's statement and in Peter's claim. Each had looked at his ability, strength and determination and had given himself too high a grade.

What bitter disappointment awaited Peter. He was to find out that his love for the Lord Jesus Christ was not as great as he had believed. Difficult experiences are ahead for those who declare their independence from the people who love them most. And bitter lessons can come to the one who says, "I will never fall prey to immorality like David did." Pride in one's self is the first step in the fall of a person who vows such will never happen. Christians should use their full spiritual armor to ensure purity of life. The failure to see that within each of us is an enemy—our sin nature—is blindness that can result in a fall (Prov. 16:18).

The most godly men, the most selfless Christians and the excellent leaders of fine churches have confessed that though they have been enabled to be solid soldiers of the cross, they still feel the downward pull of sexual attraction. All of us would do well to practice Galatians 6:1: "Brethren, if a man be overtaken in a fault, ye which are spiritual, restore such an one in the spirit of meekness; considering thyself, lest thou also be tempted."

Second Samuel 11 humbles us all! Let us approach it with humility, aware that we are not above repeating its tragedy.

In this chapter we are warned about our own sinful nature. We learn that no situation in life, no office to which even God may call one, no depth of spirituality or any admiration from others can make one immune from the attractions of sin. Though he knew union with God, even in the writing of sacred Scripture (the psalms), David plunged into sin.

David committed adultery. And then to try to cover it, he committed murder. If we turn away in disgust from David's sins, we profit little. Consider carefully the full harvest of David's actions and be warned. And as we study, we will gain encouragement to draw near to God when we are equally undeserving. We will be more patient with others who sin against us, knowing that we could have just as easily sinned against them—but for the grace of God.

David's Personality. Taylor has pointed out that some people are well-thought-of and get credit for good moral character, when the truth is that they are blameless because of their timid personalities. They are too cautious and weak to go very far toward either holiness or wickedness. This does not describe David. There was nothing "halfway" about him. His personality carried him to the top. But though a God-given temperament has the potential to lift a person, it also has the potential of bringing one very low. David was aggressive and wholehearted in whatever he did. He had known great height. But now, a great chasm yawned in front of him.

The Situation. David is about fifty years of age. For the last twenty years, he has experienced unbroken success. He has been constantly praised and admired. He was as popular with his people as any ruler, pastor or executive could be. Possibly, this prosperity had loosened his mental grip on the lessons of the fugitive years. They were fuzzy in his memory.

A Dangerous Period

We often think of youth as the time of life that is the most critical. And, indeed, it is a very important period in life. Once-in-a-lifetime decisions are made in one's youth (life partner, occupation). Habits and viewpoints are established that will likely be with one throughout his life. I suppose for every message one hears in church about the dangers of middle age, a dozen on the traps that teens are apt to fall into are heard. However, 2 Samuel 11 shows that the middle-aged saint has temptations as well. Sometimes, teens assume that all adults are responsible, godly, content and living within their means. But older people do sin. Noah and Lot were well into the "Geritol generation" when they fell into sin.

Second Samuel 11:1: "And it came to pass, after the year was expired, at the time when kings go forth to battle . . . David tarried in Jerusalem." The "and" shows chapter 10 is connected to chapter 11. Joab had defeated the Ammonites in the previous chapter. Winter passed, and in 2 Samuel 11, hostilities were renewed. Kings normally went to war at this time of the year. But, for some reason, David did not. Many writers suspect that he preferred the comforts of the palace to the hardness of camp. He was not in the place of duty.

Another factor is that David had many wives.

Michal, Abigail and Ahinoam had been with him for a long time. When he became king at Hebron, he added four more wives. And he took more wives and concubines when he became king over a united nation. God had warned against having many wives; and kings, in particular, were warned (Deut. 17:16, 17).

The Sin. One evening, David took a stroll on his rooftop. He saw a beautiful woman bathing on a distant roof. The woman was Bath-sheba, the wife of Uriah, the Hittite, one of David's "thirty mighty men."

There is danger in some of the things we see. And the danger may increase the longer we gaze at them. We cannot avoid seeing some improper things, but we can refuse to look a second time. James tells us, "Every man is tempted, when he is drawn away of his own lust, and enticed. Then when lust hath conceived, it bringeth forth sin: and sin, when it is finished, bringeth forth death" (James 1:14, 15).

Again, David faced a moment of spiritual challenge. He had exercised self-control in the past, when he had opportunities to kill Saul and did not. He had proved his integrity. In that instant when he first saw Bath-sheba, he would either turn away to safeguard himself, or he would "get an eyeful" and bring darkness into his soul.

Job struggled with the same challenge. His conclusion was "I made a covenant with my eyes not to look lustfully at a girl" (Job 31:1, NIV). Advertisements, clothing styles and television constantly focus on sex today. Cars, cosmetics, beverages and football are hawked with seductive women. Men and women alike flaunt their bodies through immodest clothing.

Christ said that the eye is the light and lamp of the body. If the eye is used for pure purposes, one's outlook will be proper, but if the eye is used to receive lustful things, the whole life becomes dark, and spiritual well-being is at risk (Luke 11:34).

David's glimpse of Bath-sheba was unfortunate,

but not sinful. He *continued* to gaze at her. When he realized who she was, he sent for her and committed adultery with her. David went to his grave regretting this sin and all the misery it brought to his life.

Many Wives: Sexual Safeguard or Fuel for the Fire? Pride played a part in the acquiring of many wives, since, normally, the king's prestige was measured by the size of his harem.

But sexual appetite also played a part in the sin. One would think that with so many wives to choose from for an evening's companionship, David would be satisfied. Since his wives had different temperaments, there would be a woman for each of his moods. We also are told that Abigail was a beautiful woman. And the others likely were not ugly. Instead of making him rich and full in this significant area of life, David's multiple wives made him even more susceptible to the charms of the mysterious beauty bathing next door.

God wants us to learn the easy way that sexual happiness is not finding Miss Universe or Mr. America. The ideal body and the ultimate sexual experience constitute a fantasy our sinful nature is apt to chase. Joy and richness come to the degree that we work diligently at being good lovers.

In 2 Samuel 12:7 and 8, when Nathan rebuked David, God put an astounding statement in the prophet's mouth. Paraphrased, he said, "I anointed you [David] king; I delivered you from Saul; I gave you Saul's throne; and I gave you your *master's wives . . . and if all this had been too little, I would have given you even more.*" What would "even more" include? God had given David safety, material possessions, wives and political power. And if what He had already given David was insufficient to offset the pressures of office—the burdens of making awesome decisions, the loneliness of leadership—He would have given David even more in each of the above categories and in other areas. Surprisingly, any additional wives David might want (except married women) came within the scope of what God offered him.

The Cover-Up

The "Developments." In the weeks that followed David's adultery, he thought that his sin would be forgotten. The more time that passed, the more secure he felt. But he could not continue to hide his sin, for there were further developments inside Bath-sheba's body—she was pregnant. When she told David, his world blew apart. Numbers 32:23 warns, "Be sure your sin will find you out." The "bills" for the king's lack of self-control were coming due. And David decided to cover up the matter.

How and Why Christians Sin. Satan makes his appeal to Christians where passion is greatest and principle is weakest. Besides the devil's temptations, every believer has an "old sin nature." This fallen nature is wicked, sin-prone and unchangeable. It is no different in the Christian than in the non-Christian. It never gets better or less selfish and never becomes subject to God. The apostle Paul spoke about his own struggle in these words: "But I keep under my body, and bring it into subjection.... For the flesh [the old sinful nature] lusteth against the Spirit, and the Spirit against the flesh" (1 Cor. 9:27; Gal. 5:17). There is a war going on inside the believer. Jesus Christ did not come to save that old sin nature but to (1) enable us to see ourselves as sinners and (2) to overcome our old sin nature by the power of the Holy Spirit.

Sinning with the "Best of 'Em." When a believer yields control of his life to his sin nature, he can be just as conniving, ruthless and self-serving as any non-Christian. David's old nature surged past his spiritual nature, carrying it along like a damsel in distress. He was indistinguishable from those who claim no spiritual orientation in life.

David was in a fix. Uriah was away at war and

would know in a few months that he was not the father of the coming child. The king had a great deal at stake—his reputation, his kingship, maybe his life. He wanted the matter hushed up.

Gross Hypocrisy. David called Uriah home from war and pretended to be very interested in how things were going. Having received Uriah's report, David dismissed him, encouraging him to go home. Sending some food delicacies to Uriah's home in an effort to promote merriment and lovemaking, David hoped the whole thing would blow over and that Uriah would think he was the father of Bath-sheba's child.

God's Perspective on Hypocrisy. A young lawyer, wanting to impress those in his waiting room, carried on an imaginary phone conversation about being unable to accept an important case because he was already too busy. But, like most hypocrites, he got caught. The telephone repair man who had come to hook up the phone was in the waiting room.

Consider several facts about hypocrisy.

First, there are degrees of hypocrisy. (1) There is the comparatively harmless kind, which leads to disrespect, as with the lawyer. (2) Then there is the person who blunders, perhaps seriously, like David does here, but whose life as a whole is characterized by walking faithfully with God. (3) In the worst degree of hypocrisy, a person is justifiably called a "hypocrite" because his lifelong pattern is one of inconsistency.

Second, Christians acknowledge that they are not what they want to be. Some believers have greatly embarrassed the One they represent. However, God has committed Himself to deal with His own in due time. The hottest words of condemnation from the Savior's lips were directed toward hypocrites (see Matt. 23:13–36). The Bible tells us that some people's sins are exposed in this life, some in the next life (1 Tim. 5:24). Judgment will begin at the house of God (1 Pet. 4:17).

Third, many nonchurchgoers say churches are full of hypocrites. God is accused of having poor representatives. But many who are thought to be believers may not be believers. Some people imagine they are Christians because they are sincere, try to live by the golden rule, keep the Ten Commandments or watch Billy Graham on TV once in a while (see Matt. 7:21, 22). Beware of blaming God for having poor representatives, when such people may just be going through the motions and not be true Christians.

Fourth, all people are inconsistent to some degree. Every parent knows and speaks more truth to his children than he practices!

Fifth, the watching world must realize that much is "lost in translation" when God seeks to show Himself through His people. Much of the Creator is missing in the creature. Believers in Christ are not photocopies of Him. Christians know they are inconsistent; that is why they have turned to Christ for forgiveness.

Sixth, people must keep their eyes on the Lord, not on His followers. David gave "the enemies of the LORD great occasion to blaspheme . . . " (2 Sam. 12:14). Undoubtedly, some were shattered by the news of what their king had done. Nations that had watched Israel decided that Israel's God could not be very concerned with high standards. Today, people judge the Savior by those who claim to be His. And they excuse their own sinful lifestyles on the basis that Christians are inconsistent. To so judge the Savior by the Christian is like comparing rhinestones with diamonds and refusing both, claiming, "They both glitter, don't they?" It is like lumping Schuler's (a very plush, expensive and quality restaurant) with White Castle's 19¢ burgers and deciding, "They are both eating places, aren't they?"

A parent does not want a child to use the disobedience of an older sibling as an excuse to disobey also. The disobedience of one child does not excuse the other child. And the inconsistencies of the Chris-

230

tian do not make the non-Christian exempt from "Ye must be born again" (John 3:7).

We may have eaten at a restaurant that we later found out had a dirty kitchen. But we don't stop eating out. And we have shopped in stores that cheated us. But we still buy things. Some businesses steal from employees, but we still work for a living. Yet some give up on Christianity altogether because of hypocrites. That's inconsistent!

Seventh, God is God. In David's day, God gave clear direction about Himself that was available to seekers of the truth. We are prone to look at others to measure spirituality. Instead, we should look to God. His Book will tell us what a Christian is.

Some people, knowingly or unknowingly, order God around. Their attitude is, "If there were not so many 'phonies' around, I might go to church. If God would just 'zap' a few of 'em and get 'em straightened out, I would believe in Him." But God refuses to come into the courtroom we set up for Him, He will not respond to what people think He should be doing.

The previous observations are not intended to condone David's sin, but rather to set it in perspective. David's mistake was serious, and he accordingly paid a high price for it.

David Plays Saul; Uriah Plays David. When David was heading into the fugitive years, Saul played the hypocrite and lied to David, hoping to lure him to his death (see commentary on 1 Sam. 18:17–25). David stood before Saul's servants in transparent innocency as he was urged by them to risk his life. How guilty they felt, especially since they liked David and were weary of Saul. But now David is the deceptive one. He strangely resembles Saul. Uriah, one of David's "thirty mighty men," acted like David used to—loyal and disciplined. One of the things making David's deed so foul is that Uriah was loyal to him. Undoubtedly, Uriah had earned his rank by valor beyond the call of duty. He was an outstanding fellow! Sterling quality had been pressed into his being by years of living on the run, by knowing that one mistake could result in the death of all, by the rigors of strenuous service. Uriah's iron-like discipline and loyalty that had flowered amidst oppressive circumstances in the fugitive years kept him unknowingly from accommodating David. When Uriah refused to join his wife because Joab and his fellow soldiers were suffering the hardships of the camp, David got Uriah drunk. But even when intoxicated, Uriah would not go home to his wife. In spite of being urged to relax and take a couple of days off, Uriah would not go home. David was violating the principle of loyalty he had drummed into his men, and he felt the sting of his hypocrisy. He was rebuked.

Now desperate, David sent Uriah back to the battlefront with a letter. Certain of the man's loyalty not to open the message, David allowed his servant to carry his own death orders. The letter told Joab to place Uriah in a dangerous part of the battle and to retreat from him so he would be killed. Again, David was counting on Uriah's loyalty to keep him at the very front of the battle even when others withdrew. His allegiance was the agency of his doom.

Joab, the general, and David, the man after God's own heart, were not normally on the same moral and spiritual plane, but this time David sunk to Joab's level. The general's character may have brought to David's mind the plan for disposing of Uriah. His ruthlessness commended him to the king as an able instrument. There had been a time when the tender conscience of David troubled him for rendering King Saul the slight discourtesy of cutting off some of his royal robe. Now he planned the death of a loyal soldier without apparent remorse.

The last incidence of hypocrisy on David's part occurs when he tells the messenger to return to Joab and console him with words to the effect, "That's the way it goes—these things happen."

Did David Know Bath-sheba Before?

Three factors suggest David had some awareness of Bath-sheba before his evening stroll on the roof:

First is the fact that Uriah was one of the king's "thirty mighty men." His frequent association with these leading soldiers makes it almost certain he did know of this man's gorgeous wife prior to seeing her bathing on the roof. David's question about the identity of the woman he had seen on the roof does not mean he had never seen her before. The question deals with positive identification.

Second, Joab's response to David after he received the death order strongly suggests David knew Bath-sheba before. Joab accomplished the grizzly task. Uriah died in battle. As the general reports back to David by means of a messenger, the form of the response shows Joab knew David had an interest in Uriah's wife. His response is taunting. He rehearses with the messenger exactly what to say to David. The messenger was to describe the general progress of the war, including the fact that Joab's plan called for several men to get very near the wall of the city being attacked. Joab anticipated what David would say. He even knew the historical example David would use to show that Joab used poor military judgment in getting so near the wall. The messenger was carefully instructed to let David get irritated and go through his whole angry tirade. Then he was to balance the king's displeasure with one simple statement: "Thy servant Uriah the Hittite is dead also." David said exactly what Joab had expected. And his anger melted away when he learned Uriah was dead. When the messenger delivered the "punch line," David would realize that Joab had let him dangle. The general may have found some grim humor in this.

Later, Joab pieced the whole thing together. He wanted the situation to yield as rich a power dividend as possible. He must wring from it advantages for himself. F. B. Meyer put these thoughts into

Joab's mind when he received the death order: "This master of mine can sing psalms with the best, but when he wants a piece of dirty work done, he must come to me. He wants to rid himself of Uriah—I wonder why. Well, I will help him do it. At any rate, he will not be able to say another word to me about how I killed Abner. I shall be able to do almost as I will. He will henceforth be in my power."[1]

Third, that David knowingly called down upon himself the awful wrath of God to get this woman indicates that he knew the value of what he was reaching for. It is likely that he had previously been attracted to her charming personality, quick mind and beautiful face. The sight of her on the roof was the last attraction that pushed him over the brink. David's grab for this woman cost him dearly, but it should be noted that she did become the woman of his life. Henceforth, the text mentions no other women in the king's life.

How Long Was David Backslidden? How much time elapsed between the time David spotted Bathsheba on the roof and when he was confronted by Nathan and wrote Psalm 51? William Taylor and Alan Redpath suggested about one year.[2] I believe it was not more than ten months at the longest or ten weeks at the shortest. Even ten weeks is much too long to be out of God's good grace.

It has been assumed that David was not confronted by Nathan until after the child was born, because 2 Samuel 12:15 records both Nathan's departure from David and the fact that the child became ill. However, there is nothing in this or other verses that precludes the possibility that Nathan rebuked David long before the infant was born.

Physical Effects on David. Psalm 32 describes the physical effects of the king's unrepentant condition: "My bones wasted away" as a result of groaning; that God's pressure was "heavy upon me"; that his strength was sapped as in the heat of summer. His body fluids were drained off, making his mouth dry—day and night. Clearly, there are physical side effects of spiritual rebellion. When one is out of fellowship with God, life gets downright miserable!

David is Confronted; He Confesses and Is Restored

Authors Meyer and Redpath attributed a harshness to David toward the conquered Rabbahites because of his guilt and turmoil of soul. They say he more than made up for the leniency he allowed himself by taking it out on the captured people of Rabbah. They claimed he treated them with cruelty, dealing out the stiff penalty he should have given himself. While often a guilty person will excuse himself from judgment by heaping wrath on others, Redpath and Taylor appear to have based their view on a disputed translation of 2 Samuel 12:31. The King James Version, which both authors used, conveys that David killed people by sawing them up, axing them, mauling them to death with iron and by making them walk through fire. But the New International Version and the New Scofield Bible state that David put the people to work as slaves with picks, axes and iron, and that they made bricks in the fire.

The Confrontation. Nathan was commissioned by God for the distasteful, hard task of rebuking the king. Who would want to face a monarch who had the power of life and death over his subjects—especially after being informed he had recently used such a power against one of his own "thirty mighty men"? The business of being a prophet could get rough! No one had faced the king about any wrongdoing on his part for nearly two decades.

For Nathan to be entrusted with this assignment shows that God thought highly of him. Nathan was ready to vindicate that trust. Because of his wise handling of this ticklish matter, the prophet endeared himself to both David and Bath-sheba, and was associated with them long into the future.

235

Nathan's Parable. Pressing his way through the people in the outer chambers of the palace, Nathan angled for the door to David's private quarters. A story he told roused David's keen sense of justice. Very likely, God had given the parable to Nathan in advance. It was too critical a matter for any ragged edges; there could be no slips! The prophet must pierce any excuses, shatter any defense. The parable was an ingenious way to ensure clear and decisive results from the meeting.

Since David prided himself on dispensing justice, the story was tailor-made to trap him. Nathan told him about a rich man who had treated a poor man unjustly. Without knowing he was "swallowing the bait," David pronounced the death penalty for the rich man.[3] In a flash of prophetism, Nathan crushed the real person of this story. "Thou art the man!" Nathan fired. He went on to name the sins of the king. Down came the hammerlike blows on the heart of David. He had despised the commandment of the Lord, caused Uriah to be killed and had taken Uriah's wife. These were not small matters, and God's judgment upon David corresponded with the awfulness of the sins. The sword, or conflict, would be a part of David's family for the rest of his life; God would take David's wives from him, allowing them to be given to another publicly; and the child of Bath-sheba would die.

A Harvest of Misery. A horrible catalogue of misery followed in David's life in fulfillment of God's pronounced judgment: a son raped a daughter; another son who was in exile long after David had forgiven him killed the rapist; when finally welcomed home, that son led a revolt that nearly hurled his father from the throne; then that son was killed; a third son was killed for his attempt to gain the crown; and David's infant son died. The misery produced by David's acts of adultery and murder should instill fear in us all.

Private Battle; Public Effect. David's great actions for self-control in his treatment of Saul had been largely private. When he proved himself, unobserved, God sent far-reaching blessings to all he ruled over. Private victory brought public progress. In like manner, the sin with Bath-sheba had been private, but it would have long-range, public effects.

Confession. The king had listened to Nathan in stunned silence. Guilt melted him. He did not deny the charges; he was caught, and he knew it. "I have sinned against the LORD," he admitted. What relief he felt! Bearing the weight of this secret had worn him out.

Though relieved, David knew that Scripture (Lev. 20:10) required his death. The law was clear: though he was king of Israel, David was to die by stoning. But God graciously spared his life.

Prayer and Fasting. When his child became ill, David fasted and prayed in hope that he might live. The illness lasted seven days, and we can assume David invested the whole time fasting and praying to show God the depth of his remorse and repentance.

The illness was hard on both the king and Bath-sheba. They knew they had caused it. And little babies cannot tell caring parents where they hurt or how to help. The parents were under great strain. Taylor said, " . . . each pleading look of the upturned eyes would go like a dart to the mother's heart, and each convulsive tremor of the infant's body would send a spear of anguish through the father's frame."[4]

The Child Dies. David's servants did not understand the depth of his spiritual life, and they became concerned about his praying and fasting. He seemed to be acting strangely. So when the child died, they were afraid to tell him; he was already on the verge of desperate behavior. As they whispered to one another, David sensed what had happened. But to the surprise of the servants, once he confirmed the death of the child, David rose, washed, dressed and went to worship God. Remember, David had not eaten for seven days. The worshiping David is the genuine David.

Repentance. Psalm 51, written by David, captures his wholehearted repentance. In abject spiritual poverty, David cast himself on the mercy of the Lord for the forgiveness and restoration he desperately needed. Life for him would be a prison of guilt and shame unless he experienced God's forgiveness.

David sinned, in spite of being "a man after God's own heart," as the apostle Paul described him one thousand years later. The fact that he turned from sin shows that he normally obeyed God.

What is the real difference between the godly and the ungodly person? Is the "righteous" person full of "rightness"? Not necessarily. The difference is that when the godly person sins, he cries out to God in repentance. The non-Christian does not. And he is not conscious of needing God's help. The unsaved person may be driven farther from God by acts of discipline, such as the death of David's infant. Since David normally functioned on a "spiritual wavelength," he was drawn nearer to God through discipline. He was like a child who, when getting a spanking, buries his face in the parent's garments. He hides himself from God in God.

Acceptance. While some Scriptures (Matt. 7:1; Luke 13:1–5; John 9:2, 3) forbid us to judge the motives and actions of others or conclude that they suffered a tragedy because they committed a specific sin, it is clear that David's child died because of David's and Bath-sheba's sin. And the grieving parents accepted this, not with stoic resignation, but with belief in God's justice. They could not logically resent God's judgment. When a believer sins, he has no control over the price God exacts.

Was David's Prayer Answered? Yes. But God

did not spare the infant's life. We do not always get exactly what we pray for. Even so, valuable things come from diligent, fervent praying. As one prays, he sees the perspective of God more clearly. Prayer changes the thing being prayed about, and it changes the one who is praying.

Though David's tearful prayers did not cause God to spare the child, they did bring down the strength of God to move along in life and not be consumed with regret. The turmoil of his soul was soothed. This is the value of prayer.

When David's little son died, he was awakened to what is really important in life, and he was rebuked for his sin.[5] Through any kind of crisis, God may be correcting His own, getting the glitter of materialism out of his eyes, generating spiritual growth or arousing an unconverted person to come to Christ for salvation.

When an infant precedes a family into eternity, those left behind prepare more earnestly for the next world. The reunion is looked forward to. All people labor under the curse of selfishness—but a tragedy can break its grip. If a stubborn sheep will not follow the shepherd to better pasture, what should be done? Get behind it and push? Tie a rope around its neck and pull? No. Pick up its little lamb and march off. It will follow.

When a Baby Dies. Second Samuel 12:23 is the vital verse in answering the important question of where a baby goes when it dies. Every family that has lost a little one will eagerly welcome the truth presented here. David's statement, prompted by the Holy Spirit, will bring comfort and encouragement regarding the eternal destiny of the souls of departed little ones: " . . . the child is dead, wherefore should I fast? can I bring him back again? I shall go to him, but he shall not return to me." If David would "go to the infant," where would David go when he died? According to Hebrews 11—the great "roll call of the faithful"—David went to Heaven. Since David was to join the infant and David went

239

to Heaven, we know that infants who die before they become knowledgeable of sin go to be with the Lord. This is a precious truth.

David's Future: Atonement or Discipline? David was forgiven. The Lord reversed the death penalty. He was restored to God's favor, instantly cleansed, but he would still suffer the consequences of his actions. However, David's future hardships were not payment for sin. In allowing David to harvest what he had sown, God was acting as the just and loving Heavenly Father, not as the eternal Judge, trying to bring a sinner to repentance or exacting from a debtor what was owed. No amount of human suffering could meet the requirements of the Holy God with Whom we have to do. Only the God-Man, Jesus Christ, could atone for human sin.

Suppose a mosquito carried some disease and caused a person to die. Would it satisfy the relatives of the departed person if all the mosquitos in the world were rounded up and killed to make up for the loss of this person? No. Why? Because insects are not worthy to be compared to human beings. Likewise, no suffering on David's part could atone for his sins—what he suffered was the discipline of God. And it reminded him to avoid such sins in the future. It also serves as a warning to all that God will not condone evil. We reap what we sow.

Bath-sheba

Although David's and Bath-sheba's relationship began sinfully, Bath-sheba became *the* woman in David's life. He had a colorful, dynamic personality. One expects to see beside him an equally distinguished woman. There was no such woman until David met Bath-sheba. His other wives disappear from the Bible narrative after Bath-sheba is introduced. She was David's companion the rest of his life. Adam sinned and knowingly identified himself with Eve as she called the wrath of God down upon herself (1 Tim. 2:14). David, likewise, knew what he was getting into. His attraction to Bath-sheba can be measured by his choice to get her and to ignore the plain command of God. Only God's grace made it possible for this relationship, which started in the flesh, to end in the spirit.

Nothing indicates that Bath-sheba compromised her faith in marrying the foreign-born Uriah. He seems to have been a worshiper of the one true God.

Upon David's invitation to the palace, Bath-sheba was probably flattered to have the attention of the king. Some suggest she was innocent because the king's word was law. Not so. That she suffered the consequences of the adultery shows that she was guilty of it. And how foolish to bathe where she could be seen.

Bath-sheba knew days of anguish over her pregnancy before Uriah died. She was more in danger of death (by stoning) than David was. She would not have been aware of Uriah's presence in Jerusalem when David called him home. She waited for her husband to come home. She knew how Uriah felt about the unwritten code of the soldier (you don't allow yourself the comforts of home if your comrades are in the fields; 2 Sam. 11:11), but she hoped he would come home anyway. But when Uriah left the capital, nothing had been accomplished to protect her from the shame. Soon everyone would know.

Bath-sheba probably knew nothing about the plan to kill her husband, but she became suspicious when news of his death arrived. She seems to have loved Uriah. She likely became aware that David had arranged his death, and we are surprised this did not put up a wall between them.[6] Being able to overcome her husband's death assumes Bath-sheba had a very strong attachment to David.

Bath-sheba shared Nathan's rebuke and repented along with David. Her close association with the prophet from then on shows genuine repentance. Rising to become the king's spiritual equal over the years, Bath-sheba qualified to be the king's companion. And her greatest influence came through the birth of her son Solomon. Nathan, incidentally, shared in his training.

Healing. David and Bath-sheba were married. David comforted his wife and tried to heal their relationship. As the *improper* use of sex brought great devastation, the *proper* employment of this blessed gift brought a restoration of emotional, marital and spiritual health. And the arrival of Solomon was tangible evidence of God's forgiveness. A rich sex life in the bonds of marriage is one of God's best gifts to a couple. Friction is reduced to a fraction when this area of a marriage is one of delight and satisfaction.

Psalms. Placing the psalms written during this period of David's life in chronological order, they would appear as follows: 38, 2, 51 and 32.

Conclusion

Peter made a painful discovery—he did not love the Lord Jesus as much as he liked to think. Likewise, it was hard for David to sense the evil lurking within himself.

Most of us make this same discovery. God told us through Jeremiah that our hearts are desperately wicked, and that we do not know them. We do not know our own potential for evil. Sadly, through life, we discover again and again our sinfulness. It is for this reason that we should handle David's sin with a brokenness of spirit. Paul wrote some excellent counsel: "Brethren, if a man be overtaken in a fault, ye which are spiritual, restore such an one in the spirit of meekness; considering thyself, lest thou also be tempted" (Gal. 6:1).

End Notes

1. Meyer, *David: Shepherd, Psalmist, King*, p. 160.
2. William M. Taylor, *David, King of Israel* (New York: George H. Doran Company, 1916), p. 270. And Alan Redpath, *The Making of a Man of God*

(Westwood, New Jersey: Fleming H. Revell Company, 1962), p. 200.

3. While I disagree with Taylor and Redpath regarding David's supposed cruel treatment shown the Rabbahites because of an uneasy conscience, I feel Taylor is correct about David's guilty conscience showing in his harsh judgment of the rich man in Nathan's parable. The levitical law covering such cases as Nathan described require a fourfold payment, not the death penalty.

4. Taylor, *David, King of Israel (1916)*, p. 258.

5. A case presented in 1 Kings 14:13 is opposite the one here. In the Kings text we are told that a child died, not because of its own wickedness or because of the parent's sin (though they were evil), but because of the child's goodness.

6. This is additional evidence that David and Bath-sheba were aware of each other prior to their adultery. David's confidence that his killing of Uriah would not shatter his relationship with Bath-sheba presupposes a substantial familiarity with her.

CHAPTER TWENTY-ONE

AMNON: IRRATIONAL, ISOLATED AND ANNIHILATED

2 Samuel 13

A young girl is pregnant or a man ends his twelve-year marriage. The details are different, but the grief is the same. Sex is the common factor; misery is the experience.

The second consequence of David's loss of self-control with Bath-sheba is recorded in 2 Samuel 13. What David had done with another man's wife, his son Amnon did to his half sister Tamar. Though he was forgiven in the court of Heaven, David's sin produced a harvest of heartache. Jeremiah 2:19 applies to David's situation: "Thine own wickedness shall correct thee, and thy backslidings shall reprove thee: know therefore and see that it is an evil thing and bitter, that thou hast forsaken the LORD thy God, and that my fear is not in thee, saith the Lord GOD of hosts."

Arthur Pink made this observation: " . . . It is ... deeply instructive and unspeakably solemn to observe the *method* God used in bringing to pass the ghastly prophecy about evil coming out of his own house. David's palace was not suddenly consumed with fire from Heaven; the Philistines did not march upon him in a devastating surprise attack; his family was not swallowed up in an earthquake; nor did a cyclone level the city. Instead, the influence of David's sinful actions brought hardship into his life as a natural outworking of God's moral law."[1]

Nathan had predicted that trouble would arise in David's house, and David must have constantly wondered, "Which son or which daughter will rebel? When? What will happen?" Such mental stress exacted a high price.

David was too "easygoing" as a parent. He had allowed himself to be stymied by Joab (2 Sam. 3:39). He took no action against Amnon for raping Tamar, nor against Absalom for murder. And, just before the end of his life, David failed to rebuke Adonijah's independence: " . . . his father had not displeased him at any time in saying, Why has thou done so?" (1 Kings 1:6).

Israel's Golden Era. Though the Spirit of God in the Biblical narrative shifts the focus to the consequences of David's sin, keep in mind that this was Israel's golden age. With the exception of Absalom's conspiracy (which happened some years later after this time, affecting less than half of the nation), there was peace. Prosperity and culture flourished.

Amnon Rapes Tamar. It is said that a man does not hear until his own voice echoes back to him. Through Amnon's actions, David painfully listened to that echo. David's failure to control his own sexual desires rendered him unfit to lead his sons to a way of purity. David's oldest son Amnon followed his father and exceeded him. While David was basically a godly man, Amnon was not. He was irrational, then isolated and finally annihilated.

Irrational

Since David had had children by several wives, rivalry was inevitable. Unhealthy competition occurred between Amnon, David's oldest son, Absalom, Amnon's half brother, and Tamar, Absalom's full-blooded sister.

David lavished his fatherly affection and enthusiasm on Amnon, his precious firstborn. Amnon could expect to ascend his father's throne. In view of the wealth that Solomon inherited, one can imagine Amnon's eagerness. Amnon grew up knowing of his father's love for the Lord, but he reached early manhood without being strongly attracted to God.

But Amnon was drawn to his beautiful half sister Tamar. He probably had more than one half sister. He was so enamored with her; yet so unapproachable did she seem, that he got sick from his desire for her.

When Amnon's slimy cousin Jonadab saw his haggard appearance, he asked what was wrong. And led by his cousin, Amnon schemed to get alone with Tamar.

Finally alone with her, passion carried Amnon beyond reason. As he started to rape Tamar, she said, "Please speak to the king; he will not withhold me from being married to you." Tamar was not saying "no"—she was urging Amnon to get what he wanted "through channels." A wedding could be arranged to legitimatize Amnon's desires.[2] What an amazingly self-sacrificing attitude on Tamar's part; she is poised and has excellent clarity of mind despite the fact that she is being raped. But Amnon did not listen to anything except his animal instincts. How stupid! How shortsighted!

This situation raises the question, How can we get things from God in a proper way? It also warns against the power of sexual attraction. Ironically, people run desperately after the things God promises to give those who follow Him. Two main reasons that people do not get what they want is that they look to the wrong source, and/or they want their desires met immediately.

The Wrong Source. The most valuable things in life—loving and being loved, peace of mind, purpose and security—are obtainable *only* from God.

Year after year, radio and television programs hold their audiences with the theme of boy-gets-girl or girl-gets-boy. Our desire to be loved is insatiable. And God promises His enduring love to all who will seek it. But people continue to seek from others the things God has a monopoly on.

Consider another highly valued aspect of life—security. God wants us to be secure. But where is security found? People build their lives around money, fame, health, power and friendships to protect themselves from insecurity. Bill Gothard points out that security comes from building one's life around things that can *never* be destroyed. Beauty can fade, health can be lost, money can become worthless, houses can burn down and children can leave. Only our relationship with God is beyond the grasp of the destructive forces of human sinfulness. God wants us to be secure *in Him*. He is the true Source of love and security.

It is normally God's will for people to marry and to have the privilege and challenge of raising a family. But many young people do not seek the right Source to find the ideal mate. Their scheming excludes the Holy Spirit's direction.

God wants people to be able to cope with life, to be able to handle the "daily grind." Too often, when problems surface, people look to psychologists, alcohol, friends, drugs, hobbies or a "good time" for solutions. Gothard defines idolatry as looking to people, things or events to supply what we should be getting from God.

Waiting in Faith. Those who are wise enough to turn to God may still not get "normal" life accomplishments, comforts or luxuries. Waiting for what we want is not easy. And it doesn't seem to get easier as we get older.

We may wait on the Lord for a month or a year, but if our patience and faith fail, we are tempted to get what we want on our own. And we may abandon God just before He is ready to supply what we want, substituting friends for God to get what we

248

desire. Using the failures of others to excuse ourselves from doing what is right is something we sinners are apt to do. We are skilled at avoiding "death of self." And "reasons" for halfhearted spiritual efforts come readily to mind.

God has a monopoly on the love and the feelings of worth and purpose that the world desperately needs. He offers these freely to all who will walk with Him.

A Warning about Sexual Attraction. In the weeks before Amnon arranged to be alone with Tamar, a moral struggle was going on in his mind. We can understand Amnon's struggle, but we must not excuse his losing. Holmes Rolston correctly observed that Amnon revealed his character in making an intimate friend of such a "dirt dealer" as Jonadab.

The intensity of Amnon's struggle against temptation shows that he was not "all bad." He was torn between what he wanted and what he knew was right. But he gave way to his thirst for Tamar's beauty. At times, Amnon was likely a reasonable, fairly likable person. But under the pressure of sexual passion, he changed. And grabbing for the rose of sexual ecstasy, his hand was torn by thorns. Satan hides those thorns from us so effectively.

Many young people have been persuaded to yield sexual favors by the old ploy, "If you really loved me, you would. . . . " But true, Biblical love is different. Love meets the basic needs of others. Love can wait to give; lust cannot wait to get.

Isolated

Unreasonable and impatient, Amnon took what he wanted. Then, with awesome potency, the spiritual counterattack started. The bloodhound of guilt began its relentless pursuit. "Then Amnon hated her [Tamar] exceedingly; so that the hatred wherewith he hated her was greater than the love wherewith he had loved her. And Amnon said unto her, Arise, be gone," (2 Sam. 13:15). It is natural for a person to want to be alone when he feels ashamed. But it is a time when friends, family and forgiveness is needed most of all. The time when a person is the least lovable is when he most needs love.

When Amnon ordered Tamar out, she responded maturely: " ... this evil in sending me away is greater than the other. . . . " Her statement is a significant psychological truth: "Isolating yourself will bring greater harm upon you than your having raped me." Tamar is to be highly commended for having a clear mind, control of herself and Amnon's well-being in mind. She knew that if his life were to be salvaged, he would need supportive counsel.

Unheeding, Amnon multiplied his problems by pushing Tamar away. He isolated himself and hardened the circumstances that called for revenge.

Absalom's Reaction. David's third son was the vain Absalom. Absalom and Tamar shared three things: blood, beauty and a home. They were born to David by Maacah. Since both of their parents were excellent physical specimens, it is no surprise that both were good looking. Absalom was admired for his beautiful long hair, and Tamar was gorgeous. Absalom and Tamar lived in the same house after she was raped. This allowed constant opportunity for Absalom's sympathies to be aroused on his sister's behalf. Absalom favored his sister; it is very likely he named his daughter after her (2 Sam. 14:27).

David's Reaction. News of Amnon's wicked deed made the king angry. David was the chief officer of justice and was, therefore, obliged to set the matter right. But fearing that his own past deeds would be thrown up to him, David did nothing! Several authors on the subject state that David's hands were tied; in keeping with the mercy he had received, he could do nothing. Not so! There is a vital difference between David's sin and Amnon's sin. David repented; Amnon did not! The king was free to press his son for a confession and repentance.

David's inactivity hardened Absalom in his resolve to take vengeance on Amnon. Ecclesiastes 8:11 says, "Because sentence against an evil work is not executed speedily, therefore the heart of the sons of men is fully set in them to do evil."

Annihilated

Revenge smoldered in the mind of Absalom— and two full years did not extinguish the fire. The opportunity to kill Amnon presented itself when Amnon was lured out of Jerusalem to a sheepshearing feast. After he killed Amnon, Absalom fled to his mother's home country of Geshur.

Amnon's course had spiraled downward: from passion to irrationality, to isolation, to death.

David did not attend the sheepshearing feast, so he was in Jerusalem when the hysteria of the "massacre" was received: "All the sons of the king have been killed!" Then Jonadab, David's nephew, informed him that only Amnon had been killed.

Remember that it was Jonadab who had suggested to Amnon that he get alone with Tamar. Yet Jonadab was also in Absalom's confidence sufficiently to know that he would seek revenge. Know-it-all Jonadab pushed his way through the crowd to inform David that only Amnon was dead. And he told the reason for the murder. Did he expect such information to endear him to the king? In David's former days, he would have killed such a scoundrel for not having prevented the assassination.

Absalom stayed away for three years because he feared his father. This isolation of son from father was a serious problem for Dad.

Conclusion

I recently talked with a pregnant teenager. Her embarrassment, tone of voice and manner said, "The world is against me—I want out." A cloud of isolation was settling over her, which could be as destructive as the original sin. In avoiding the people who really cared about her, she was cutting off the means God would use to heal her.

Amnon suffered a similar fate. He expected peace, joy and ecstasy. Instead, he faced a greater struggle than he had had before he raped Tamar. He suffered more from having fulfilled his desires than from wrestling to control them. The price of self-control is never as great as the price for sin.

Paul wrote that it is God's will for one to "know how to possess his vessel [know how to handle one's body] in sanctification and honour" (1 Thess. 4:3, 4). Self-control is one of the highest virtues a believer can cultivate.

Amnon arranged the circumstances that led Absalom to kill him. Absalom was wrong to kill him, but Amnon would have died anyway. Amnon did not know what would happen to him when he took Tamar, as David had not known what would happen to his family when he took Bath-sheba.

End Notes

1. A. W. Pink, *The Life of David,* vol. 2 (Swengel, Pennsylvania: Reiner Publications, 1971), p. 72.

2. Holmes Rolston, *Personalities around David* (Richmond, Virginia: John Knox Press, 1946), pp. 115–120. Holmes Rolston maintains that Tamar's appeal was meaningless, since both she and Amnon knew that David would not allow such an incestuous marriage. I disagree. Her offer was valid, and Amnon should have acted on it.

CHAPTER TWENTY-TWO

AGONIZING CHOICES

2 Samuel 14

Most of us have been in "no-win" situations. No matter what choice is made, things still look dark and as if they were not going to get better. I believe the American presidency is a constant experience of this. The problems are of such a long-standing, complicated nature that there are no simple solutions.

There are many times when one is "cursed if he does and cursed if he doesn't." David was in such a situation in 2 Samuel 14. His heart was broken. He was reconciled to the loss of Amnon and, after three years, he forgave Absalom. And he wanted him back home. But justice had been outraged; there was a cry for vengeance from some quarters of the nation. Should David bring Absalom home or leave him in exile? It was an agonizing choice for David.

The content of this chapter is as follows: (1) Absalom was in voluntary exile; (2) the king accepted Amnon's death; (3) Joab sensed David's desire and skillfully employed a woman to that end; (4) Absalom returned to Jerusalem but did not see the king; (5) Joab ignored Absalom after he came back from exile; (6) Absalom burned Joab's grain field to force his participation in obtaining a full restoration to the king; (7) David and Absalom were reunited.

The Last Twenty Years of David's Monarchy. From this point on, the life of David becomes increasingly complex. Awesome, mind-boggling, emotion-packed, life-wrenching events fall on him in hammer-like blows. Life-threatening changes had to be absorbed by a man whose physical and emotional energies were declining. David became locked into situations that totally exposed him. The whole nation looked on as disaster undressed him. When pushed to the breaking point, it "all hung out"—exactly what he was and what he wasn't. Someone said, "What you are in a crisis is what you are." Life yields us a thorough examination. These are humbling chapters for us to read. Who can read them smugly, certain such things won't happen to him?

The Author of Scripture—the Holy Spirit— has raced past the pleasant years of David's monarchy (ages thirty through fifty) and saved a larger amount of space in the Bible to report his closing years, where his life seems to spiral out of control.

The motives and actions of leading people in 2 Samuel 14 and 15—Joab, Absalom, Ahithophel, Bath-sheba, Hushai and Ziba—become complex. Tense, dramatic circumstances develop. Why would Joab be so concerned about getting Absalom back? Once he was home, why did Joab ignore him? How could David welcome Absalom home with a clear conscience? Was Absalom repentant? How would his return affect the nation? With Absalom home, was David better or worse off? Did David make the right choice?

At the beginning of 2 Samuel 14, David is about fifty-eight years old. He would rule for another twelve years. During those years, he would need to draw heavily on his remaining spiritual reserves.

Absalom in Exile

Having avenged his sister by killing Amnon, Absalom fled to Geshur, the homeland of his mother Maacah. Geshur had been conquered by David, so his marriage to the king's daughter had a good deal of poison in it from the beginning (see 1 Sam. 27:8; 2 Sam. 3:3). Absalom stayed with his grandparents or relatives for three years. During this time, David was able to accept Amnon's death and gradually to forgive Absalom. Affection for Absalom swept into his heart and drove out anger and hurt. David longed to see him. But he was in a bind. Justice must be done! The murderer must be punished! Could David dare be lenient with his son while the whole nation looked on?

Joab's Plot. Joab sensed that David wanted his son home. Perhaps he noticed the king's energies were being drained—he was increasingly unable to administer the large empire they had forged together. Joab came to see that it was time to bring Absalom home—right or wrong.

It is likely that Joab knew of Nathan's method of using a story when he confronted the king years before. So he found a capable woman who would not melt in the king's presence—and primed her with what to say to David.

Only the most important cases were put on the king's docket. What energy he had was carefully hoarded for matters of prime importance. One day, however, a brokenhearted woman arrived at the palace and insisted on having the king render her a verdict. Joab may have swung open a few doors for his accomplice—and see the king she did!

Prostrating herself before the king, the woman begged for his help. Her story was that one of her two sons had risen against the other and killed him. The townspeople were now calling for the murderer's death.

Since he was a man of deep feeling, David's sympathies were aroused on behalf of the woman.

After hearing her story, he dismissed her, promising that a ruling would soon be forthcoming.

But the woman knew that Joab's purposes had not yet been accomplished, so she appealed for further discussion. The case before David was more ticklish than we might realize at first. It pitted the just punishment of a murderer against the strong Hebrew concern that a man's family not die out. Great public disgrace was associated with the extinction of a name. And it was a major tragedy for a man's land to be sold out of his family. Laws in Israel safeguarded the handing down of land from one generation to the next.

The king told the woman he would have to think about it.

But she was not about to let go. She did not have what she had come for, and she pled with the king! By pressing for a ruling, she was maneuvering David toward a principle that could serve as the basis for the return of Absalom.

As the woman appealed to his fatherly heart, David finally guaranteed the son's safety at the expense of justice. Then the woman was quick to apply the ruling to the king's family. She said, in effect, "Since you have been merciful to me and my son, why don't you apply the same principle to yourself and bring home your son Absalom? We will all die—we will all one day be like water spilled on the ground that cannot be gathered up [she was referring to Amnon]. You cannot bring him back. It is true that God plays no favorites and renders justice, but He finds ways to restore *His* banished. Why don't you bring back *yours?*"

David was awestruck. This was a new approach to his own problem. He had not seen it in that light before. Composing himself, David pierced the facade of the whole charade. When questioned, the woman admitted that Joab was behind the whole thing. After dismissing the woman, David called for Joab. Though apprehensive, Joab had read the king's spirit correctly. He was ready and willing to bring Absalom home.

A Defense of David's Actions. David had to weigh *justice* and *mercy* in this case. Many authors say David was wrong for showing mercy to Absalom. Three factors indicate that David was very concerned with *justice* in this agonizing choice.

First, half of 2 Samuel 14 shows David having to be persuaded to bring Absalom home. This side of the problem was no trifling matter, and David did not ignore it.

The *second* factor is that David had to be *tricked* into seeing his situation in2 Sam a new light. Even though he wanted Absalom home, he held off until others urged him.

Third, Absalom's restoration was only partial. He was welcome back in Jerusalem, but he would not have the privilege of seeing the king. This was very difficult for David—that's what he wanted most of all! Later events show that Absalom did not really care about seeing his father—so the restriction penalized only David.

Were David's Hands Tied?

Some Bible teachers maintain that David was hopelessly bound by his past sins. They say he could not logically judge the sins of others since he had been guilty of the same. While it is true that David harvested what he had sown, some make it sound like David was accountable for every sinful action of people around him.

David's hands were not tied. The Bible teaches that every man is responsible for his own actions. Joab, Amnon, Absalom, Adonijah and everyone else were directly responsible to God for their sins. Let's not hang them all on David!

Also, while Absalom was never interested in spiritual things and did not repent of having killed Amnon, David was totally repentant. He was crushed by his sin, and he turned wholeheartedly to God. And because of this, David received a personally spoken pardon from God. He was free to rule the government and lead his family.

Oh, the importance of repentance! It lifts a person up. Repentance is the only basis on which we can stand before God.

As David's position had many taxing responsibilities, he needed a personal pardon from God if he were going to be able to march forward in life victoriously. God saw he needed such a word, and He gave it. David was free to be God's man.

How, then, do we account for the misery of David's family? Some percentage of his troubles came as a fulfillment of God's punishment stated through Nathan.

Also, the life that David lived is almost more than a mortal can handle. Guiding the destiny of a nation is a huge responsibility. And David neglected the critical area of his own family.

It could be argued that David gave his whole life to the well-being of Israel, but no one reciprocated by raising his children for him. As you look at capable and gifted people who are serving the church, doesn't it seem that they could hope others would invest time in their children? God raises up some who are gifted in writing, preaching, teaching, leading or singing, and they make major contributions to the Christian world. But some of these neglect their primary responsibility in the home. Right or wrong, David may have felt that others had failed his family.

Some of what is attributed to the aftereffects of David's adultery should be attributed to his failure to give strong direction in his home. David loved his children to a fault. He did not rebuke them when they needed it. This failure had nothing to do with the consequence of his adultery. While we can understand how David's past sins would make him sheepish about judging the sins of others, there was nothing preventing him from being all God wanted him to be.

David's Forgiveness of Absalom. Alexander Maclaren provided some valuable insight about the *kind* and *quality* of forgiveness that David extended to Absalom.[1] It made him only angry and rebellious toward his father.

Healing, Biblical forgiveness must insist that sin be admitted and forsaken. Anything short of this does not maintain the wide gulf between the holiness of God and the sinfulness of man. If God forgave without demanding repentance, His holiness and justice would suffer. Man's sinful nature wants God to act as though sin does not matter and costs Him very little. Redpath noted that people want a "sunny and syncopated gospel that says, 'Fly now and pray later!' "[2] Because forgiveness cost God the life of His Son, He maintains His separateness from sin by demanding acknowledgment of sin in exchange for forgiveness.

Absalom was restored to the good graces of the king at the expense of justice. Absalom got what he wanted—restoration without admitting he had done wrong.

Life-changing forgiveness involves a change in the sinner. A person must want to avoid the same sin in the future. Sometimes a person cannot forgive himself. The basic cause for this fact is that one has made no effort to change his thinking and behavior patterns.

David, Absalom and Joab: Their Views on the Restoration of Absalom

Let's look at the situation from David's, Absalom's and Joab's views. Each of these men knew each other well. If David were about fifty-eight years old, as suggested, Absalom was twenty-eight and Joab was forty-eight. David and Joab had been working together for at least twenty-five years.

David's Viewpoint. One can imagine David praying, "Lord, I have been so sick lately. When will I get well? Thank You for my wife Bath-sheba and our precious son, Solomon. Lord, I cannot work as hard as I used to—I wish I had greater energy. You know I miss Amnon, and Absalom is not doing well.

My children are so dear to me! I know you are watching over me, but I feel overwhelmed. I know you have forgiven me for my sin with Bath-sheba, but I am the song of drunkards (Ps. 69:12). They mock me and call me a hypocrite. But I am in Your hands. I know You will give me the grace I need."

Psalms 41 and 55 indicate that David was ill near or during this time. He speaks of this time of illness as a low point in his life. Since God has designed us as three-part beings (body, soul and spirit), it is hard for two parts to be spiritually victorious if the third part is hurting. A sick man is apt to be discouraged—even the great psalmist and king was no exception to this rule.

David's viewpoint was also colored by the loss of two sons and the alienation of a third. Bath-sheba's first child had died. That son was special because of David's fervent love for Bath-sheba. The loss of Amnon before this had been a blow. He had been special because he was the king's firstborn. One's first child is an exciting experiment, an adventure. A parent sets out to be the perfect parent. A mother or father notices the failures of other parents and vows to do better than they did. Young parents resolve to make good; they are willing to invest any amount of love and self-sacrifice to guide their sons and daughters properly. But often—as in the case of Amnon—as the years wear on, the child grows up and pulls away from the guidance and love the parents offer.

The king may have become overprotective of the remaining members of his family. Having lost some sons, the rest became doubly precious. This is especially true of David's relationship with Solomon, Bath-sheba's second son. For seven years, David lavished all his affection on the son of his favorite wife.

Absalom's Viewpoint. We can imagine Absalom thinking: "If only Dad had dealt with Amnon! He was always the favorite. But now I'm clearly the front-runner for the throne. Just because my mother is from a conquered area of the empire, I should not be kept from the throne. I must take strides to achieve the monarchy, or Nathan, Bath-sheba and Zadok will convince the king to make this passive, 'culture-vulture' Solomon the next ruler. Without a strong man like me, the empire will fall apart. Life owes me something good for those crummy years I had to spend in exile. The nation needs me! The people think I'm dashing! Besides, I have no sons and I must make my mark on the world, or my name will die out."

A significant portion of the nation felt that Absalom did not do such a horrible thing in killing Amnon. They believed he did the messy job his father was unwilling to do. Since Amnon was gone, and David's second son, Chileab, had disappeared, Absalom did seem to be the logical choice for the throne to many Israelites. Absalom was about thirty years old. Solomon, however, could have been only six or eight years old because he was born at least nine months after Nathan rebuked David.

Everyone would like to be remembered after they die, but Absalom had an extreme desire for this. Second Samuel 18:18 says he had no son to carry on his name. Apparently, his three sons, mentioned in 14:27, had died. Absalom erected a pillar to himself to guarantee that he would be remembered. This indicates his great vanity.

Absalom was a methodical, calculating worker. The assassination of Amnon shows these traits. This deed was not hasty, fired by the passion of anger. Absalom planned for two years to accomplish it. Absalom was also very handsome. No one was as praised for his appearance as he was. When Absalom cut his hair—of which he was very proud—the portion that was cut off weighed five pounds.[3]

David's treatment of Absalom could have aroused antagonism. First, he likely had learned that Joab had to resort to a trick to convince his father to bring him home. Second, when he returned to Jerusalem, he got a cold reception. Third, he knew that pro-Solomon supporters had monopolized the

king for seven years. And, fourth, Absalom believed his father was inconsistent in bringing him
home but refusing to see him. If the king were still
outraged, he should have left him in exile. Knowing
human nature, we can assume Absalom blew these
inconsistencies out of proportion.

Joab's Viewpoint. Mulling over the situation,
Joab likely had these thoughts: "I am concerned
about David's successor, for I will outlive the king
by fifteen or twenty years. Absalom has a strong
personality—he can hold the empire together. Solomon is far too young now, and he is weak and timid.
The task is far too demanding for a personality like
his. I will bring Absalom into David's favor so that
both will be indebted to me."

Joab is hard to understand. He does some vicious things (murdering Abner and a second man
named Amasa [2 Sam. 20:10]). But he also does some
commendable things (calling David to come and get
credit for a victory he was on the verge of winning:
"Come and take the city, lest it be named after me"
[2 Sam. 12:28; and 2 Sam. 10:12]) showing he under-
stood God's part and man's part in accomplishing a
task. Scripture also shows he had faith in God. But
Joab was not likely to do things without a reason.

Israel's monarchy had not existed long enough
for a pattern to be established for naming the next
king. People expected David to announce his choice.

When God refused David the privilege of building the temple, He promised that one of his sons
would be king—but which one? When Solomon
("the peaceful") was born, God sent his prophet to
name the child Jedediah ("loved by the Lord").
Although this was God's direction regarding a
successor, it would not have been so apparent to
David and others that this was *the* son to be king.
With the whole Bible in front of us, it is easy for us
to see. We wonder, Why didn't they see that Solomon was God's choice? But there were logical con-
siderations at the time that made it tough! Absalom's rebellion would soon come, and he would

disqualify himself; but at this time, the problem of succession was very thorny!

Solomon—the Heir Apparent

While Absalom was in exile, the faction at court that supported Solomon for the throne—Bath-sheba, Zadok the high priest, Nathan and Benaiah, the leader of the king's bodyguard—had the king's ear for seven years.[4] They felt their candidate was comfortably entrenched in David's favor. They enjoyed watching the king lavish all his attention on Solomon. But David still loved lively Absalom. Slaughter pointed out that Solomon's supporters could not be certain that David would feel bound by his promise to name Solomon king if Joab or others persuaded him that Solomon was not strong enough to hold the nation together. Next to being right with God, David regarded his leadership of the nation as a sacred responsibility. The unity of the country depended on the right choice for the successor. One can imagine the political intrigue and the calculated action to support one candidate or another.

We do not know when David settled on Solomon, but it is clear that he was the king's choice. Later, when Adonijah made a bid for the throne, Bath-sheba and Nathan reminded David of his promise to Solomon, of which he had spoken himself (1 Kings 1:11–13, 17, 29 and 30). Another indication that Solomon was David's choice is that when Adonijah gathered leading people to his coronation, Solomon was conspicuously uninvited.

Joab was in a hard situation. He was justifiably concerned for the nation. Anarchy could break out if David died without making his choice for a successor clear. And if Solomon was to be king, a period of coregency was a must. Absalom, on the other hand, was old enough to take the reigns of the nation.

Absalom presented a dilemma for David. We cannot understand how heartrending it was for David to decide how to treat this brash young man.

What price should he demand of Absalom to balance the scales of justice?

I believe it would have been best for David to have left Absalom in exile. He had chosen to leave. True, David's heart ached, but it was nearly destroyed by what was to come. David thought his loneliness for his son was a great burden—and it was. But it was nothing compared to seeing his nation plunged into a civil war in which more than twenty thousand people died!

God once taught me that the present could be unpleasant, but the future could be much more miserable if the wrong choice were made. Just out of seminary, I served as an assistant pastor in a large Baptist church. The church had no senior pastor during the four years I was there. An excellent interim pastor moved the church forward. As various candidates declined the pastorate and the process of looking for a pastor continued, there rose a feeling in the congregation that nothing was happening. Though the offerings were as steady as ever and the attendance remained high, a negative mood settled over the church family. A great church got an inferiority complex. A pastor finally came, but he left after five disastrous years. Both the church and the man were scarred. Then the people looked back upon the previous pastorless days as the glory days. The people thought that things were bad before, but when a bad decision was made, things got worse.

Before taking action to change our circumstances, we should think carefully, pray earnestly and obey Colossians 1:18: " . . . that in all things he might have the preeminence."

End Notes

1. Alexander Maclaren, "2 Samuel," *Exposition of Holy Scripture* (Grand Rapids: Eerdmans, 1938), p. 79ff.

2. Redpath, *The Making of a Man of God*, p. 210.

3. The weight equivalent of the King James Version's "two hundred shekels" is given by the

New International Version as being five pounds.
For his hair to weigh this much, it must have been
very thick and come down to the middle of his back
or even lower.

4. This seven-year figure is arrived at as follows:
Absalom lived in his own home for two years while
he planned to avenge his sister; he was exiled for
three years; and when brought back to Jerusalem,
he was still separated from his father for two years.

CHAPTER TWENTY-THREE

DAVID'S GETHSEMANE

2 Samuel 15 and 16

T he night before Jesus was crucified, He prayed in a garden named Gethsemane. While He was there, Satan attacked Him, seeking to turn Him from the cross where He would purchase our redemption. Our Lord was under tremendous pressure. This withering attack of Hell caused Jesus to be "sorrowful, even unto death" (Matt. 26:38).[1]

In the lives of most godly people—especially those whom God plans to entrust with great spiritual influence and power—there is such a "Gethsemane experience."

The apostle Paul had a similar experience in Acts 21:27 and through the book of Acts. Second Corinthians 1:8 is most significant! Elijah had a "Gethsemane experience" (1 Kings 19:1–18). What exactly is the "Gethsemane experience"? It is coming to the end of one's self and depending totally on God. It is being weak, weary, attacked, pressured and overwhelmed to the limit of one's physical, emotional and spiritual reserves. And it is finding out that God takes care of those who turn to Him when they are backed up against problems they cannot solve.

Second Samuel 15 through 19 recounts David's Gethsemane. God allows his choice servants to speak of His faithfulness, sustaining power and comfort from firsthand experience. The greater God's plans are for a believer, the deeper his Gethsemane.

Absalom: Home and Active. During the two years before David allowed Absalom into his presence, he longed for his son. Maybe he looked out the palace window and caught sight of him every now and then—quickly drawing back when his son caught his eye. Painful days for David!

But they were productive days for Absalom. The years at Geshur had not mellowed him. In a characteristically vain act, he hired fifty men to attend him wherever he went. This provided an air of importance and urgency to his presence. He served in the government and pretended to be a man of the people.

Public Opinion

Of Absalom. The king, happy to have his colorful son home again, was blind to the purposes of his overaggressiveness. While Absalom built a power base of public opinion, David dismissed troubling thoughts and warning signals. This follows from the fact that Absalom's activities were too widespread to be kept secret. Either people feared to warn David, or he ignored what was happening.

Personal magnetism and beauty drew people to Absalom. Knowing what people wanted, he put on a good show. By hiring a large entourage—bigger than the king's—he impressed people. As Slaughter pointed out, to the young and untutored he seemed only a bit less important than the king himself.

While David was ill and secluded, Absalom made it his business to mix with those who were available. Many felt that he had been right to avenge his sister's honor by killing Amnon.

Currying the favor of all who would give him a hearing, Absalom weaned the people away from their loyal devotion to his father. He assumed the posture of a ruler vitally interested in people. By intercepting people with problems before they could get to David's officials, Absalom stole the hearts of the people away from his father. He was disloyal, telling the people how much better things would be if he were in charge. Thus he injected division into the nation. With false modesty, he refused to allow people to render him customary homage. He would embrace them and act like they were "long-lost friends."

And people swallowed it! Imagine the effect when the king's own son said that the government was not meeting their needs! When David was not able to handle all the cases in court that clamored for his attention, Absalom seemed the only one who would go out of his way to see justice done. The king did not seem to care!

To the disgruntled, to those who had lost their cases, to those who were ready for something new, Absalom offered words of sympathy. He told them what they wanted to hear. As in political rhetoric today, the man out of the office can promise people the moon without fear of having to make good on his word.

Absalom appeared to be taking over more and more aspects of the government from his ailing father. It was generally accepted that he would take over the king's responsibilities and power.

Another fact played into Absalom's hands to make his popularity rise. It is a fact that the longer a government leader, pastor or director has held power, the more enemies he has. All leaders become less popular as time passes, no matter how good, diligent and brilliant they may be. When two people came to court for a verdict, one of them lost and became a ready market for Absalom's campaign of subterfuge.

If Absalom had just waited, the kingdom might have come his way. But he was impatient and convinced of his cleverness. Without consulting Joab, the one who had originally befriended him, he laid plans for a revolt against his father.

Of David. David was not what he had been when people rallied to him thirty years earlier. He was ill, and the problems of the past sapped his vitality. To some, he had come to appear as a retiring old man. He had retreated from public life to some degree. But godly, responsible people still looked to him as their leader and loved him deeply.

Other people, who were less charitable, felt he was a worthless hypocrite. Taylor wrote that if David had made no claim to spirituality, people would not have held him to such a high standard. But since he claimed to be walking with God, some thought he must be hiding wickedness behind a cloak of religion. His steady efforts to accumulate materials for the temple, attendance at worship, pious actions and even his writing of psalms were suspect. Some continued to view him as an adulterer and murderer, worthy only of condemnation.

David had openly confessed *his* sin. But to those who were not about to repent of *their* sin, David's past provided a constant excuse. They mocked his efforts to please God. Their unwillingness to get right with God made them angry at David. And some likely resented God's mercy to him, while they secretly envied his courage and humility. Those who lived in the "gutter" were glad the hero of the nation had fallen briefly to their level.

If David had been an out-and-out scoundrel who claimed no allegiance to God, the nation would have accepted him as being "up front" and "standard fare" for the realm of politics. Cynical people saw further evidence of weakness over the question of Absalom's restoration.

The Revolt

After four years of going up and down the lanes of shady behavior in semi-seclusion, rebel Absalom felt the time was right for his revolt to surface. Knowing that he had greater support in Hebron than in Jerusalem, Absalom invented a clever excuse to be absent from the capital. His line was one the king could hardly refuse: "I promised God while I was in exile that if He ever brought me home, I would pay Him this vow." What a lie! Absalom *never* had a spiritual thought in his head!

Arriving in Hebron, Absalom spread the word to his dissident supporters—and the revolt was on. A considerable number of the citizenry supported Absalom as he had himself crowned. This indicates that there was some legitimate dissatisfaction in the nation. Leon Wood suggested that taxes may have been high, or that the king had been distracted from domestic issues as he focused on foreign policy and the guiding of his far-flung empire. With his new followers behind him, Absalom marched on Jerusalem to take the throne of his father by force.

Absalom's Deception. Absalom was constantly deceptive! He pretended all was well toward Amnon so he could lure him away from the protection of Jerusalem to kill him. He had tricked two hundred people into going to Hebron—they did not know he was starting a revolution. But it would appear that they were supporting him. He was disloyal, using lies and half-truths to get a following.

How shortsighted it is to be deceitful! How destructive! It can take years to rebuild what has taken only minutes to ruin!

People Are Easily Deceived. As Leon Wood pointed out, history shows that a substantial segment of almost any population can be fooled. Many people are attracted by outward appearance and high-sounding promises. All too often, careful reasoning cannot compete with these. Glib lies sound more exciting than common sense (which is not so common). People were fooled by Absalom's apparent generosity—he got a large following in a hurry! While David had endured eleven years of difficult character-building before becoming king, Absalom elbowed his way to the top in four years *without* God. People were unwise to follow this loud-mouthed kid! Though David led the finest government the world had ever seen, many of his people were ready to turn him out for this fast-talking young man!

The King Evacuates the Capital. As David left his beloved Jerusalem, he was entering a deep "Gethsemane experience." He was crushed in spirit. Since he was ill, he was already "down." How utterly humiliating! The whole nation watched this tragic spectacle of a son battling his father.

Several factors inclined David to flee Jerusalem. First, by his leaving the city, the loyalty of the people would be tested. It would cost them something to be faithful; they would have to leave their homes. David had to know who he could count on in the critical battle ahead.

Second, he may not have had enough soldiers to make the city secure.

Third, he may have been concerned for the well-being of the city. Absalom might destroy it to dethrone him.

Fourth, in the past, David had never fought using fortress walls.[2] His forte had always been the open-field strategy. Thus, he withdrew from his beloved capital—like his great descendant the Lord Jesus Christ one thousand years later—in rejection and exile.

The Positive Aspects of David's Situation

In spite of this being an extremely difficult moment in David's life, there are some things to put on the plus side of the ledger.

The People. The king's heart was warmed to know that when put to a stiff test of loyalty, many, many stood with their king. And they had no way of knowing if they would ever come back to their possessions in Jerusalem. There was no guarantee David could pay them back. Seeing a long, plodding column traveling east toward Jericho and the Jordan River had to lift the king's spirits. He stood erect as the long line filed past him out of the city. Great emotion swept the people over this horrible thing: "And all the country wept with a loud voice" (2 Sam. 15:23). It encouraged David to know that his exile affected others.

Joab. Joab's faithfulness also cheered the king. Though Joab had greatly embarrassed David by killing Abner, he had served with distinction over the years. Since he was instrumental in bringing Absalom back, the king assumed he would side with the rebel. It strengthened David to have Joab stand with him. Had he joined Absalom, he would have been a critical factor against David.

The Cherethites and Pelethites. David's personal bodyguards marched out of the capital to continue their steady service to the king.

David's 'Six Hundred.' These mighty men also stood with David, as they had since the fugitive days at the cave of Adullam. The men had never lost a battle in the half-century they served David. The closest thing to defeat they ever experienced was this strategic withdrawal. These dedicated ones lifted the sagging king. David hoped it would be like the old days when his inspiration and military genius stirred his men and brought victory after victory. Like it or not, David could not afford to be old and bent now. He must rise and lead a great campaign.

Ziba. Ziba was a servant of Saul. He had accompanied the lame son of Jonathan, Mephibosheth, to David's palace and had tended to his affairs. As David was leaving Jerusalem, Ziba sought him out. He brought a timely gift: animals and food. David gratefully acknowledged the valuable gift—which he may never have been able to repay.

Hushai. He had been with David for a long time and was older than the king. David declined to have Hushai to come with him. Instead, he asked him to serve as a spy. Hushai had served with dedication; he would prove of immense value to David as a spy, feeding Absalom poor counsel and smuggling intelligence information out of the city to the exiled king.

Ittai of Gath. This man was willing to follow the monarch into exile. Along with his six hundred men, he stood true to David. Though David pointed out that he had just recently been exiled from his own country, Ittai insisted on joining the departing column. This was most heartening to the king. Choked with emotion, the battered old man waved them on, unable to say anything more than " . . . go and pass over" (2 Sam. 15:22).

God's Promise. God had promised that one of David's sons would build a temple and reign on his throne. So David got the promise down off the shelf and dusted it off—he needed to draw strength from it now. Satan tried to convince David that all his family troubles made the promise void. But the king's faith strained to believe that God would keep His word.

Zadok and Abiathar. These two were the high priests who brought the ark of the covenant along as they left the city. Not only had they put aside dispute about who was *the* high priest, they sought to encourage David by bringing that which would remind him of God's presence. But David was unwilling to make the ark a "lucky rabbit's foot," as Hophni and Phinehas had (1 Sam. 4:3, 11). Instead, he told them to carry the ark back into the city, remain there and funnel information to him by means of their sons. They obeyed him, with great benefit.

Loyalty can be demonstrated *only* under trying circumstances when there is some other attractive alternative. These people sided with David when his back was against the wall, when following the king was dangerous, when the future was uncertain and when others found it convenient to leave him for the upstart rebel. They did not decide to be loyal in a moment of euphoria when all was going well. Rather, their pledge came at a time when everything was going wrong. David's kingship and authority were in question, and joining him meant rough surroundings and battles.

To some people, it appeared that David was the king as always—solid and steady, able to handle this crisis as he had so many others in the past. The people thought, "He is doing fine!" But the truth of the matter was that David had every reason to see himself as a failure in two great areas of responsibility—parenthood and kingship.

It does not cost money to speak encouragingly to others. It requires only the thoughtfulness to look at things from other people's perspectives. God brings strength to His servants through knowing others understand their hurts, frustrations and disappointments. Paul wrote that we should "weep with them that weep." You never know when the encouragement you could bring to your leaders may provide the motivation to continue in a difficult situation. Ittai was especially uplifting to David in this respect.

The Negative Aspects of David's Situation

Along with the positive things in the king's situation, an abundance of negative things descended upon him:

Absalom. The most crushing factor in the rebellion was that his own son led it. How shameful! How shattering! How humbling to have the whole nation watch as one tries to straighten out his son!

Ahithophel. As the king climbed the Mount of Olives, barefoot and weeping, a devastating piece of news arrived: Ahithophel, David's long-time confidant, counselor, battle commander and friend, had defected to Absalom's cause. David was shocked!

Psalm 41:9 almost certainly refers to Ahithophel: "Yea, mine own familiar friend, in whom I trusted, which did eat of my bread, hath lifted up his heel against me." Psalm 55 also refers to Ahithophel's betrayal: "For it was not an enemy that reproached me; then I could have borne it: neither was it he that hated me that did magnify himself against me; then I would have hid myself from him: But it was thou, a man mine equal, my guide, and mine acquaintance. We took sweet counsel together, and walked into the house of God in company" (vv. 12–14). This betrayal was a part of David's Gethsemane.

That David then prayed specifically that God would defeat the wise counsel of Ahithophel shows how seriously he regarded his defection. And he set in motion the machinery to defeat his counsel of Absalom. Some people would have naively said, "I am invincible until 'my number' is up," and do nothing. Others would say, "I'm safe until a bullet has my name on it." Not David! In the providence of God, Hushai came to David just after he received the news about Ahithophel. "Hushai could possibly defeat the counsel of Ahithophel," David thought. He set up a system of getting intelligence information. And he opened channels through which God's deliverance could flow. He did not merely claim Romans 8:28: "And we know that all things work together for good to them that love God, to them who are the called according to his purpose," and sit down to do nothing. The time to claim Romans 8:28 is after you have done all you can do; then yield the matter to God, knowing that He will rule according to His sovereign will.

Hushai stole back into Jerusalem and made himself ready to appear before Absalom.

Ahithophel was in his hometown of Giloh, so he

could receive word of the revolt promptly and join it.

What swept Ahithophel into the ranks of the conspirators? The answer seems to lie in those seemingly dry, meaningless genealogical tables in the Bible. While the genealogies may look like phone directories, they contain valuable information. Ahithophel was the grandfather of Bath-sheba. The only reason scholars have produced for his defection was that he resented how David destroyed either Uriah, his granddaughter's first marriage or both. William Taylor pointed out that the strength and brains of Absalom's rebellion came to him as a direct result of David's sin with Bath-sheba.[3]

Ahithophel was not a man to change sides rashly. His decision to side with Absalom must have come out of smoldering resentment against David. He would make David pay for his past sins.

That Ahithophel was wise is shown from what follows. Absalom rejected his strategy. And when he saw that the plan Absalom accepted had no chance of success, Ahithophel left and committed suicide. One has to be very certain that disaster is coming to decide to die in advance!

Ziba's Lie. Another negative factor that David had to overcome was the information brought by Ziba about Mephibosheth. Mephibosheth was a descendent of Saul. David, because of his former friendship with Mephibosheth's father, Jonathan, had been gracious to his lame son. Cheered by Ziba's timely provision and apparent loyalty, David reeled when he heard about Mephibosheth. But Ziba lied about the man, slandering him to his benefactor.

Ziba claimed that Mephibosheth had stayed behind in Jerusalem because he expected to become king of the nation. David was stretched to the limit of his endurance. Vulnerable! He was not thinking clearly. Normally, he would have seen through Ziba's lies. The claim that Mephibosheth expected to be made king was absurd in light of his personality and abilities. For years he had eaten at David's table. He was seen as one who needed to receive, not as one who could give the nation anything. He had been lame since he was five years old. The flimsiness of the lie is also seen in that the rebellion was clearly led by Absalom. Mephibosheth had no reason to think that this selfish, vain man would share the fruits of his victory with him.

But David was not his normal, keen self. He was wounded—and he was occupied with his own problems. On impluse, he took everything he had given to Mephibosheth and gave it to Ziba on the basis of his word alone!

Shimei. Another negative factor arose from a man still loyal to the house of Saul—Shimei. Some distance down the road, a ridge came close to the route of retreat, running parallel to it for a considerable distance. Shimei walked along the ridge, showering rocks and insults on the fleeing king. He shouted false accusations at David. Now David was very pleased that he had had nothing to do with the death of the former king. Shimei accused him of foul treatment of Saul. But David restrained his men from silencing the fool.

David's Testimony

The most precise information about this trying hour comes from the king himself. The psalms he wrote express the feelings that raged within him.

Two things must be kept in mind as we read these psalms: First, we are apt to think only of our Savior's sufferings at Calvary when we read these poems, so we are in danger of forgetting their original setting. While it is true that these psalms speak of David's greater Son, the Lord Jesus Christ, David also experienced some of the awesome, crushing things that wrung from his soul the immortal words in his psalms. Second, God allowed David to pass through some events that would parallel the things Jesus suffered during His betrayal and crucifixion.

Our Savior certainly suffered more than David. But the fact that any of what David went through prophesied the things that would befall the Messiah helps us measure the severity of David's hardship. The following psalms are attributed to this time in David's life:

Psalm 3. Authors E. W. Hengstenberg, Charles Spurgeon and H. C. Leupold attribute Psalm 3 to this occasion. The morning after crossing the Jordan River, David wrote, "LORD, how are they increased that trouble me! many are they that rise up against me. Many there be which say of my soul, There is no help for him in God." Others thought that he had gone beyond the range of the forgivable. David knew that and had no right to hope that God would help him.

Psalm 4. The same authors also attribute Psalm 4 to David's flight from Absalom. It tells that people wanted to shame David, but he slept in peaceful safety.

Psalm 22. Though much of Psalm 22 is purely prophetic, speaking exclusively of Christ's death experience, and much of it could not have been literally fulfilled by David (such as "all my bones are out of joint," and "my heart is like wax; it is melted in [me]"), it is logical that David identified with the suffering person in this poem. The following phrases from Psalm 22 are applicable to David's Gethsemane experience: "O my God, I cry in the daytime, but thou hearest not; and in the night season"; "I am . . . a reproach of men, and despised of the people"; "All they that see me laugh me to scorn"; "Be not far from me; for trouble is near"; and "I am poured out like water."

Psalm 55. The following phrases in Psalm 55 speak David's feelings as he was driven out of Jerusalem: " . . . the terrors of death are fallen upon me"; "fearfulness and trembling are come upon me, and horror hath overwhelmed me." Verses 12 through 14 speak of Ahithophel. Leupold translates one of the verses: "I toss about in my anxiety"; and "I am quite distracted by the voice of the enemy, by the pressure of the wicked." The song of the "sweet singer of Israel" was a troubled one. "The terrors of death" were upon him—a most punishing kind of distress.

Psalm 63. David was understandably angry at liars and wrote in verse 11: "The mouth of them that speak lies shall be stopped."

Some Bible students say other psalms—41, 61, 109 and 143—are also connected with this time in David's life.

David's Attitude. Our hero had a very admirable perspective toward all the things that rained upon him. His gracious, godly attitude is seen when he restrained Abishai, who wanted to kill the mocking Shimei. At a moment when we would expect the weary David to tolerate nothing more, he was unspeakably kind to the foolish man. He met the cursing and pelting stones with poise and greatness of heart.

David also recognized the hand of God in the events unfolding against him. He knew that some of what he suffered was fulfilling Nathan's prophecy that trouble would arise out of his own house. His view was, "I believe God's prompting Shimei and others to persecute me, and I shall not resist the agents of God's chastening." Believing that God would remove these thorns when He saw fit, David showed his trust in the Lord by not retaliating.

Also, David expressed great confidence in God. He spoke in Psalms of ultimate victory:

But thou, O LORD, art a shield for me; my glory, and the lifter up of mine head (3:3).
I will not be afraid of ten thousands of people, that have set themselves against me round about (3:6).
. . . the LORD will hear when I call unto him (4:3).
Thou hast put gladness in my heart (4:7).
By this I know that thou favourest me, because mine enemy doth not triumph over me. And as for me, thou upholdest me in mine integrity, and settest me before thy face forever (41:11, 12).

280

This was an agonizing time for David. But he came through the Gethsemane experience with the proper attitudes: (1) He was gracious to others who afflicted him. (2) He saw the hand of God in his hardships. (3) He trusted the Lord for ultimate victory.

Bitter people have failed their Gethsemane experience exam. They say, "I can prove God does not love me—look what He allowed to happen to me!" They put God on trial by dictating how He must show them love.

Hebrews 12:15 says that bitterness is basically a failure of faith. We fail to see how God's plan for us could be good and yet include some very distasteful things. Bitter people cannot see how God can take the hard, hurtful events of one's life and weave them into a fulfilling, spiritually effective life. David was not a faith dropout. And we can learn through his experiences how to be triumphant in testing.

End Notes

1. See Dr. Leon J. Wood, *The Significance of Gethsemane*, for an excellent treatment of this subject.

2. Only four times does Scripture record that David was involved in siege-type warfare (Keilah, 1 Sam. 23; the Jebusite stronghold of Zion, 2 Sam. 5:6–10; Rabbah, 2 Sam. 12:26; and the occasion of Uriah's death, 2 Sam. 11:17–21). On all of these occasions, David was attacking from outside the walls; never did he decide to make a stand inside a city.

3. Second Samuel 11:3 tells us that Bath-sheba was the daughter of Eliam; 2 Samuel 23:34 adds that Eliam was the son of Ahithophel the Gilonite. Eliam, Ahithophel's son and Uriah were among David's mighty men. Ahithophel may have felt indebted to Uriah if he had been a positive influence on his son.

CHAPTER TWENTY-FOUR

GOD'S PROVIDENCE

2 Samuel 16:15—19:8

A woman named Carol, whose father had suddenly died, chose to roam around the country rather than being with her mother, who needed her. After she had "worn out her welcome" with all the relatives out west, she came home—pregnant. Carol's baby was unnamed for several days at the hospital because her mother's insurance would pay the hospital costs only if the child carried the grandmother's name. The father of the baby was long gone. Nineteen years old, Carol had thought it would be exciting and fulfilling to travel and be "free." How different life looked now that she had a child to take care of twenty-four hours a day. God, in His providence, gave Carol something quite different from the excitement and glamour she had expected.

A young man named Bob thought he could skip much of his final semester of high school and still graduate on schedule by taking the Graduate Equivalency Diploma test. So he lied to his mother who was trying to cope with a divorce, to make a living in downtown Detroit and to make a home for them.

Since she left for work before he usually left for school and he came home before she did, it was a long time before his mother got wise to what was happening. Bob thought he had it all figured out. But the school informed his mother that he needed a certain number of credit hours, plus a G.E.D. test, to graduate. Bob didn't know that God overrules. He wants to make sin expensive to keep us from its destruction.

These two negative examples of God "catching up" to people should not cause us to think of God's providence as negative. He controls all things—that's a favorable fact that brings great security to the Christian!

My favorite illustration of God's wonderful providence concerns a poor widow and her eight-year-old son who were being evicted from their home. Though she had made the house payment that would keep the house in her possession, she had lost the receipt. The day arrived for the foreclosure. As the banker came into the house with the paperwork, so did a butterfly. The boy collected butterflies and noticed it immediately. It flew behind the sofa, and he asked the man to help him move it. As they moved the sofa, the missing receipt fluttered to the floor. God had sent the butterfly into the house at the right moment and to the right spot!

Now back to 2 Samuel, where the Holy Spirit focuses our attention on Jerusalem. Absalom has recently entered in triumph. It will become clear, as we study the passage, that God was controlling events to defeat sin and honor righteousness.

Absalom Takes Command. Once inside the palace, Absalom faced the need of consolidating the nation under his leadership. The impression we get from the text is that he immediately sought the counsel of others about how this could be done. He had not thought very far ahead, and he leaned heavily on others—particularly Hushai—who had just joined him. Even if his father's departure from Jerusalem had taken him by surprise,

Absalom's shallowness is evident.

Ahithophel's Counsel. Securely entrenched in the city, Absalom sought counsel from Ahithophel, whose first piece of advice was about the ten concubines David had left behind. He said Absalom should have sexual relations with them, thinking, "David violated my granddaughter through sex; I will strike back with the same weapon." Ahithophel said that this would make David hate him and convince everyone that Absalom was determined to carry the revolt to its fullest extent. Ahithophel had come out openly as a rebel, and he did not want Absalom to have a sudden change of heart. If Absalom turned soft on David, Ahithophel was a dead man.

It was made sure that all Absalom's people knew of his treatment of the women. Ahithophel had said this would make "the hands of all that are with thee strong." And he was right.

Ahithophel's Counsel about David. In the evening of the same day that David had evacuated the city, Ahithophel offered to take the men with Absalom and pursue David. He argued that David was weary, weak and unprepared to fight. That he offered to "choose out ten thousand men" implies that there were more than that in Jerusalem. He promised Absalom that he would kill only David, and that all the others—once David was dead—would become loyal to him.

The plan was brilliant! Ahithophel knew David's fighting style—*how, when* and *where* he would fight. Those listening were immediately impressed with Ahithophel's tactics. Maybe there was a chorus of "amens" and smiles of confidence on their faces. If this counsel had been followed, the revolt would have succeeded.

God's Overruling Providence

The Lord stepped in to overrule the counsel of Ahithophel. God always invades human affairs when *He* decides critical things are hanging in the balance. There may be many times when we regard something as critical, but He does not. God may allow your father to die, a loved one to be crippled or a brother to go bad. But when, *from His vantage point*, God sees that Romans 8:28 would otherwise not be true, He intervenes. The text says, "For the LORD had appointed to defeat the good [for Absalom] counsel of Ahithophel, to the intent that the LORD might bring evil upon Absalom" (2 Sam. 17:14).

Hushai's Counter-Counsel. Hours before, as David was leaving the city, Hushai had reached him just after the news of Ahithophel's defection. And David had sent him back into the city to counterbalance shrewd advice Ahithophel would provide the new king. Hushai was also to feed intelligence information to David via the sons of the two high priests.

In the providence of God, Hushai came into the presence of Absalom, who was surprised that he would join his revolt. Hushai's love and loyalty to David were well-known. Hushai's answer to Absalom can be taken two ways. He did not declare unqualified support for Absalom, though he wanted Absalom to believe he was now on his side.

When Hushai was told of Ahithophel's counsel, he recognized it as an excellent plan. It likely sent a shudder through him. He must foil it somehow!

Hushai knew that David was not in a position to fight. Therefore he stalled, buying time. David needed adequate time to get across the Jordan and regroup. And Hushai wisely gained time by appealing to Absalom's vanity.

He claimed that Ahithophel's advice was unwise. He said, "David is angry—like a mother bear who has just been robbed of her cubs. He is too smart to stay right with his men, so he would not be found if you went after him now. He is hiding in some cave."

Hushai warned: "If even a few more of our men get killed, word will spread that our forces are being slaughtered and people will desert our cause. David is a mighty man, and seasoned soldiers are with him. We need a large force of soldiers to ensure victory!" Instead of an immediate attack, Hushai suggested that men be gathered from all parts of Israel to enable Absalom to lead a vast army. This appealed to the new king's vanity. Knowing that it would be the quality, not the quantity of the soldiers that would decide the coming battle, Hushai was being faithful to David in his advice to Absalom. Being outnumbered was nothing new for David.

Hushai undoubtedly stressed that Absalom must be patient, saying that patience is a virtue of all good leaders. In skillful fashion, he painted in glowing terms the victory that would be Absalom's—but he must wait long enough to gain the massive force necessary to ensure victory.

First Chronicles 27:1–15 says David had an army of 288,000, of whom 24,000 were on active duty any given month. Absalom was told to wait until these soldiers could be appealed to.

Ahithophel's Response. Ahithophel saw that men who had been loyal to David and had fought many successful campaigns under his direction would not make an effective fighting force against him. When it became clear that his counsel had been rejected, Ahithophel knew the revolt was doomed. He came to see himself as a fool for trusting foolish Absalom. Withdrawing in disgrace, Ahithophel set his house in order and killed himself. Ahithophel's certainty of the failure of the rebellion shows what great perception he had. Some of the success David had enjoyed in former years was due to this brilliant man, Ahithophel.

Leaving Absalom, Hushai sent a message to David to move safely beyond the Jordan River. This shows he still feared Absalom would see through his scheme and pursue David for a quick kill.

We cannot know how soon David found out about Ahithophel's suicide, but he, no doubt, received the news with mixed emotions. David rejoiced to see God's overruling hand in Absalom's refusal to follow Ahithophel's advice, but he also felt sorrow. True, Ahithophel had deserted him, but as loyal and tender as David was, the defection had not made void all the splendid victories, the joyous times, the friendship and the mental stimulation they had brought each other over the years.

David Prepares for Battle. A second providential factor in the situation that cheered the king was the devotion of his men. This trying hour brought their love for him to the surface. Some of them had seen him slay Goliath; others remembered his sparing of Saul's life. Their admiration for David was so great that his momentary slip into the mud of immorality could not extinguish it. They had never met a man like David.

David Refused. Along with the others, David got dressed for battle. But many objected to his marching out with them. They said, "Thou shalt not go forth: for if we flee away, they will not care for us; neither if half of us die, will they care for us: but now *thou art worth ten thousand of us*" (2 Sam. 18:3). Great insight and devotion were in their response. They could have easily stepped out of the way in this father-son battle. And their love must have thrilled the old king.

Once before,[1] the men had refused to allow David back on the battlefield. In that encounter he had become faint, and Abishai had saved his life. When David readied himself to return to the conflict, his men refused to let him go, saying, "Thou shalt go no more out with us to battle, that thou quench not *the light of Israel*" (2 Sam. 21:17). Usually, men going out into war want their leaders to share the risk. We want others to have only the safety, ease or comfort we have. David's men called him the "light of Israel." Few leaders have been given such praise by their followers. David was a *great* man!

David had a special reason for wanting to go out with his men; he hoped to protect Absalom from being killed. However, he saw the unreasonableness of this personal motive and agreed to remain behind to direct the campaign.

David's policy of graciousness to conquered enemies now paid off. Machir of Lo-debar, Barzillai of Rogelim, and Shobi, a son of the Ammonite king, brought to David supplies, which were of immense help.

Gathering his entire force, David gave final instructions. He ended with an appeal to be gracious toward Absalom "for my sake." All David's men were present to hear this charge. This is clear, for the one man who eventually came upon Absalom by chance was aware of David's admonition (2 Sam. 18:10–13).

The Battle. Absalom was foolish to go after David. This allowed David to pick the battle site. He and Joab selected a wooded area to aid their style of fighting. Here numbers would not be a great advantage, but skill and experience would.

Dividing his men into three groups, David watched them disappear into the "wood of Ephraim." Joab took the veterans; Abishai the lesser proved men; and Ittai the men whose fighting skill was undetermined. In the pitted and hilly terrain, David's men took on the hastily mustered troops of Absalom. By cutting Absalom's larger force into small, conquerable units, Joab's men were able to match the enemy, soldier for soldier. Though outnumbered, David's lion-hearted, battle-hardened veterans knew how to fight. Soon the outcome was clear.

Absalom Dies. As his forces began to break and run, Absalom joined the stampede. In the providence of God, his long hair got caught in a low branch.[2] One of Joab's men found Absalom and reported it to him. Joab rebuked the man for not killing him. The soldier's response to Joab reveals what people thought of the general: "Though I should receive a thousand shekels of silver in mine hand, yet would I not put forth mine hand against

289

the king's son: for in our hearing the king charged thee and Abishai and Ittai, saying, Beware that none touch the young man Absalom. Otherwise I should have wrought falsehood against mine own life: for there is no matter hid from the king, and thou thyself wouldest have set thyself against me" (2 Sam. 18:12, 13).

The man's response indicates that though Joab was a skilled general, he also was self-serving and could not be trusted to defend his men to David. Joab's parting comment to the soldier ignores the accusation—he storms off, saying, in effect, "I am wasting my time with you. Let me at what's important."

Joab found Absalom. One swing of his sword through the entangled hair would have cut him free. But Joab saw more clearly than David what needed to be done. And he was not squeamish about it. This young man had plunged the nation into a civil war that cost the lives of more than twenty thousand men. He deserved to die. The nation was better off without him. At one time, Joab had favored Absalom for the throne. But he had invested too much sweat and had "slugged it out" in the trenches too many times to let a vain fool like Absalom destroy everything he and David had accomplished for the nation.

Joab took a heavy dart and hurled it at the dangling rebel. A second and a third were thrown. Then Joab's men finished the job. With convulsive thrashing, Absalom ingloriously departed this life. His body was thrown into a pit and covered with a heap of stones—a vastly different memorial than he had built for himself in the king's dale (2 Sam. 18:18).

David Receives the Word. The results of the battle reached David by means of two runners. One of the runners was Ahimaaz, the son of the high priest. He had been most helpful to David during the retreat from the capital, bringing word to hurry across the Jordan. The second runner was Cushi (or the Cushite).

When Ahimaaz asked permission to run to the king, Joab refused. The calculating general knew Ahimaaz was a sympathetic man, highly favorable to David. He did not want emotionally distorted information to reach the king about his son's death; he was in enough trouble as it was.

So, Cushi was sent. After a few minutes, Ahimaaz asked again if he could go. Believing that Cushi would get to the king first, Joab allowed Ahimaaz to go.

David had been anxious to hear from the battle-front. When the lookout spotted a runner, he was excited.

Ahimaaz loved David, so he ran very fast. Besides taking a route different from Cushi that would get him to the king first, he ran with all his strength so he could cushion the blow for David.

David took Ahimaaz's coming as a positive sign, since he knew the man's heart. He reasoned that if his forces had been defeated, the road would be full of retreating soldiers.

The breathless runner said David's men were making good progress, but just as he was leaving the front, the battle was intensifying. Ahimaaz pretended not to know the details of Absalom's death.

News of the battle was nothing to David compared to the information about his son. When Cushi arrived, he was quizzed about Absalom. At this moment, David was more a father than a besieged king. Cushi was not sympathetic like Ahimaaz, and he bluntly told David that Absalom was dead.

The Mourning Father. The dreaded news had come. David was crushed! Unrestrained sorrow gushed out of him. He fled upstairs crying, "O my son Absalom, my son, my son Absalom! would God I had died for thee, O Absalom, my son, my son" (2 Sam. 18:33). Every parent can understand the agony of David. He was overwhelmed. Taylor suggested: "There are griefs, as well as joys into which a stranger may not delve; let us shut the chamber door and withdraw, lest we improperly gawk at David's wounds."[3]

Joab's Rebuke. Soldiers returned to the fortress of Mahanaim following the victory. David had abandoned himself to his sorrow. When people became aware of the king's reaction, they slipped in quietly, as though they had lost the battle and were ashamed. So great was their love for the king that his reaction colored the whole event.

Swallowed up in grief, David did not have the initiative to cinch the victory. Absalom's beaten forces were retreating across the Jordan River to safety. The situation was becoming critical; no direction was forthcoming from the king.

Into this tender situation stepped Joab. He rebuked David: "If you do not get out to the gate and welcome your loyal soldiers, things will get worse. You are shaming the men who risked their lives for you. You act as if you would be happy if your men were dead and Absalom alive!"

This took courage on Joab's part. He knew he was already out of the good graces of the king. Even though David may have hated Joab at this moment, he saw that he was right. Though numb and wounded, David made a public appearance to show his gratitude to his men.

Conclusion

God Rules the Affairs of People. While there are some mysteries about this, Proverbs 16:9 says that in the heart a man plans his course, but the Lord determines his steps. Proverbs 16:33 adds that the lot (dice, "drawing straws") is cast into the lap, "but its every decision is from the LORD" (NKJV).

Rebellion Leads to Disaster. God's providence is wonderfully comforting to those who love and obey Him. But it also means that sin cannot be hidden from God's laser-beam eyes. And one of His laws is that what a person sows, he reaps.

The rebellion of Absalom led to his death. David had waited years for God to lift him to the throne; Absalom thrashed his way to the top in about four years. But the *way* he got there ensured he would not stay long.

How many others grab what looks exciting and fulfilling, only to end up in total defeat? Pride hardens a person in his rebellion, so he must pretend he is happy to be away from parents, church and neighbor—the very ones who are most often God's agents to heal. Young people are not the only ones in danger of rebellion. Adults also resist God's shaping influences, and the results are equal to the disaster that befell Absalom.

Lost Opportunity. Absalom is an example of a wasted life. As Judas Iscariot was no better for having been associated with Jesus, so Absalom was unresponsive to the example of his great father. Humility and submission to his father would have made him great. But he threw away his life.

Pride. Few things anger God more than pride. Satan fell because of his pride. Paul asked, "And what do you have that you did not receive? Now if you did indeed receive it [health, salvation, good children, money, keenness of mind, spirituality, faith, wisdom, a loving spirit], why do you glory as if you had not received it?" (1 Cor. 4:7, NKJV). Absalom was proud and vain. He never showed an interest in spiritual things. One can hardly find a clearer example of a person's pride becoming the cause of his downfall than Absalom's treasured hair, which ultimately caused his death.

There's No Substitute for Obedience. David knew that he was partly responsible for Absalom's rebellion. His sin with Bath-sheba had set a poor example. There was no way he could make up for it.

A sign in a dentist's office said, "There is nothing the dentist can do for what you won't do." There is no way for a father who is absent during his children's formative years to go back and shape them for God once they are grown.

Parents Are Creating Equals. David felt defeated about Absalom. Many parents, like him, have raised a child that brought them shame. Parents create an equal when an infant is conceived. A child is his parent's equal in power of choice, potential and having a sinful nature.

Parents should not play into the hands of the Devil by walking around in a continual state of self-reproach if they fail to be perfect. They should ask forgiveness from God and their children, then march forward for God. One must believe God for mercy and progress spiritually—because He rules and overrules.

End Notes

1. The events of 2 Samuel 21 are generally believed to have taken place prior to Absalom's rebellion, though they are not recorded until afterward.

2. Both the King James text and the New International Version say that his head was caught in a tree. This is best taken to mean that his head was caught by his hair. Apparently, he was suspended too far below the branch to free himself. This indicates that his hair was quite long—maybe as long as four feet.

3. Taylor, *David, King of Israel* (1916), p. 371.

CHAPTER TWENTY-FIVE

BRINGING BACK THE KING

2 Samuel 19:9—20:26

T he rebellion against David collapsed with the deaths of Absalom and Ahithophel, but the nation was in a precarious position. Division, weariness and uncertainty hung over the country. Many of the soldiers who had served David for years were in the embarrassing position of having sided with Absalom. They felt dispossessed. And it was certainly an awkward moment for the king! He wondered where he stood in the hearts of those who had been defeated.

For a while, the popular, glamorous son of David had been attractive. But his defeat slapped the people back to reality: David was the better man to be king—and had been for thirty years. The pendulum of their loyalty was swung back to its proper place.

David was shattered, emotionally drained. Still, people looked to him to take the initiative to heal the nation's wounds. Such are the burdens of leadership.

Church members may give lip service to the thought, "The pastor is not perfect; he is only human"; but it takes maturity to allow him mistakes.

David was viewed as stronger and wiser than average; so, with little allowance made for his humanness, he was expected to lead.

A sizable portion of the country had followed Absalom, so future reign for the grand old monarch depended on the consent of the subjects.

Judah and Israel were understandably uncomfortable in arranging reconciliation. Many of the tribes had sided with a "loser," so they made no effort to bring back the king. David was humiliated—turned out by his own son and tribe.

An overture had to be made! And being the leader he was, David made it. Judah was the key group for three reasons: (1) they knew him best; (2) he knew them thoroughly; and (3) his relatives were there. Their allegiance was essential.

In the message David sent to the elders of Judah was the offer of generalship to Amasa. This was more a punishment of Joab than a wooing of Judah, which it also accomplished. Joab had disobeyed the order to be merciful to Absalom.

Though Amasa had been second to Joab in battle, he might prove a powerful adversary in the future. And David wanted him in his camp.

Amasa's Promotion Unwise. Several factors made the promotion of Amasa unwise: (1) David acted when he was emotionally down; his main purpose was to wound Joab. Most people do not make wise decisions when they are experiencing inner turmoil. (2) Amasa was of questionable military value—Joab had just shown himself to be superior. (3) Though Joab had acted decisively in disobeying the king, in so doing he had served the best interests of both David and the nation. (4) Joab was not apt to stand idly by and be replaced.

Judah's Response. The elders of Judah yielded to the appeal of David. The text says that David "bowed the heart of all the men of Judah, even as the heart of one man . . . " (v. 14).

Shimei, Mephibosheth and Barzillai

Shimei. One thousand Benjamites came to the Jordan to welcome David home and formally conduct him across the river. The first to speak to David after crossing was Shimei, who had cursed and thrown stones at him as he retreated from Jerusalem (2 Sam. 16:13). With his fellow Benjamites watching, Shimei knelt down to beg forgiveness of the king.

Shimei remained loyal to the house of Saul. So who knew what he might do next? He was a continuing threat to the royal family. Abishai again asked permission to kill him—and the king would have been just to allow it.

However, Abishai sounded too much like his aggressive older brother. With the slaughter of Absalom still fresh in the king's mind, David overreacted to Abishai. His statement was a reference to Joab's callousness, more than a pardon of Shimei. His anger flared out at Abishai and he rejected the idea that Shimei should die. David forgave Shimei and took an oath that he would not be punished in the future. Later, when he had cooled down and saw things in perspective, David realized the foolishness of his mercy on Shimei. Years later, he left instruction with Solomon to have Shimei killed (1 Kings 2:8.9), unadmirably breaking his word.

Mephibosheth. David's treatment of Mephibosheth also showed that he was not himself. In retreating from Jerusalem, David had been vulnerable. Ziba had used this chance to full personal advantage, lying about Mephibosheth. The food-laden animals had been more than David was able to resist. They convinced David that Ziba was telling the truth that Mephibosheth had deserted him. David responded: "Ziba, I give you everything I had previously given Mephibosheth."

On his return to the capital, Mephibosheth met the king, wanting to be on good terms with him. He was sure Ziba had slandered him, and now he gave David his half of the story. Three factors pointed to Mephibosheth's innocence:

His Grooming. The Holy Spirit informs us about Mephibosheth's appearance before he spoke to David. He had " . . . neither dressed his feet, nor trimmed his beard, nor washed his clothes" since David had been driven out of the capital. This is significant because it declared his loyalty to David throughout the exile.

By remaining in a condition of mourning, Mephibosheth was doing what he could and declaring his loyalties to the point of endangering himself. The text does not say that Mephibosheth had help in coming to David; nor does it prove he could have gone with him into exile.

Partial Reversal. Mephibosheth convinced David that what he was saying was true. He had meant to bring the food to David, but Ziba had stepped in at the last minute, leaving him behind so he could get the credit. David's partial reversal of his previous decision shows he believed Mephibosheth.

It is surprising that the monarch did not punish Ziba for lying to him and taking advantage of his distressful situation for personal gain.

Why did David restore to Mephibosheth only half of what he had taken from him? Perhaps David was embarrassed for being fooled so easily by Ziba, ashamed he had made a quick decision when he was hurting. He wanted to put the whole thing behind him (2 Sam. 19:29). I imagine that with a dismissing wave of his hand, he continued up the trail.

Putting the Matter to Rest. David's reaction points to more innocence on Mephibosheth's part than he seemed willing to voice. In spite of David's dismissal of the matter, Mephibosheth wanted the last word: "Let Ziba have it all. Your return is all the reward I want," he said.

Frederick William Krummacher and William M. Taylor point out that this reveals the true attitude

298

of the man. Mephibosheth knew he was still welcome at David's table. He was back in the good graces of the king. By saying this—if the king took him at his word—he had everything to lose and nothing to gain.

Taylor says that that situation is similar to the one Solomon later faced. Solomon had to decide which of two women was the mother of an infant. He ordered the living child cut in half to give each woman half of what she claimed. He wisely knew that by watching the reactions of both women, he could determine which one was the mother. The real mother would rather give up her child than have it killed. She did, and Solomon awarded her the child. Mephibosheth yielded to Ziba in the same way. His very willingness to suffer loss demonstrates his sincerity.

David felt especially embarrassed about having believed Ziba that Mephibosheth hoped to have the kingdom restored to him by Absalom. It was such a trumped-up, unbelievable tale! David now saw how low he was to be taken in by such an unreasonable claim. To punish Ziba would be to admit how foolish he had been, and the king wanted to forget the whole mess.

Barzillai. This eighty-year-old man was of great help to the exiled king. Seeing that David was safely on his way to being reenthroned, Barzillai felt his task was complete. He withdrew from the growing throng.

David became aware that his ancient servant was leaving. His appreciation for Barzillai's help can be measured by the invitation to be his guest at the palace for the rest of his life. However, the grand old gentleman declined—he wanted to die in familiar surroundings. Apparently, he saw the grave as a pleasant resting place. His cup was full. In sight of all, David embraced and kissed him, and they parted.

Bringing Back the King

Heated Words. As David traveled southwest

toward Jerusalem, the ranks of his followers swelled.

David actually crossed the Jordan River early in 2 Samuel 19—at verse 18. But something important happened that is not recorded until verses 41–43.

Arriving at the Jordan River, David allowed himself to be conducted across by the men of Judah. Many of the representatives of the northern tribes (Israel) had not yet arrived. Since bringing the king to the west side of the Jordan (land more distinctly Hebrew) was equivalent to an official reception as king, the northern tribes felt slighted.

When the northerners arrived, they accused Judah of "stealing the king away." They had been the first to want David back as king.

Judah retorted that David was a member of *their* tribe! And they denied the insinuation that they profited by bringing the king back, such as receiving free meals or other hospitality from David.

Israel argued that since they were ten times as numerous as Judah, they had ten times the claim on David. The text says "the words of the men of Judah were fiercer than the words of the men of Israel."

Leon Wood suggested that David passively listened to the two sides argue, rather than acting to reduce the friction of the moment. To the initial mistake of not waiting for the northern tribes to arrive before crossing the river, David compounded the error by remaining passive. But we can understand David's reluctance to act. He had been bruised by the revolt and was about to find out if either of these factions would accept his leadership, so he did not exert authority.

Many northerners were offended. They withdrew from the restoration ceremony to follow a hotheaded man named Sheba. David continued toward Jerusalem, and he assumed power there. Concerned for the unity of the nation, he knew that he must deal with Sheba quickly and decisively.

The Spirit of God interrupts at 2 Samuel 20:3 to inform us of David's attitude toward the ten concubines he had left behind when he went into exile— the women Absalom had presumptuously violated.

Having just eaten a large portion of the bitter fruit planted by his immorality with Bath-sheba, David wanted nothing more to do with extra wives. He continued to provide for them, but he "went not into them."

Amasa's Leadership. Once back in Jerusalem, David made good on his promise to make Amasa his new military strongman, removing Joab.

David instructed his new general to gather as many troops as possible in three days. But he did not have three full days. By Jewish reckoning, he could have had as little time as (1) the remaining part of the day; (2) the next full day; or (3) the early morning of the third day before he was to meet David.

To the king's amazement, Amasa failed to show up at the appointed time. Characteristically, Amasa continued seeking more men after David's deadline passed. He thought superior numbers would ensure victory, even though this was the fatal flaw in Absalom's tactics. Amasa was foolishly willing to sacrifice speed and the element of surprise.

The few things we know about Amasa help us understand his behavior. *First,* he was an "underdog" all his life. As the illegitimate son of Jether an Ishmaelite (2 Sam. 17:25; 1 Chron. 2:17), he suffered constant social stigma. His cousins Joab and Abishai were achievers, while Amasa does not appear in the Biblical narrative until middle age. *Second,* he revolted with Absalom. *Third,* he had been the losing commander when he fought against Joab. Certainly, this was one reason soldiers were reluctant to follow him as David's general, and he labored under a sense of rejection.

The Mistake Repeated. Did Amasa realize that waiting for more men had been the reason Absalom's rebellion failed? The difference between Ahithophel's and Hushai's counsel dealt with this factor. Ahithophel argued for a quick kill even if it meant going with fewer men. Hushai argued that a larger force would surely triumph, but it would require time. Amasa repeated the same strategy that proved disastrous against Absalom. Did he not realize what we know—that this delay would be fatal?

When Amasa failed to show up on time, David sent his veterans, the "mighty men," and his bodyguard under the direction of Abishai to pursue Sheba.

Meanwhile, Joab had been waiting outside the city for a chance to redeem himself. Once the force was clear of the city, he joined his brother at the head of the column.

When Amasa heard of the troops leaving the city, he hurried to intercept them. He met with them at the spring of Gibeah, six miles north of Jerusalem. His goal was to assume command since he was David's general.

Joab's Perspective. Being replaced was a bitter experience for Joab. But to be replaced by the man he had defeated was unbearable! Joab had been faithful to David when others found it convenient to break away. He had won an excellent victory—only to be replaced. Some gratitude! Although he had violated David's order to have mercy on Absalom, he acted to benefit the nation and the king at a time when others lacked the courage.

Amasa Killed. It was a tense moment when Amasa tried to assume command. What would happen? The soldiers knew Joab well, and his family was prominent in Judah. Respectfully sweeping Amasa's face with one hand to distract him with a customary greeting, Joab stabbed him with the other!

The soldiers looked on numbly. When someone shouted, "He that favoureth Joab, and he that is for David, let him go after Joab," the shocked men continued north.

Sheba Killed; Joab Reinstated. Most of those who had joined Sheba at the river crossing reception/revolt did not follow him very far. They did not fully support this new rebel. The heated exchange near the Jordan River did not nullify their long-standing interest in having David as king. When Joab surrounded the city where Sheba was making a stand, Sheba's head was tossed over the wall and the revolt ended.

Joab returned to Jerusalem as the reestablished general. David was again in the awkward position of continuing disciplinary action against this man who had been valuable.

Conclusion

Reinstating the King. As David was driven from his rightful place, so the Lord Jesus Christ has been temporarily robbed by Satan of His rightful property—humanity. Each person bears the unmistakable trademarks of the evil one—selfishness that permeates every aspect of one's being and a determination to be the god of one's own life.

The Bible teaches that every person must see himself as God does, believe in Jesus Christ as his Savior and repent of sin. Today, Jesus is going quietly through the world, setting up His reign of peace and love in the lives of people who yield themselves to Him. He brings joy, peace and fulfillment.

In the future, Jesus Christ will stop being patient with humanity. He will return to earth, shedding the meek and beaten aspect of His first coming. The God-Man will come "in flaming fire taking vengeance on them that know not God, and that obey not the gospel of our Lord Jesus Christ" (2 Thess. 1:8). Please, "bring back the King" in your life before that awesome day.

Disobedience Is Expensive. Amasa had no idea that his delay would set up the circumstances for his death. His failure to submit to David's wiser military counsel cost him his life.

David's Responsibility. David's family failures

had put him on display for the nation to gawk at. He was crushed, humiliated, worn and tired. His son was dead, and he had a general he could not control. Who had the energy to rise and bind the nation's wounds? David was expected to do so. One of the heaviest burdens of leadership is that initiative always rests on the leader. No matter how defeated, embarrassed or down their leaders are, the "follower types" sit back and wait to be led. This is a major reason why leaders wear out!

Don't Make Decisions When Discouraged. David made an unwise decision in promoting Amasa over Joab due to discouragement.

Israel had made a poor decision in turning out the king for his flamboyant son. It cost the country about twenty-five thousand lives—a high price, indeed.

CHAPTER TWENTY-SIX

IS GOD CONCERNED WITH JUSTICE?

2 Samuel 21

Headlines scream the latest murder, rape and white collar crime. Politicians and university professors are no longer respected because of the shady and un-American things they have done. Hard-working, godly people are trampled, while the wicked ever prosper. Hollywood celebrities flaunt their immorality, proud of what they should be ashamed of (Phil. 3:19). Is God concerned about injustice? What is He doing to maintain righteousness?

Second Samuel 21 is evidence that God is very much concerned about justice, honesty, morality and order. In this chapter we see the hand of God straightening out an injustice over a three-year period. Only after things were made right did God heal the land.

The Situation. It is questionable whether the events of 2 Samuel 21 took place before or after Absalom's rebellion. But since it is independent of surrounding events, it does not matter.

A famine arose in the country. People hoped

that the next year would be better, but the famine continued into the second and third years! Starvation and hardship stamped a gaunt impression on the land. And some people died. The people were in despair.

Though many think there is no connection between the morality of a country and the weather, this passage shows there is!

When David realized his nation was under God's judgment, he sought the Lord. For this he is to be credited. Many people turn away from spiritual remedies when a trial comes. They are hardened by their problems into further resistance instead of being softened by them. David was wise to seek the Lord: He sent the famine, and only He could remove it.

God informed David that the famine came because Saul had broken the promise of safety to the Gibeonites extended by Joshua three hundred years before.

God had told Joshua not to make any pacts with the inhabitants of the Promised Land. The Gibeonites appealed to Joshua, coming with moldy bread, worn-out shoes and tattered clothing, and they tricked Joshua into believing they had traveled a great distance to see him. Actually, they lived in the path of the conquering Israelite soldiers. And they chose to sue for peace and to be slaves rather than risk annihilation.

The chapters of the Bible that cover Saul's life do not tell of his violation of this covenant. We read of it in 2 Samuel 21, some thirty years after Saul was buried. Saul had killed many Gibeonites and had apparently taken their possessions and land.

David's Dealing with the Gibeonites. David asked the Gibeonites how the situation could be made right. They asked that seven male relatives of Saul be put to death and their bodies "[hung] up unto the LORD in Gibeah of Saul" (2 Sam. 21:6). This type of revenge was accepted in that day. The grizzly task of picking the victims fell to David.

Because of David's promise to Jonathan, Mephibosheth was spared. Two sons of Saul by Rizpah[1] were selected; five sons of Merab, the daughter of Saul, completed the required number.[2] The reason such an awesome price was exacted was that God's reputation had suffered because Saul violated His word. Other nations expected Israel to be different! God is serious about His public image because all must know the truth about Him and obey it, or perish forever in the Lake of Fire.

Was Justice Done?

Leon Wood has excellent insight on this question.[3] It could be argued that God was unfair to penalize these seven men. Had they done anything wrong? Saul had led in attacking the Gibeonites, and he was dead; so perhaps the matter should have been dropped.

However, we can always trust God to be fair. He is infinitely just! He directed the selection of those to be judged through David. They must have been guilty in some degree—likely profiting at the expense of the Gibeonites. There is a hint of this in 1 Samuel 22:7. Saul kept a grip on those around him by passing out lavish rewards for loyalty: "Hear now, ye Benjamites; will the son of Jesse give every one of you fields and vineyards, and make you all captains of thousands, and captains of hundreds?" Where did Saul get such things to pass out? He had won precious little from the Philistines, and his own estate was modest. The land and possessions of the Gibeonites would have been a source of the booty he needed to remain popular.

God Keeps His Own on a Short Leash. This chapter teaches that the Lord's reputation is "on the line" in the behavior of those who claim to follow Him. He expects us to keep our promises—even when we have been deceived, as Joshua was. Scripture warns believers against close business relationships with unsaved people, committing resources to cover the responsibilities of unbelievers and being "unequally yoked together with unbelievers" (2 Cor. 6:14). God demands quite a bit, but He gives much more than He asks.

Ironic though it seems, God will tolerate sin, inconsistency and rebellion in unbelievers more than in believers. Two Bible illustrations show this to be true:

Saul's Massacre at Nob. When Saul killed everyone at the priestly community of Nob, there was no immediate divine reaction. Nor did God ever take Saul to task for this sin. The Bible attributes Saul's death to his disobedience (1 Chron. 10:13, 14), but nothing is mentioned about the massacre. The reason was that only believers were involved. In contrast, God brought judgment upon the nation over the breach of promise with the Gibeonites.

Those Who Abused the Ark. When the Philistines abused the ark, no great devastation came upon them. But when the curious residents of Beth-shemesh—who knew better—treated the ark irreverently, many died (1 Sam. 6:19).

God keeps His own on a short leash. Sometimes a believer gets a spiritual spanking right in front of an unsaved person. Paul wrote that dedicated Christians are made " . . . a spectacle unto the world, and to angels, and to men" (1 Cor. 4:9).

Why does God supervise His own so carefully? He wants Christians to be models of what He is like to an unbelieving world. While our best efforts may produce only a faint reflection of God, we are still His blood-bought trophies of grace.

God also deals promptly with His own so that sin will not accumulate. Unbelievers pile up their sins and will be accountable for them all on Judgment Day. The apostle Paul put it this way: "But after thy hardness and impenitent heart treasurest up unto thyself wrath against the day of wrath" (see Rom. 2:5). God keeps His children on a short leash, but that is so much better than being headed for

Hell! And the rewards for cooperating with God are unspeakable wealth, in terms of fellowship with the true and living God, joy and satisfaction, purpose, a high quality of life and eternal bliss.

Conclusion

God is concerned about justice! But during this present age, there is a greater emphasis on mercy, salvation, love and grace. Even the God-Man, Jesus Christ, did not receive justice in this world—He did not deserve to die. In the next world, however, justice will be much more evident. And while we wait for justice to be done, God would have us concentrate on being holy.

End Notes

1. Poor Rizpah! She had been a wife of Saul, though her status as a concubine meant she was not awarded the honor of full wifehood. Then Saul was killed. A few years later, she was in the middle of a power struggle between Abner and Ishbosheth (2 Sam. 3:7). She had been violated by Abner. Now, two of her sons were killed to expiate the guilt of their father. Second Samuel 21:9 informs us *when* these seven men were killed, so that we can measure this woman's devotion to her sons. For at least six months ("the beginning of barley harvest" until "water dropped upon them," meaning the fall season), Rizpah stayed with the decaying corpses of her sons to keep animals away from them. Merab, the mother of the other victims, did not do this, though her absence may have not been because of lesser love.

2. Wood's footnote regarding the identity of the mother is excellent: "According to 2 Samuel 21:8, five of these sons were of Michal. If so, they must have been born when she was married to Phalti, for she was barren with David as a result of her criticism of his dancing before the Lord (2 Sam. 6:20-23). However, there is textual evidence of a copyist's error in which 'Michal' was substituted for 'Merab.'

Also, the husband cited in 2 Samuel 21:8 is Adriel, whom Merab, Saul's oldest daughter, married (1 Sam. 18:19). It is, of course, possible that Michal raised these children for Adriel (Merab perhaps having died). If so, David's action in taking them from her was difficult for the king as well as for her; for though they had quarreled, she likely still lived in the palace." *Israel's United Monarchy*, p. 252.

3. Taylor, *David, King of Israel (1916)*, p. 371.

CHAPTER TWENTY-SEVEN

ATTITUDE SINS

2 Samuel 24

Many Hebrew students in seminary were relieved when the professor said that in the past the ones who had done the best in his classes had not always made the best pastors. That meant there was hope for those of us who found the language difficult. Basically, the professor was saying that *attitude* is more important than *aptitude*.

While the businessman is tremendously concerned with a prospective employee's ability, the Lord places greater value on a person's outlook on life. Attitude counts more than I.Q. Second Samuel 24 shows how important it is to avoid attitude sins.

Pride. Second Samuel 24 deals with the sin of pride in the nation of Israel and in King David. The nature of the temptation sent to David shows this was the basic sin God was dealing with.

God had blessed Israel for nearly four decades. It was a great time to be an Israelite; victory and convenience were standard. But the people had slipped spiritually.

The degree of greatness God grants becomes the measure of responsibility. God's blessing should make one all the more contrite before Him, since accountability comes with blessing.

Though David's strength lay in being faithful to God, he chose to number the people. But the number of fighting men at his disposal meant nothing apart from God's sustaining grace. Likewise, our talents and accomplishments are useless unless submitted to God. Jesus said, "Without me ye can do nothing" (John 15:5).

Israel was put on trial through their king. While David bore the brunt of the test, it is clear that the people were on trial by proxy; the attitude of the people was similar to David's.

We do not know when the events of 2 Samuel 24 took place. A census is normally taken when a young king is flexing his military muscles, not when he is old. This event is recorded just before David's death. But it is likely that it had occurred earlier in David's reign than its placement would indicate. Possibly it is significant that the writer of 1 Chronicles placed this event earlier in the book instead of later as the writer of 2 Samuel did.

Who Is to Blame? Both 2 Samuel 24 and 1 Chronicles 21 indicate that displeasure was directed toward Israel. The former attributes the anger to God, while the latter says the provocation came from Satan.

Coordinating these two Bible passages is not difficult when we take into account the teaching of Scripture that a person must bear the consequences of his sin. Also, God does not lead men into sin (James 1:13). Both David and the people provoked the Lord with their pride. God responded by allowing Satan to tempt the king. When David responded to Satan's temptation, God brought punishment on him and the nation for their pride.

The Devil cannot make people sin. He brings to mind the pleasures of sin, but the person yields his will.

A census is amoral—neither good nor bad in and of itself. But in this case, Hell's archfiend tempted David to count his fighting men. As this appealed to the king's sinful nature, he sinned in doing so. The spirit in which it was initiated by David and received by the people was wrong. Israel must have been more to blame than the king, since God punished the people while bypassing David.

God moved only when provoked by the pride of His nation. This is not immediately apparent. William Taylor stated, "The meaning is that God permitted Satan thus to move David, in order that through this act an opportunity might arise for the punishment of Israel's sin."[1]

The Target. Leaders of all kinds—administrators, pastors, missionaries, Sunday School teachers and deacons—are always Satan's targets. Let us pray for our leaders instead of criticizing them. The tendency is to speak against leaders. That comes easier than praying for them. Counsel should be given to leaders in private when one disagrees with them. And encouragement should be regular and sincere.

The Census. When David issued the order that all the fighting men be counted, even normally unspiritual Joab tried to dissuade him. The captains of the host also opposed the project.

After the census was taken, David lost interest and sensed the displeasure of God. Exodus 30:12 directed that when a census was taken, a half-shekel offering was to be given to the Lord. This was possibly neglected by David and brought some degree of disfavor. Leon Wood suggested the census may have been the basis for increased taxes—beyond what was acceptable to God. Or the census may have been the basis for a forced labor program—what Solomon was later hated for.

Judgment Options

God gave David three punishments to choose

from: seven years of famine, three months of military defeat or three days of plague. Of these, two would come directly from God (famine and plague) without human instrumentation. Military defeat would come through people of another country.

David was wise to entrust the nation to God for two reasons: (1) If the punishment came via people, the basis for a bitter feud would be laid; and (2) God is more merciful than people. Notice that David did not actually answer God's question. He stated his desire to be in God's rather than man's hand and gave the matter back to the Lord.

The Plague. God selected the plague as a punishment. Within minutes of its descent upon the nation, news of dying people flooded the capital. Knowing the disease must last three days, nothing could be done except wait it out and hope it did not strike one's self or loved ones.

Near the end of the three days, David toured the land. He is to be given credit for not isolating himself in the sterile shelter of the palace. Doubtless, he tried to bring comfort to the ravaged people he met.

Returning to the city, he saw an avenging angel poised over Jerusalem! David fell on his knees and interceded for his people. He nobly pled that he had sinned, not the people. Apparently, because of his humility, he did not know that the sin of the people was greater than his own.

Deliverance. The prophet Gad instructed David how to stop the dreaded plague. He said that David should build an altar and offer a sacrifice. Quickly, the king purchased the necessary property.[2] Though the owner was in harmony with David and offered the land free, David insisted on paying full price. With an excellent spirit, David said, "Should I offer to God that which costs me nothing?" To the degree that service to God is costly in terms of time, love, self-denial and effort, it is valuable and lasting. A mother must give freely of herself. To do so grudgingly would be to forsake the potential benefit. A

father, also, must spend that most precious commodity—time—with his child. And the pastor must
labor diligently to bring forth a spiritual advance on
the Lord's Day. Serving God costs something. One
may have to sacrifice ease or convenience. But such
interruption is not without value. Even Jesus could
have found something else to do the day He died on
the cross. There is no cheap way to gain something
of great value. And being a servant of the living God
is something to value highly. Too many people
value careers, houses and hobbies more than spiritual things. Some make gods out of their children,
spending all their energy on them, while never
lifting a finger to serve the Master. How shortsighted! Serving God will cost, but in the end it will
pay!

David confessed his sin (the reason he remained
high in God's estimation). The Lord dramatically
answered his plea, consuming the offering with fire
and stopping the plague instantly!

The nation suffered more than David did, which
indicates God saw them as being more sinful in this
matter of national pride. Though accountability
ends when someone repents of sin, the immediate
consequences run their course. Ironically, when
David wanted to know how many soldiers were at
his command, God promptly removed seventy
thousand from the national arsenal via this plague.

Conclusion

Attitude sins can be very costly. Lack of faith
caused the Israelites to wander in the wilderness
forty years. Lack of love for others cheats one out of
the joy of giving, and isolates one's self.

We can compare the consequences of physical
and attitude sins we have looked at in this chapter.
When David sinned with Bath-sheba, he paid fourfold, as the prophet Nathan had predicted. Added
to that was the miserable civil war that killed at least
twenty thousand people. But this did not even come
close to matching the destruction that came upon

315

Israel through the sin of pride. Self-pity, lack of faith, nervousness, indifference, ingratitude, resentment and other attitude sins are as deadly to a believer's spiritual life as an assassin's bullet. Guard your spirit; attitude is much more important than aptitude.

End Notes

1. Taylor, *David, King of Israel* (1916), p. 371.

2. The temple was built on the same site (or very near it) by Solomon a few years later. Many scholars teach that this location was where Abraham had brought Isaac a thousand years before.

CHAPTER TWENTY-EIGHT

THE LAST DAYS

1 Kings 1:1—2:11

The snows of seventy winters had fallen on David and some of the white remained—in his hair. Our bodies are frail and perishing robes that we use for a while. They are vehicles we use to travel through this life. David's body was worn out. His circulation was so poor that he "gat no heat" and he was warmed by a beautiful young woman. (Nothing sexual was involved.) David was ready to be promoted. His colorful career of leadership was nearly over.

Forbidden to Go. A few years before, David had become faint on the battlefield. A Philistine giant named Ishbibenob was on the verge of killing him when trusty Abishai stepped in to defend the tired monarch (2 Sam. 21:15–22). Thereafter, David's men refused to let him go into battle. "Then the men of David sware unto him, saying, Thou shalt go no more out with us to battle, that thou quench not the light of Israel. " What great love was expressed in this order. Most leaders become less popular with time, but not David.

One Last 'Bill.' Though loved and protected, David was not shielded from the awful prophecy of Nathan. Trouble continued to stir his house. One more grizzly fulfillment of this prophecy came before David rested in the grave.

Adonijah's Reach for the Throne. Solomon had not yet been named as successor to the throne. Because of the weakened condition of the king and the undisciplined manner in which Adonijah had been raised, he made an effort to gain the throne.

David had never rebuked his son Adonijah or given him proper guidance to curb his selfish nature (1 Kings 1:6). What a price David paid for his leniency with his sons! Adonijah is an example of what a son or daughter will do when allowed to pursue his own inclinations.

Like his older brother, Adonijah hired a team of attendants and chariots to make himself look important. And Joab joined his cause. Previously Joab seemed to favor Absalom and then swung back to David. Now, with David older and death in view, and with the bitter experience of having been turned out twice by David (2 Sam. 19:13), Joab was ready to take a chance. An uneasy truce had existed between him and David ever since Joab put down Sheba's revolt.

Abiathar, one of the high priests, also sided with Adonijah. This was sad, for he had been with David since the days at the cave of Adullam—more than forty years. He had given vital assistance in defeating Absalom. Zadok remained faithful to the king. Since he is mentioned first, when the names of both priests appear, we may assume that David favored him over Abiathar. This may account for Abiathar's defection.

Possibly, Bath-sheba and those who favored Solomon kept David's other sons away from him. This surely would have heated up resentments and multiplied political maneuvering.

While Joab and Abiathar supported Adonijah, Bath-sheba, Nathan, Benaiah and the majority of the "mighty men" (2 Sam. 23) favored Solomon.

The Secret Coronation. Adonijah arranged a pre-crowning feast, keeping it secret from all who favored Solomon. All of David's other sons were invited—except Solomon—which shows that Adonijah knew Solomon was David's choice of successor.

Solomon Crowned. When news of the clandestine meeting spread, David was alerted. This brought swift action from the king. In a flash, David had Solomon crowned. Authoritative orders were sent to Zadok, Nathan and Benaiah, showing that "even in the smouldering ashes of the old man, something of the ancient fires still burned."[1]

The parade that followed Solomon's coronation and the cheering people alerted Adonijah's guests to declare their loyalty to Solomon, or suffer the consequences. When the shout "God save King Solomon" was heard by those at the feast, Adonijah's support melted away.

The National Coronation. Although Solomon was crowned king, the tribes or representatives still had to approve him, formally swearing their allegiance to him. Most of the influential leaders of the nation were David's old friends, and he knew he could count on their cooperation.

What a moment for the departing leader! David stood face to face with those who had traveled with him from obscurity to fame. It was his last formal address to his precious people. They had been much truer to him than his own family. Deep emotion welled up in the grand old king! It was a more positive "good-bye" than Moses' (Deut. 31–33) or even Samuel's (1 Sam. 12).

David used the occasion to accomplish three things: (1) to publicly charge Solomon with his responsibilities; (2) to urge him and the nation to build a temple to honor God; and (3) to lead the people in worship.

The Charge to Solomon. David urged Solomon to obey, trust and faithfully serve God. He charged him to be strong and of good courage (1 Chron. 28:9, 20), as the huge load was placed squarely on his shoulders. Solomon was about twenty years old.

David's admonition to Solomon is excellent for any believer. But *how* does one "be strong"? How will God add His strength to ours?

We must be willing to invest our time, effort and love, trusting that God will add whatever is needed to gain victory. At the graveside of Lazarus, Jesus instructed those with Him to do two things within their power: to remove the stone and to remove the grave clothes of Lazarus. Then Jesus did the thing they could not do—He raised Lazarus from the dead.

So silently and humbly does the Lord add His might to ours that it is often indistinguishable from our own. The blending of the human and the divine in daily accomplishments is one of the mysteries of the Christian life.

The Temple

The retiring king's comments about the temple were addressed to all the people, not just Solomon. David challenged the people to be fully committed to the building of a temple. With tender affection and bold commands woven together, the aged king urged the building of a fine temple. In that day, people measured a nation's affection for their God by the magnificence of the temple. And the Lord allowed His people to show the world their attitude toward Him.

David unfolded some personal history, telling that God had refused to allow him to build the temple. And he earnestly coaxed them to reach his cherished goal. He emphasized to Solomon the importance of this task. In the last months of his life, David likely intensified his efforts to accumulate the needed materials. What attention he paid earthly things was focused on insuring the swift and careful building of his cherished temple. David was so set on having this temple built that a similar desire in the prospective king was likely a major consideration to David.

The text seems to convey that architectural details for the temple were received from the Lord by David in the closing months of his life (1 Chron. 28:19). If so, it would have been especially meaningful to the old king. It showed God's approval of him and rewarded him for not turning sour when God refused to let him build the temple.

David gave a large amount of money to help finance the temple construction. Theodore Epp claimed that the figures given in the King James Version convert to $87 million in gold and $12.5 million in silver.[2] Having endorsed the project with his own resources, David challenged the people to give: "And who then is willing to consecrate his service this day unto the LORD?" (1 Chron. 29:5). They responded with $145 million in gold and $20 million in silver.

Worship. This enthusiastic financial outburst was a gratifying moment for David! It was the finale to the determined effort he had put forth as ruler of the nation for forty years. This unified, spiritual, smooth-functioning nation did not just happen!

As the nation listened, David blessed the Lord. He acknowledged the Lord's goodness, greatness, power, loving-kindness and faithfulness. David's love for God made him great. He spoke glowingly of God, and he predicted the great future reign of the Messiah.

How important worship is! It is refreshing and absorbs one into God's Person. David knew what it was to worship God. As a family reflects the attitudes of the father, as a church mirrors the values of its pastor, so Israel was now like David. I can imagine a chorus of thousands of "amens," as the people rallied to support this significant project. A national feast followed the coronation.

Final Instructions. David instructed that Barzillai's son was to be shown kindness and that Shimei was to be killed. This violated David's word to Shimei, but we can understand it. King David also urged that Joab be killed. But why?

If Joab could have defended himself, he would have made these points: (1) "I have been loyal to David fifty years—does that count for nothing? Is my disagreement about his successor sufficient reason to kill me?" (2) "I have risked my life on countless occasions to advance the king's reputation, power and wealth. He should reward me, not kill me!" (3) "Even my killing of his spoiled son Absalom was for the king's own safety. I did what he was too weak to do." (4) "David led me to believe that my past crimes were forgiven. To punish me now would be the same crime he is putting me to death for."

If David could speak to us, how would he justify having Joab killed? (1) "Joab is an opportunist. Perhaps he would ride roughshod over my inexperienced son for his own gain." (2) "He murdered two men—a great embarrassment to me! How do I know he won't kill Solomon?" (3) "I have been criminally weak for too long. I was weak with Amnon, with Absalom and with Joab when he killed Abner and Amasa. I will be weak no longer! I do not want Solomon to think that a ruler does not deal with criminal acts just because they are done by powerful, useful people." (4) "Solomon is a peaceful man. I must give orders to remove Joab, who could threaten his rule. Men like Joab could do him great harm before he is strong enough to deal with them." (5) "I may bring disaster upon the whole nation by failing to dispense justice. Look what happened when Saul slaughtered the Gibeonites—three years of famine and the lives of seven of Saul's relatives. It looks like we favor the rich and powerful." (6) "Joab killed my son in cold blood, as he dangled helplessly in a tree." (7) "He showed his lack of loyalty in siding with Adonijah."

If David gave this directive out of revenge, it

was the first time we see this characteristic in his life. I believe there must have been some solid reasons behind what he did. Both David and Joab had their strong points. It is good that we do not have to decide who was right—that is God's responsibility.

The King Is Promoted

Now we meet David walking " . . . through the valley of the shadow of death." Death is the common experience of humanity, whether one has worn royal purple or beggar's rags.

The attendants at court stole through the halls silently, lest they disturb the king. Faces were downcast, for David was failing. The palace had previously belonged to generals, merchants and diplomats. Now doctors, nurses and aides made the important plans and orchestrated the king's care.

After seventy years of "eating the fat and drinking the sweet," David, the greatest monarch ever, was "gathered to his fathers." He went out full of love and good works for God and His people. Oh, happy rest—no more fighting with a sinful nature.

David's Greater Son. What an honor for Jesus Christ to be identified with a mere human being. Jesus used his ancestral relationship with David to confound the Jews (Matt. 22:43–46 quotes Ps. 110:1). People who knew the prophecies about the Messiah called Jesus "the son of David."

God chose David. And God has chosen you also. How? To be able to read puts you in a select group of human beings. Likely, you live in the United States, which enjoys a standard of living that has been unheard of in human history. Third, God has chosen you to live in a day when spiritual truth about Himself is available. What a privilege! And if you are a believer in Jesus Christ, or want to be, you have been chosen for even greater fulfillment and satisfaction in life. Jesus Christ is the Savior of the world. All who believe in Him, repent from sin and obey Him are "born again." Everyone must repent and accept the salvation Christ bought on Calvary's

323

cross, or suffer the terrifying consequences of eternity in Hell. David's greater Son, the Lord Jesus Christ, said, "I am the way, the truth, and the life: no man cometh unto the Father, but by me" (John 14:6). The God David served is wonderful, merciful and loving. You, too, may serve and enjoy Him.

End Notes

1. Taylor, *David, King of Israel* (1916), p. 401.

2. Theodore Epp, *David, Man after the Heart of God* (Lincoln, Nebraska: Back to the Bible Broadcast, 1965, n.p.), p. 199.

Subject and Scripture Text Index